MAX WEBER'S VISION OF HISTORY

We know of no scientifically ascertainable ideals. To be sure, that makes our efforts more arduous than those of the past, since we are expected to create our ideals from within our breast in the very age of subjectivist culture; but we must not and cannot promise a fool's paradise and an easy street, neither in thought nor in action. It is the stigma of our human dignity that the peace of our souls cannot be as great as the peace of one who dreams of such a paradise.

Weber in 1909

MAX WEBER'S
VISION OF HISTORY
Ethics and Methods

Guenther Roth and Wolfgang Schluchter

UNIVERSITY OF CALIFORNIA PRESS

BERKELEY • LOS ANGELES • LONDON

University of California Press
Berkeley and Los Angeles, California

University of California Press, Ltd.
London, England

First Paperback Printing 1984
ISBN 0-520-05226-9
Library of Congress Catalog Card Number: 77-20328
Printed in the United States of America

1 2 3 4 5 6 7 8 9

In memoriam
BENJAMIN NELSON,

single-minded partisan of scholarship
*February 11, 1911 †*September 17, 1977*

CONTENTS

ABBREVIATIONS

AJ

Ancient Judaism. Trans. and eds. Hans H. Gerth and Don Martindale. Glencoe: Free Press, 1952. A translation of Part III of "Die Wirtschaftsethik der Weltreligionen," first published in *Archiv für Sozialwissenschaft und Sozialpolitik,* 1917–19; reprinted, with a posthumously published study, "Die Pharisäer," as vol. III of *Gesammelte Aufsätze zur Religionssoziologie.* Tübingen: Mohr, 1920–21.

"Author's Introduction"
Introduction to vol. I of *Gesammelte Aufsätze zur Religionssoziologie,* trans. Talcott Parsons, in *The Protestant Ethic and the Spirit of Capitalism* (see below), pp. 13–31. (Note that this text is not part of *The Protestant Ethic.*)

China

The Religion of China. Confucianism and Taoism. Trans. and ed. Hans H. Gerth. New edition, with an introduction by C. K. Yang. New York: Macmillan, 1964 (1st ed. Free Press, 1951). A translation of "Konfuzianismus und Taoismus." Part I of "Die Wirtschaftsethik der Weltreligionen," first published in *Archiv für Sozialwissenschaft,* 1916, extensively revised in vol. I of *Gesammelte Aufsätze zur Religionssoziologie.*

EH

General Economic History. Trans. Frank H. Knight. London: Allen & Unwin, 1927; reissued New York: Collier, 1961. A translation of *Wirtschaftsgeschichte,* eds. S. Hellmann and M. Palyi (Munich: Duncker und Humblot, 1923), a posthumously transcribed lecture series. (Third German edition 1958, ed. Johannes Winckelmann.)

ES

Economy and Society. Eds. Guenther Roth and Claus Wittich; trans. E. Fischoff et al. New York: Bedminster Press, 1968; reissued Berkeley and Los Angeles: University of California Press, 1978. Based on the fourth edition of *Wirtschaft und Gesellschaft* (Tübingen: Mohr, 1956), ed. Johannes Winckelmann. First published in 1921–22.

India

The Religion of India. Trans. and eds. Hans H. Gerth and Don Martindale. New York: Free Press, 1958. A translation of "Hinduismus und Buddhismus." Part II of "Die Wirtschaftsethik der Weltreligionen," first published in *Archiv für Sozialwissenschaft*, 1916–17, vol. II of *Gesammelte Aufsätze zur Religionssoziologie*.

"Introduction"

"The Social Psychology of the World Religions," *From Max Weber.* Ed. and trans. H. H. Gerth and C. W. Mills. New York: Oxford University Press, 1958, pp. 267–301. A translation of "Einleitung" to "Die Wirtschaftsethik der Weltreligionen," first published in the *Archiv für Sozialwissenschaft* in 1916, reprinted in revised form in vol. I of *Gesammelte Aufsätze zur Religionssoziologie*.

PE

The Protestant Ethic and the Spirit of Capitalism. Trans. Talcott Parsons. New York: Scribner, 1958 (first published in 1930). A translation of "Die protestantische Ethik und der Geist des Kapitalismus," *Archiv für Sozialwissenschaft*, 1904–5; reprinted in revised form in vol. I of *Gesammelte Aufsätze zur Religionssoziologie*.

"Politics"

"Politics as a Vocation," *From Max Weber,* pp. 77–128. A translation of "Politik als Beruf," *Gesammelte politische Schriften* (1921); 3rd rev. ed. by Johannes Winckelmann (Tübingen: Mohr, 1971), pp. 505–560.

PS

Gesammelte politische Schriften, 3rd rev. ed. (see "Politics" above).

"Science"
"Science as a Vocation," *From Max Weber,* pp. 129–156. A translation of "Wissenschaft als Beruf," *Gesammelte Aufsätze zur Wissenschaftslehre* (1922); 2nd rev. ed by Johannes Winckelmann (Tübingen: Mohr, 1951), 4th ed. 1973.

"Theory"
"Religious Rejections of the World and Their Directions," *From Max Weber,* pp. 323–362. A translation of "Zwischenbetrachtung: Theorie der Stufen und Richtungen religiöser Weltablehnung," *Archiv für Sozialwissenschaft,* 1916; reprinted in revised form in vol. I of *Gesammelte Aufsätze zur Religionssoziologie,* pp. 536–573.

WL
Gesammelte Aufsätze zur Wissenschaftslehre, 2nd ed., 1951 (see "Science" above).

Note: The publication dates of the *Archiv für Sozialwissenschaft* refer to the year of the volume. The individual issues, however, were delivered two to three months ahead of time, so that the first issue of 1916, for instance, went out in October 1915, the second in December 1915. The dates on p. 60 below refer to the delivery dates.

INTRODUCTION

These essays are about matters left unfinished or insufficiently elucidated by Max Weber. During the first half of the 1970s about one hundred publications a year dealt with Weber, articles as well as chapters and sections in books, not counting major monographs and ignoring textbook summaries or ritual references.[1] In spite of this wealth of publications, we have felt for years that two central issues deserve much more attention than they have received in most of the literature: on the level of social philosophy the elaboration of Weber's theory about the appropriate relation of science, politics, and religion in a rationalized world, and on the level of historical inquiry the articulation of Weber's substantive theories and practiced methodology in distinction from his contribution to the debate on the nature of the social or cultural sciences. Especially since the sixties much has been written about value-neutrality or, better, freedom from value judgment, both in critique and defense, but few positive attempts have been made to go beyond Weber's explicit position toward a systematic construction of a theory of science and politics. An exception is Hans Henrik Bruun's *Science, Values and Politics in Max Weber's Methodology*.[2] Many publications have also dealt with the feasibility of interpretative sociology and

1. See Constans Seyfarth and Gert Schmidt, *Max Weber Bibliographie: Eine Dokumentation der Sekundärliteratur* (Stuttgart: Enke, 1977). For a review of major publications and translations since 1960, see my introduction to Reinhard Bendix, *Max Weber: An Intellectual Portrait* (Berkeley and Los Angeles: University of California Press, 1977).
2. Copenhagen: Munksgaard, 1972.

1

the logical status of ideal types, but few writers have addressed Weber's actual research practice.

For several years the authors have tried to do something about these gaps in the Weber literature and have come to feel that their efforts complement each other. Schluchter, a student of the philosopher Dieter Henrich—who was the author of the well-known *Die Einheit der Wissenschaftslehre Max Webers* (1952)—has worked on both a philosophical and a sociological level, as reflected in his two German books, *Decision for the Social Rechtsstaat* and *Aspects of Bureaucratic Domination*.[3] Roth, a student of Reinhard Bendix, has approached Weber on the historical and sociological levels, first in *The Social Democrats in Imperial Germany* and then in his introduction to Weber's *Economy and Society*. In *Scholarship and Partisanship* he expanded some of his observations on Weber's practiced methodology.[4] In the meantime both authors have carried their work further, and the result is the essays assembled here. Schluchter's two closely related investigations reflect the evolution of his thinking on religion, science, and politics in the disenchanted and rationalized world. Roth's essays attempt to clarify the levels of historical analysis—configurational, developmental, and situational—implicit in Weber's research and that of historians in general. The authors believe that they have now reached a point where their complementary efforts should be viewed together. They want their writings to be understood as "essays" in the literal sense of "attempts" to come to terms with unresolved issues not only in Weber's work

---

3. See W. Schluchter, *Entscheidung für den sozialen Rechtsstaat: Hermann Heller und die staatstheoretische Diskussion in der Weimarer Republik* (Cologne: Kiepenheuer & Witsch, 1968); *Aspekte bürokratischer Herrschaft: Studien zur Interpretation der fortschreitenden Industriegesellschaft* (Munich: List, 1972).

4. G. Roth, *The Social Democrats in Imperial Germany: A Study in Working-Class Isolation and National Integration* (Totowa, N. J. Bedminster Press, 1963); Max Weber, *Economy and Society,* ed. G. Roth and Claus Wittich (New York: Bedminster Press, 1968; reissued by the University of California Press, 1978); Reinhard Bendix and G. Roth, *Scholarship and Partisanship: Essays on Max Weber* (Berkeley and Los Angeles: University of California Press, 1971).

but also in the methodology of the social sciences and in the theory of modern society. In the first chapter Schluchter identifies the kind of rationality that is at the core of modern society and the kind of ethical life-style adequate to it. Weber's approach is interpreted as a viable alternative to systems theory and the Marxian perspective. Schluchter examines Weber's sociology of religion in *Economy and Society* and his essays on the economic ethics of the world religions, focusing on the world views or cosmological orders. Particular attention is given to Weber's "Intermediate Reflections: Theory of the Stages and Directions of Religious Rejections of the World" in his *Collected Essays in the Sociology of Religion*. Two dimensions are explored in order to systematize Weber's analysis: monism and dualism, on the one hand, and theocentrism and anthropocentrism, on the other. Along these two dimensions three constellations are treated: (1) ethico-religious forms of world rejection: the Indian and Judeo-Christian tradition; (2) ethico-religious forms of world mastery: Catholicism and Protestantism; and (3) the dialectical development of the rationalism of world mastery: religion and science. The conclusion: not only did Weber himself affirm an ethic of responsibility, but this ethic, properly reformulated, can also be regarded as the basis of an ethical life-style capable of coping with the problem of meaning in modern society. For practical reasons the chapter limits itself to the dimension of world images, but this implies neither an idealist interpretation of Weber nor the view that for him religion was the ultimately decisive factor in the course of Western rationalization.[5]

In the second chapter Schluchter analyzes Weber's famous speeches "Science as a Vocation" and "Politics as a Vocation," which contain a profession of his views on the relation of

---

5. Schluchter has dealt with Weber's "materialist" analysis of agrarian capitalism in Imperial Germany in "Das Wilhelminische Deutschland in der Sicht eines Soziologen: Max Webers Kritik am Kaiserreich," in his *Rationalität in Perspektive: Studien zu Max Weber* (Tübingen: Mohr, 1979).

science and politics in a rationalized society. Here Weber's values are more visible than elsewhere in his work. Schluchter critically examines the notion that Weber tended toward a decisionist position in defining the relation between science and politics. It has been alleged by Jürgen Habermas and Herbert Marcuse that, on the ethical level, Weber limited the role of scientific knowledge in political decision-making to technical critique and, on the institutional level, propagated an organization of science that made it serviceable for any political end. Although these assertions find limited support in some of Weber's formulations, they fail to do justice to the subtlety of his reasoning. The chapter demonstrates this failure by detailing the different shades of meaning inherent in the concepts of freedom from value judgment and of the ethic of responsibility. By clarifying the complex meaning of these two concepts, the chapter shows that Weber does not naively identify or totally separate science and politics on the ethical and institutional levels. Rather, he demands a relationship of political action to science through which cognition and decision can be mutually corrected. The chapter presents two arguments: first, on the ethical level there is a necessary inner connection between freedom from value judgment and the ethic of responsibility; second, on the institutional level the subsystems of science and politics have equal rank. Both aspects converge in the conception of value analysis, on the basis of which it can be shown that Weber's vision of the relation of science and politics is more pragmatic than decisionist.

The first essay was written after the second one to provide a historical perspective for it. The earlier one pointed to the external and internal connections of Weber's two speeches with "The Religious Rejections of the World" of 1915, an earlier version of the "Intermediate Reflections," and to the significance which the analysis of the relation of ethics and world has for our understanding of Weber's basic position. In the four years between the writing of his two essays Schluchter realized that "Science as a Vocation" is temporally closer to "The Religious Rejections of the World" than was previously

known. Contrary to the old assumption in the Weber literature, it has recently been established that "Science as a Vocation" was given as early as November 7, 1917, not close to the
date of "Politics as a Vocation," which was almost certainly
delivered on January 28, 1919. The new dating suggests that
Weber's basic outlook on the epoch, unlike his political views,
was not decisively affected by the events of 1918.

Like Schluchter, Roth links Weber's studies on politics with
those on religion, but he approaches them more on the
methodological than the normative level, although both authors are concerned with Weber's substantive historical
theories. The purpose of chapter three is fourfold: (1) to
clarify Weber's distinction between history and sociology; (2)
to elucidate a basic distinction in his work, and generally in
historical analysis, between socio-historical models and developmental or "secular" theories; (3) to examine two neglected
aspects of Weber's analysis of charisma, the community of
ideological virtuosi (a model), and the charisma of reason as a
revolutionary legitimation founded on natural rights (a secular theory); (4) to apply model and theory to the counterculture in order to provide a novel theoretical framework for its
further study. The youth and student rebellions of the 1960s
are viewed as the charismatic eruption of a new moral mood
reviving the charisma of reason, and the contemporary
peaceful communes and warlike groups are interpreted as the
counterculture's charismatic core.

Chapter four poses the question of how adequate Weber's
world-historical sociology of religion is in relation to our
understanding of secularization, especially the rise of quasi-
religious political movements and ideologies. It argues that,
for both analytical and historical reasons, Weber's work retains a considerable degree of conceptual adequacy in the face
of new historical developments. The chapter elaborates the
distinction between theory and model, the secular theory of
modern revolutionary beliefs and the model of ideological
virtuosi and of social marginality. Topically, the model of revolutionary religious virtuosity is applied to the Catholic oppo-

sition against church and state in the United States, and the secular theory of the counterculture is extended.

Chapter five compares Weber and Fernand Braudel, for many years the dominant figure of the French *Annales* school, which has received increasing attention in the United States in recent years and is sometimes seen as providing an alternative to Weber's approach. The chapter points to some common roots of Weber's work and the *Annales* tradition in late nineteenth-century social and economic history in Germany, but it is mainly concerned with an analytic, not a historical comparison. The chapter explores the ways in which both historians can be said to pursue a structural strategy in spite of their obvious differences—Braudel studying different "layers" of time, especially of long duration, and Weber investigating various kinds of rationalization. The relations among duration, model, and secular theory are examined, and the two scholars' distinctive views of capitalism are contrasted. Finally, Braudel's notion of *la longue durée* is applied to Weber's analysis of China and the West in terms of different outcomes of rationalization.

The epilogue moves beyond the distinction between secular theory and socio-historical model to situational analysis. In contrast to his more "academic" writings, Weber quite naturally emphasized situational analysis—the third level of historical inquiry proper—in his more political ones, since this kind of analysis is primarily concerned with the current distribution of power and its possible change, not with secular change or differences between civilizations. In his situational dissection of the first Russian Revolution, Weber recognized as early as 1906 that economic development and advanced capitalism do not necessarily favor political pluralism and liberal constitutionalism and thus anticipated the present-day critique of the optimistic American development theories popular in the 1950s and 1960s. The epilogue concludes that Weber's historical vision kept "the future as history" open to human will and resolution in spite of powerful trends toward the reduction and elimination of freedom.

Some of the rougher edges of Roth's translation of Schluchter's essays were smoothed by Karen Wayenberg, whom we should like to thank for her careful reading. Professor Caroline W. Bynum of the History Department at the University of Washington read the whole manuscript with the skeptical eye of the professional historian and offered helpful advice.

Guenther Roth
Wolfgang Schluchter

Seattle and Heidelberg
March 1978

Part I

I

THE PARADOX OF RATIONALIZATION: ON THE RELATION OF ETHICS AND WORLD

Wolfgang Schluchter[1]

Contemporary social scientists are extremely divided in their evaluation of the rationality of modern society. Two illustrations should suffice. For Talcott Parsons the system constitutive of modern societies is the most rational yet achieved in historical development. It has an unsurpassed adaptive capacity rooted in multi-dimensionality. Structural pluralism permits progressive change, and this in turn ultimately strengthens individual freedom.[2] By contrast, for Herbert Marcuse advanced industrial society is the most irrational of all societies in history. It has an unsurpassed capacity to manipulate human beings by virtue of its one-dimensionality, which permits the permanent suppression of progressive

1. Translated by Guenther Roth. In many cases quotations from the German have been newly translated. Therefore, references to previous English translations, which have not been used, are indicated by "cf."
2. Cf. Talcott Parsons, *Societies: Evolutionary and Comparative Perspectives* (Englewood Cliffs, N.J.: Prentice-Hall, 1966) and *The System of Modern Societies* (Englewood Cliffs, N.J.: Prentice-Hall, 1971). Parsons' reference point for the notion of adaptive capacity is society, but if other reference points are chosen, different conclusions are possible. Parsons' position is clearly stated also in "Christianity and Modern Society," *Sociological Theory and Modern Society* (New York: Free Press, 1967), pp. 385ff.

change. Thus, the few remaining freedoms from the era of liberal capitalism are threatened.[3] Such an extreme difference in the evaluation of our situation makes it difficult to find a mediating position. If one exists, I suspect it will be found within this difference rather than beyond it. Let me demonstrate this by reference to a fact of intellectual history. In spite of their irreconcilability, Parsons and Marcuse have a common basis: Max Weber's position plays an important role in each one's judgment about the origin and the future as well as the rationality of modern society.[4] Of course, neither man wishes to retain Weber's posi-

3. Herbert Marcuse, *One-Dimensional Man* (Boston: Beacon Press, 1964): "By virtue of the way it has organized its technological base, contemporary industrial society tends to be totalitarian. For 'totalitarian' is not only a terrorist political coordination of society, but also a non-terrorist economic-technical coordination which operates through the manipulation of needs by vested interests. It thus precludes the emergence of an effective opposition against the whole. Not only a specific form of government or party rule makes for totalitarianism, but also a specific system of production and distribution which may well be compatible with a 'pluralism' of parties, newspapers, 'countervailing powers,' etc." (p. 3).

4. In Parsons' case this is obvious, since his book on *The System of Modern Societies* "is written in the spirit of Weber's work" (pp. 2 and 139). Marcuse used his critique of Weber to specify his diagnosis of advanced industrial society. See "Industrialism and Capitalism," in *Max Weber and Sociology Today*, ed. Otto Stammer (New York: Harper, 1971), pp. 133–151, reprinted in Marcuse, *Negations* (Boston: Beacon Press, 1968), pp. 201–226; and my own critique of Marcuse in *Aspekte bürokratischer Herrschaft* (Munich: List, 1971), pp. 254ff. Parsons and Marcuse take a similar historical perspective in their analyses of modern society. Parsons notes that the most influential intellectual root of his analysis was German idealism "as it passed from Hegel through Marx to Weber." It is well known that Marcuse wrote an influential study about the transition from Hegel to Marx (*Reason and Revolution: Hegel and the Rise of Social Theory*, New York: Humanities Press, 1954, 2nd ed.). But in pointing to these similarities we do not want to deny the basic differences in premises and reception. Parsons' merits in the American reception of Weber and his relative fidelity toward his work cannot be denied. (cf. *The Structure of Social Action*, New York: McGraw-Hill, 1937, and his introduction to *Max Weber: The Theory of Social and Economic Organization* (Glencoe: Free Press, 1947). However, Parsons' interpretation of Weber has been challenged in recent years by younger sociologists (for instance, by J. Cohen, L. E. Hazelrigg, W. Pope, "De-Parsonizing Weber," *American Sociological Review*, 40

tion. Parsons wants to transcend it, Marcuse wants to go back to a position older than Weber's. I, however, believe that it has become worthwhile again to stay with Weber for some time to come. For his sociology is not only, as is every great sociology, the "articulated problematic of reality itself";[5] his problems are at least partly still ours and have not been resolved by either systems theory or neo-Marxism. Weber achieves a diagnosis of our situation on the basis of his socio-economic, political, and socio-cultural analyses of capitalism and of occidental rationalism.[6] It is the diagnosis of the disenchantment of the world which has been going on for millennia and has now been completed, the diagnosis of the rationalization of its value spheres and of the intellectualization of our responses to them. But it is also the diagnosis of the paradox of this process, which presents to modern society a problem not only of management but also of meaning.

It has often been pointed out that the issues of rationalism and rationalization are particularly well suited for an overall interpretation of Weber's position.[7] However, this requires

(1975): 229ff.). Earlier Reinhard Bendix had criticized Parsons' interpretation of Weber in "Two Sociological Traditions" in Bendix and Roth, *Scholarship and Partisanship* (Berkeley and Los Angeles: University of California Press, 1971), pp. 282–298.

5. S. Landshut, *Kritik der Soziologie* (Neuwied: Luchterhand, 1969), p. 41.

6. Dieter Henrich has identified in Weber's position the consistency of philosophical consciousness and scientific analysis of the present (in Stammer, *op. cit.*, pp. 66–78). Not only Weber's work but also his person and life have time and again been viewed as a diagnosis of the modern situation, most emphatically by Karl Jaspers: "Man who was born into the world of Homer and the Jewish prophets was not lost with Nietzsche. His last great incarnation for the time being was Max Weber, a figure of our world which changes so rapidly that the particular features of Weber's environment have disappeared in spite of the passing of such a short time. What has not passed are the basic questions of our existence, of human knowledge, of human challenges. We no longer have a great human being who could reaffirm our identity. Weber was the last one." (*Max Weber: Deutsches Wesen im politischen Denken, im Forschen und Philosophieren,* Oldenburg: Stalling, 1932, p. 78.)

7. This was true as early as the Weber interpretation of the 1920s, witness the study by Siegfried Landshut, *op. cit.*, and Hans Freyer's book of 1930, *Soziologie als Wirklichkeitswissenschaft* (Darmstadt: Wissenschaftliche Buchgesellschaft, 1964), pp. 145ff., 157f. The discussion revolved not only

that we use the concepts with precision, in contrast to Weber's ambiguous usage. I propose three usages.[8] First, rationalism refers to the capacity to control the world through calculation. Here rationalism is a consequence of empirical knowledge and know-how. Therefore, in its first sense rationalism is *scientific-technological rationalism*.[9] In its second meaning ra-

around the recognition of the connection between methodology and historical content in Weber's work, but also around the confrontation with Marx. See the unexcelled essay by Karl Loewith, "Max Weber und Karl Marx" (1932), in his *Gesammelte Abhandlungen* (Stuttgart: Kohlhammer, 1960), pp. 1–67. The Weber section has been translated in *Max Weber,* ed. Dennis Wrong (Englewood Cliffs, N.J.: Prentice Hall, 1970), pp. 101–122. In recent years Jürgen Habermas has harked back to this discussion (see Stammer, *op. cit.,* pp. 59–65). Among recent contributions is the well-researched study by Günter Abramowski, *Das Geschichtsbild Max Webers* (Stuttgart: Klett, 1966). Much attention was aroused by Wolfgang Mommsen's "Universalgeschichtliches und politisches Denken," reprinted in his *Max Weber: Gesellschaft, Politik und Geschichte* (Frankfurt: Suhrkamp, 1974), pp. 97–143. Mommsen locates Weber's implicit philosophy of history within a dialectic of charisma and rationalization and thus attempts a synthesis of Loewith and Abramowski. Reinhard Bendix, too, has remarked that rationalization is a suitable notion for an overall analysis of Weber's work, but only if we keep in mind the ambiguity and multi-dimensionality of the term (see "Max Weber's Sociology Today," *International Social Science Journal,* 17, no. 1 (1965): 9–22). With regard to the almost limitless discussion of the Protestant ethic, Constans Seyfarth has said: "Only if we reformulate the theme of the Protestant ethic in the wider but more precise context of rationalization can we productively continue Weber's work and go beyond mere citation and polemic" (see his "Protestantismus und gesellschaftliche Entwicklung," *Seminar: Religion und gesellschaftliche Entwicklung,* ed. C. Seyfarth and W. Sprondel, Frankfurt: Suhrkamp, 1973, p. 342).

8. On the multi-dimensionality of the term "rationalism" see Weber, "Introduction," p. 293; also Landshut, *op. cit.,* pp. 49ff.; Bendix, *Max Weber* (Berkeley and Los Angeles: University of California Press, 1977), p. 278; Ann Swidler, "The Concept of Rationality in the Work of Max Weber," *Sociological Inquiry,* 43 (1973): 35ff.; and Johannes Weiss, *Max Webers Grundlegung der Soziologie* (Munich: Dokumentation, 1975), pp. 137ff. My proposal differs somewhat from theirs.

9. Cf. Weber's formulation in "Science," p. 138f., which refers to empirical science of the nomological type with its mathematical foundation. I shall employ a wider notion, which can subsume "the simple empirical skills of early times" and "the superstructure of magically 'rational' science," as in China (cf. Weber, *China,* p. 199). Calculability on the basis of empirical knowledge is not specific to the Occident, but the kind and purpose of the calcula-

tionalism refers to the systematization of meaning patterns. This involves the intellectual elaboration and deliberate sublimation of ultimate ends. In this sense rationalism is a consequence of cultured man's "inner compulsion" not only to understand the world as a "meaningful cosmos" but also to take a consistent and unified stance toward it. This second type of rationalism may be called *metaphysical-ethical rationalism*.[10] Third and last, rationalism also refers to the achievement of a methodical way of life. Here rationalism is the consequence of the institutionalization of configurations of meaning and interest. Hence we may refer to this last kind as *practical rationalism*.[11] All three kinds of rationalism vary with social circumstances and are related to each other in changing ways. We are especially interested in the manner in which historical forms of scientific and ethical rationalism affect practical rationalism. For the capacity of humans to adhere to "certain kinds of practical rational conduct"[12] depends not only upon their interests and the socially defined ways of pursuing interests but also upon the interpretation of their position vis-à-vis the "gods" and the "world." In Weber's own well-known formulation: "Interests, material as well as ideal, not ideas directly control action. But world images, which are the product of ideas, have often served as the channels along which action is moved by the dynamics of interests. After all, it is in response to an image of cosmological order whence the question arises from what and towards what one needs to be saved."[13]

---

tion are (cf. Weber, "Author's Introduction," p. 13). On the complex relationship between "science" and the social development of pre-modern societies, see Joseph Needham, *Science and Civilization in China* (Cambridge: The University Press, 1956), vol. 2.

10. Cf. *ES*, p. 499. In his sociology of religion Weber speaks of goals and ways of salvation. I prefer to use the wider notion of ultimate ends.

11. Cf. *ES*, p. 528.

12. Weber, "Author's Introduction," *PE*, p. 26. Note, however, that this is Weber's 1920 introduction to vol. I of *Gesammelte Aufsätze zur Religionssoziologie*, not an introduction to *The Protestant Ethic*. Cf. Benjamin Nelson, "Max Weber's 'Author's Introduction' (1920): A Master Clue to His Main Aims," *Sociological Inquiry*, 44, no. 4 (1974): 267–278.

13. Cf. "Introduction," p. 280. On the distinction between "world" and

I shall retrace Weber's analysis of rationalization, which he develops into his theory of the disenchantment of modern occidental culture, primarily on the level of the world images. Such a strategy presupposes that this level can be isolated in a meaningful sense. In my view, this is indeed feasible without having to assert that Weber represents an idealist interpretation of history and without inappropriately "idealizing" his approach. An excursus on Weber's procedure will be useful to support my view. I shall address myself to his research program as laid down especially in the studies on the economic ethics of the world religions.[14]

Weber's procedure can be described as the attempt to demonstrate the limitations of the materialist as well as the idealist interpretation of history, without denying the relative justification for both views.[15] Social formations can be understood only up to a point with a materialist or idealist scheme of base

---

"gods" see *ES*, pp. 404 and 540f. According to Weber, world images interpret man's relation to the "world" as the cosmos of natural and social relations from the perspective of supernatural beings or supra-individual meanings. Thus, the world images are conceptions of the ultimate external and internal conditions of existence. (Cf. Robert N. Bellah, "Religious Evolution," *American Sociological Review*, 29 (1964): 358–374.) The world images contain cognitive and normative elements, hence they transcend by virtue of their symbolization a "primeval" unity of man with his environment and set him free from it. These ideas about man's position in the world are, of course, not independent of his surroundings. Since they are rooted in symbolic systems which are influenced by social-structural factors, one can assume with Turner that there is "a correlation between the dominant mode of economic production and the structure of man-god relationship" (Bryan S. Turner, *Weber and Islam*, London: Routledge and Kegan Paul, 1974), p. 52.

14. For this reason my interpretation is not fully congruous with Weber's own methodological reflections in his methodological writings. Tenbruck, in particular, has argued that today we should largely disregard Weber's methodological essays and focus on his substantive analyses (cf. F. H. Tenbruck, "Die Genesis der Methodologie Max Webers," *Kölner Zeitschrift für Soziologie*, 11 (1959): 573ff.). Reinhard Bendix seems to hold a similar view; his book on Weber does not deal with the methodological writings. Dieter Henrich continues to represent the alternative view. Johannes Weiss (*op. cit.*) has attempted a linkage of methodological writings and sociology of religion.

15. Weber, "Antikritisches zum 'Geist' des Kapitalismus," in *Die protestantische Ethik II*, ed. J. Winckelmann (Munich: Siebenstern, 1968), p. 169; *PE*, p. 183; *ES*, p. 1091f.

and superstructure—their structure is too complex for such a reduction. This does not mean, of course, that certain basic relationships are not of particular importance for their analysis. Weber distinguishes three above all: (1) The relationship among ideas themselves, which derives from the human need for a unified attitude toward the world; (2) the relation of ideas and interests, which refers to men's need to define their position in the world; (3) the relationship between ideas (or interests) and social organization for the sake of satisfying the need toward greater calculability of the world. It is primarily the last relationship which, so to speak, coordinates the other two by guaranteeing the ideological and social unity necessary for the persistence of social formations. This unity can also be viewed as the result of an elective affinity between form and spirit.[16]

This approach puts the macrosociological analysis into a dual perspective: social action can be understood as the expression of institutionalized interests as well as institutionalized ideas.[17] In both perspectives we must take into account a dialectical relationship between function and autonomy. Constellations of interests and ideas remain tied to one another: only interpreted interests and interest-laden ideas are sociologically relevant. However, both also have autonomous aspects, and herein lies the relative justification for a materialist as well as an idealist interpretation of history. Only by pursuing this dialectic in a double perspective can we serve "historical truth,"[18] only then are we able to elucidate the mediating processes among ends, means, and interests

16. *PE*, pp. 50ff., 90ff., 232; "Introduction," p. 269f; Weber, "Antikritisches," pp. 27ff., 163ff., 284f. Carl Mayer has gone so far as to link the conception of elective affinity with an ontological difference between real and ideal factors. See "Max Weber's Interpretation of Karl Marx," *Social Research*, 42, no. 4 (1975): 701–719.

17. Bendix holds a similar view; cf. *Max Weber* (n. 8 above), pp. 286ff.; he distinguishes among the three dimensions of value orientation, domination, and material interests and between interest constellation and legitimation. On the importance of organization as an intervening variable, see also Stephen D. Berger, "The Sects and the Breakthrough into the Modern World," *Sociological Quarterly*, 12 (1971): 486–499.

18. *PE*, p. 183.

within social formations. We must consider equally the center and the periphery, the elites and the masses—that is, the representatives of dominant ideas and interests and their opponents, on the one hand, and their possible following, on the other. In Weber's sociology of religion this constellation is articulated in the opposition of orthodoxy and heterodoxy as well as the juxtaposition of the religiosity of the virtuosi and the masses.[19]

This frame of reference is enlarged by two further considerations. First, social formations consist not only of classes, status groups, and parties but also of value spheres, of inner-worldly normative structures, which are subject to their own logic and hence to an elective affinity between form and spirit. Second, these inner-worldly realms have specific historical relations with one another, leading to changing primacy and also to changing dominance of life-style. Within this enlarged framework Weber analyzes the relation of religion and economy in world-historical perspective: the relation of the dominant religious ideas to the economic ideas, the relation of these economic ideas to the economic systems, and the changing primacy of the religious and economic ideas themselves.[20]

My investigation, then, deals with Weber's approach to these ideas on the basis of his assumptions about a science of historical reality. From this viewpoint world images are particularly important in their "psychological and pragmatic connections," as components of human motives, on the one hand, and as possible stimuli for action, on the other.[21] In

19. To a limited degree we can draw a parallel between this juxtaposition and that between institutionalized domination and charismatic leadership.

20. For Weber the transition from traditionalist to modern society is indicated by the change from religious to economic primacy. However, this primacy is not absolute. It is relativized by the special role of politics. In traditional society this is apparent from the precarious relation between politics and religion, and in modern societies between economy and politics.

21. This corresponds to the distinction between internalization and institutionalization of values. Bendix, in particular, has emphasized that Weber did not clearly separate psychological drives and stimuli and, so to speak, short-circuited them in the concept of ethos. This makes it clear that Weber

analyzing the world images we cannot prejudge the relation of developmental factors internal and external to them. If we take both into account, we can formulate our task in the following manner: We are concerned with the reconstruction of the origin and the present form of the "occidental ethos" (Loewith) on the basis of Weber's investigations and with answering the question about "the life-style ethically adequate" for modern society.[22]

This reconstruction requires three steps, which arise when we view Weber's studies in the sociology of religion in their unity and follow the distinctions proposed by them.[23] Weber analyzes the development of religious ideas and the resultant problematical aspects of the world views in various comparisons. If we greatly simplify, we can say that the comparisons lead to two distinctions: between oriental and occidental rationalism, on the one hand, and between occidental and modern occidental rationalism, on the other. The differences between oriental or, better, Asian rationalism and occidental rationalism are clarified primarily through the comparison of the Indian and Chinese with the Judeo-Christian tradition. In Hinduism and Buddhism, Confucianism and Taoism, as well as Christianity, stages and directions of ethico-religious conduct appear in the form of flight from the world, world adjustment, and world mastery.[24] The comparison between

---

did not have an explicit theory of socialization. See Bendix in Stammer (n. 4 above), p. 157, and in *Scholarship and Partisanship* (n. 4 above), p. 189f.

22. Weber, "Antikritisches Schlusswort zum 'Geist des Kapitalismus,'" in *Die protestantische Ethik II*, p. 286.

23. We take a unified approach that overcomes the isolated analysis of the Protestant ethic and sees it as part of a larger program for the analysis of rationalism and rationalization. This does not mean that all of Weber's studies in the sociology of religion lie on the same methodological and substantive levels. See the distinction between socio-historical model and secular theory in Roth's chapters below.

24. Cf. Weber, "Theory," pp. 323ff. We will not consider Weber's treatment of Islam, which he did not live to undertake systematically. See Bryan S. Turner's *Weber and Islam* (n. 13 above). We must also disregard Weber's detailed analysis of the various Asian religious movements. We will select Hinduism, the orthodox variant of Asian salvation religion, and *Gesin-*

Hinduism and Christianity is of particular interest, for both tend toward world rejection on the basis of their world image, whereas Confucianism tends toward world affirmation.[25] In this regard Hinduism and Christianity, but not Confucianism and Christianity, operate on the same wavelength, for Confucianism represents, among the important religions, that ethic which reduces "the tension vis-à-vis the world, both its religious devaluation and its rejection in practice, to an absolute minimum."[26] Thus, our first step must consist primarily in confronting the Indian and the Judeo-Christian tradition. They constitute forms of religiously motivated world rejection, which lead to world flight or world mastery. The difference between occidental and modern occidental rationalism can be approached by comparing the Catholic and the Protestant tradition: Catholicism, Lutheranism, and especially Calvinism represent different stages and directions of ethically interpreted world mastery. Thus, our second step must contrast the variants of the Judeo-Christian tradition, which articulate the Christian world image in such different ways. However, the peculiarity of modern occidental rationalism is only partially elucidated through such a comparison. Modern occidental rationalism appears *in statu nascendi* in these various forms of the Christian tradition. Its full development becomes visible only when we look at its transformation from a religious to a non-religious world image. Part of this transformation lies in the dialectical relationship of religion and science. This will be the third step in our analysis.

---

nungsreligiosität. Weber classified the Asian religions along the dimensions of orthodoxy and heterodoxy and of salvation and magic. Thus, Hinduism is an orthodox salvation religion, Confucianism an orthodox magical religion, Buddhism a heterodox salvation religion, and Taoism a heterodox magic religion.

25. Weber says of Hinduism that it belongs, "both theoretically and practically, to the most world-rejecting forms of religious ethics ever created" (cf. "Theory," p. 323). This is true also of Buddhism, especially early Buddhism, which was even more world-rejecting than Hinduism. However, I will focus on Hinduism, since it is the orthodox position for Weber.

26. Cf. Weber, *China*, p. 227.

These remarks should make it clear that Weber's sociology of religion contains not only a model of cultural differentiation, a rudimentary typology of ethical, especially of ethico-religious rationalism,[27] but also a rudimentary historical theory of the stages of rationalization, which are classified according to the systematic degree of the world image and according to the degree of its magical content.[28] The rudimentary typology of rationalism and the rudimentary theory of the stages of rationalism are related to each other especially through the disenchantment thesis and are combined into an "open-ended" theory of religious evolution.[29] For in the last analysis Weber's program in the sociology of religion is intended to make us understand the uniqueness of modern occidental culture and to answer the question of why only in the Occident did there appear cultural phenomena "which took a developmental path of universal importance and

27. Cf. Weber "Theory," p. 324.
28. Cf. Weber, *China,* p. 226. It is very important to understand that systematization of the attitude toward the world and disenchantment do not necessarily go together. There are religions that are rational on the level of systematization but not of disenchantment. This is true, for instance, of Hinduism, whereas the special character of ascetic Protestantism consists in having a high degree of rationality along both dimensions. On Weber's sociology as a theory of cultural differentiation, see Wilhelm E. Mühlmann, *Max Weber und die rationale Soziologie* (Tübingen: Mohr, 1966).
29. Besides Parsons, Bellah in particular has interpreted Weber in evolutionary terms; his essay on religious evolution can be understood as a reconstruction of Weber. A similar line is followed by Günter Dux, "Religion, Geschichte und sozialer Wandel in Max Webers Religionssoziologie," *Seminar: Religion und gesellschaftliche Entwicklung,* eds. Constans Seyfarth and Walter Sprondel (Frankfurt: Suhrkamp, 1973), pp. 313–337. Bendix has opposed the "fashionable construction of general developmental schemes" (as Weber once put it) and advocated the identification of the distinctive character of different developments. He emphasized especially the necessity of distinguishing between logical and historical validity (see Bendix in Stammer, *op. cit.* n. 4 above, p. 196). However, it seems to me that he goes too far in his anti-evolutionary stand when he writes that Weber's analysis of rationalization should free us from the assumption "that for him this process was either inevitable, unequivocal, or irreversible" (*Max Weber* (n. 8 above), p. 279). Weber does have a minimal evolutionary program (see C. Seyfarth, "Protestantismus und gesellschaftliche Entwicklung" (n. 7 above), pp. 338–366).

world-historical significance, at least as we like to think."[30] The three steps of our reconstruction, then, can be labeled in this way: 1. Ethico-religious Forms of World Rejection: The Indian and the Judeo-Christian Tradition; 2. Ethico-religious Forms of World Mastery: Catholicism and Protestantism; 3. The Dialectical Development of the Rationalism of World Mastery: Religion and Science.

1. Ethico-religious Forms of World Rejection: The Indian and the Judeo-Christian Tradition

If we want to grasp the particular structure of the religious ethics of world-rejection, we must contrast them, according to Weber, with magic, out of which they developed in historically complicated ways. The magic world view is monistic, although it is true that it recognizes a double world, the realm of things and events and the "world behind the world" of souls, demons, and deities. But the idea that there are powers behind things and events, that natural processes not only happen but also have an intrinsic meaning—in other words, that the "world" is an "enchanted garden"[31]—does not lead to a radical separation of the this-worldly and the other-worldly sphere and to an unbridgeable gulf between men and supernatural powers. Men remain close to the gods through magic, ritual, and the observance of taboos.[32] At this stage men's relation to the gods cannot yet be described as worship proper; rather, coercion is the predominant attempt to control the gods through magic or simply to win them over through bribery. Magic and magical "ethics" are still ignorant of religious law and the demand that it be observed. Cult and sacrifice as an expression of supplication and worship remain peripheral. Thus, we do not yet encounter the idea central to

30. Cf. "Author's Introduction," *PE*, p. 13. The quotation shows that Weber did not indulge in the ethnocentrism that is nowadays found so frequently in modernization theories. See the critique by Hans-Ulrich Wehler, *Modernisierungstheorie und Geschichte* (Göttingen: Vandenhoeck, 1975).

31. Weber, *China*, p. 200; *India*, p. 335f.

32. Cf. *ES*, pp. 399ff.

every salvation religion: "that whoever flouts divinely appointed norms will be overtaken by the ethical displeasure of the god who takes these norms under his special protection."[33] Therefore, what Weber asserted for Taoism is also true for the magical world view in general: "Magic, not conduct, decides man's fate."[34]

One decisive developmental factor internal to the world image is the elaboration of the idea that gods have established the rules for certain realms of action and watch over their observance. This development makes conceivable not only such notions as worship but also sin, conscience, and especially salvation. However, at the same time, such sublimation of the magical starting point through knowledge leads to an increase in the dualism between man and god, this world and the other world. Now it becomes possible to conceive not only of the distinction but also of the opposition of natural and divine claims, of natural causality and postulated compensatory causality. As a rule the monistic world view is undermined whenever a "rational metaphysic and religious ethic"[35] come into being. Then an opening is created for the elaboration of a dualist world view, of a theocentric world image which tends to subordinate the "world" to what used to be only the "world behind the world" (*Hinterwelt*). This also prepares the way for a religiously motivated rejection of the world. However, the degree of the religious devaluation of the world and the degree of its rejection in practice are not necessarily identical.[36]

One of the preconditions for such a development is obvi-

---

33. *ES*, p. 437. Weber does not keep apart primitive and archaic religion as clearly as Bellah has done. However, he distinguishes the magical phase of religious development, which is characterized by symbolism, from the phase of "pre-animistic naturalism" (cf. *ES*, p. 406). For Bellah, too, the difference between the primitive and the archaic phase is one of degree rather than of principle. If one accepts Bellah's scheme, Weber's concepts apply primarily to the historical religions.

34. Cf. *China*, p. 200.   35. *ES*, p. 427.

36. Vf. *China*, p. 227. On the difference between monistic and dualist world image, see especially Bellah, "Religious Evolution" (n. 13 above).

ously the systematization of the idea of divinity. This is brought about by the creation of a pantheon, which transforms the subordinate magical realm of spirits in the direction of anthropomorphism, specialization, and hierarchy.[37] When the three processes happen to occur together, the ideas of divinity may become not only "ethicized" but also universalized. Both elements are fused in monotheism. In the light of our perspective on evolution, monotheism is therefore an "unlikely" invention and indeed achieved historical importance only in Judaism and, partly under its impact, in Islam. In Christianity monotheism frequently became important only in relativized form. If we include Zoroastrianism, which in Weber's eyes was ultimately without historical significance, we can say that universalist monotheism has been a product of the Near Eastern and Iranian and of the Christian, but not of the Indian and Chinese, religious world.[38]

Thus, the formation of a pantheon, the rationalization of the magical spirit world, does not necessarily lead to the idea of a personal supernatural creator god who can punish as well as love. The rationalization of the magic spirit world can also take on the form of an "impersonal and immanent divine power," combined for instance with the notion that the world was not created.[39] Frequently, however, rationalization did not go far in one or the other direction, and the formation of a pantheon remained on the level of a congeries of functional and local gods. But Weber is interested in the consistent rationalizations. These are represented in Yahwe, the Jewish personal god of action, on the one hand, and in Brahma, the Indian "god" of eternal order, which is experienced only as a mental state.[40] If we assume a common origin in magic and a divergent movement toward ethical and exemplary prophecy, the rationalization of salvation results in two totally different notions of god in the Judeo-Christian and the Asian tradi-

---

37. Cf. *ES*, pp. 427ff.   38. Cf. *ES*, pp. 418, 518.
39. Cf. "Theory," p. 325; *India*, p. 167.
40. Cf. *AJ*, pp. 311ff.; *India*, p. 170.

tion.[41] In this manner, certain channels are created for the further rationalization of the theocentric world view.[42] For these two conceptions of god have an affinity not only with certain definitions of human identity, but also with the institutionalization of roads to salvation and hence with the interpretation and orientation of the believers' need for salvation. By contrast, in Confucianism rationalization leads away from the problem of salvation and aims at the "maintenance of the magic garden."[43] The idea of a god of action is paralleled by the idea of man as his tool, whereas the idea of the divine as an eternal order is paralleled by the idea of man as a vessel. The notion of being a tool, in turn, is closer to the salvational methodology of asceticism, whereas the notion of a vessel is more closely connected with contemplation and mysticism.[44] It is true that there has been mysticism in the Christian tradition and asceticism in the Indian, but they remain tied to the peculiarities of these traditions. Thus, in Christianity the idea of god forced the mystic to acknowledge that an

41. Weber perceives a decisive difference between the two developments in the fact that basically the Asian religious world did not know ethical prophecy; rather, it originated in exemplary prophecy and remained a religion of intellectuals. For this reason, among others, religious ethic could not take on the character of a radical ethic of single-minded conviction that became so important for the occidental development. Thus, in Asia no activist notion of personality could arise; instead a contemplative notion prevailed. Insofar as the Asian religions did not slide back into magic, they remained intellectual rather than ethical religions (cf. *India*, pp. 164, 171). On Weber's concept of personality and its relation to Judaism and ascetic Protestantism, see Abramowski (n. 7 above), p. 31, n. 61, and Mommsen, *Max Weber und die deutsche Politik*, 1890–1920 (Tübingen: Mohr, 1974, 2nd ed.), pp. 108ff. and n. 48.

42. Other factors that must be taken into account in assessing the different developments are, for instance, the impact of Roman law and the rational organization of the Catholic church (cf. *ES*, pp. 552ff.).

43. Cf. *China*, p. 227.

44. Cf. "Theory," pp. 324ff. Weber emphasizes time and again that these elective affinities are not necessary relationships. At the same time he points to the central importance which the institutionalization of these roads to salvation has for these connections.

"ultimate union with God" was unattainable, whereas the Indian ascetic was made to flee the world.[45] At the same time the two relations of elective affinity also differ from each other according to the realm of proving oneself (*Bewährung*): here it is sought more in this world, there more in the other.[46] Wherever such constellations come into being, we must also expect differences in the adequate ethical life-style; in one case action, in the other inaction, is the ultimate goal. Hence, the forms of practical rationalism, which correspond to these two kinds of theoretical rationalism, differ in a significant manner: here we have the "rational transformation of the mundane order on the basis of a methodical pattern of life directed toward external success"; there we have an attitude that is "relatively indifferent to the world and at any rate humbly accepts the given social order."[47] This indifference to the world is particularly likely when the religious world view is connected with an organicist social ethic, as in India. For when the relationship to the inner-worldly order is relativized in an organicist manner, the religious ethic is deprived of its claim to unify the world in principle and thus permits the isolation of the inner-worldly from the other-worldly sphere.[48]

This ideal-typical elaboration of differences in world views and of their consequences, which could be set in parallel with

45. Cf. *ES*, p. 553; *India*, p. 152; "Theory," p. 325.

46. Weber's distinction between this-worldly and other-worldly is open to misunderstanding insofar as these concepts fuse two different aspects of religious action: There is a difference between religious self-affirmation through action in the world and through taking a stand against action necessary in the world, and a difference between limiting action to the religious value sphere and extending it to other spheres. The first distinction is linked to that between asceticism and mysticism. I consider it useful to distinguish between asceticism (and mysticism respectively) that is oriented to mastery over the world versus flight from the world, and to treat separately the institutional realm, the this-worldly sphere, to which action is oriented.

47. *ES*, p. 550.

48. Incidentally, Weber explains in this way the general attractiveness of organicist social doctrines for traditionalist societies, which have a dominant salvation religion (cf. *ES*, p. 598; "Theory," p. 338).

Weber's distinction between oriental and occidental city,[49] must not obscure one consideration: the fact that there is a basic similarity between the two world images. Even though Weber demonstrates that not only Confucianism but also Hinduism remains entangled in magic,[50] we must understand Hinduism at least as a salvation religion. Hinduism, just like the Judeo-Christian tradition, must have a dualist world view—the idea that the world not only is doubled, as in the magical view, but is split into two principles.[51] Tension prevails between these principles, but its extent depends upon the manner in which the ethico-religious world view has been rationalized. The believer experiences this tension as a discrepancy, an experience not alien to the believer in magic, who, however, could resort to ad hoc solutions.[52] The believer in a salvation religion experiences a discrepancy between a postulated divine perfection and the imperfection of the "world." This issue arises with particular acuteness when intellectual rationalization, as in the Judeo-Christian tradition, has made God explicitly the creator of the "world" and given him the attributes of "absolute unchangeableness, omnipotence, omniscience, in short, of absolute transcendence."[53] In this case there is a powerful need to explain why this all-powerful god has created and governs an imperfect world. Even more, the believer must find a plausible explanation for the way in which he is affected by the discrepancy between fate and just deserts, by the unequal distribution of happiness and suffering, and by his own sinfulness and death. All salvation religions have recognized this problem and have reacted to it intellectually with the construction of theodicies.[54]

49. Cf. Turner, *Weber and Islam*, pp. 75ff.; Abramowski (n. 7 above), pp. 85ff.

50. For Weber Confucianism and also Taoism are ultimately value systems that remain completely embedded in a magical world view (cf. *China*, pp. 196ff.).

51. Cf. *ES*, p. 525f.

52. Cf. T. Parsons' introduction to Weber, *The Sociology of Religion*, tr. E. Fischoff (Boston: Beacon Press, 1963), p. xlvii.

53. *ES*, p. 518.   54. Cf. *ES*, pp. 518ff.; "Theory," p. 357.

The rationalization of the magic world view leads to a peculiar dialectic both in the Judeo-Christian and in the Indian tradition in spite of their different foundations and directions. It tears apart the magic unity of event and meaning, produces a tension-ridden dualism, and thus also destroys the "primeval immediacy of man's relation to the world."[55] The world is now partially released from its magic ties, it is partially demagicalized, and it can also be freed for the autonomous rationalization of its realms (*Ordnungen*) according to rules of experience. When this happens, religious metaphysic and ethic are confronted with a problem that propels them further on the road toward intellectual rationalization. Now men, and especially intellectuals, feel an intensified need to find a plausible answer to the metaphysical question: "If the world as a whole and life in particular are to have meaning, what might it be and what must the world be like to correspond to it?"[56] The problem, therefore, is one of conceptualizing the unity on the basis of the dualism embraced by the believer. Finding an answer is more urgent, the more freely the mundane realms are rationalized according to their own laws—that is, the more apparent the discrepancies become between religious postulate and empirical realities. However, the further the disenchantment of the world advances, the more difficult and intellectually demanding it becomes to construe a unity, and the more consistent the solution, the more does it contribute in turn to progressive disenchantment. This peculiar dialectic need not but can lead to a total collision between world and religious postulate. For the more religion devalues the world, the more resistant the world becomes to religious claims and the greater is the compulsion to find a religious compromise and to limit the religious claims institutionally.

Let us look once more at this connection by comparing the Christian and Indian traditions. Intellectually they have reacted differently to the basic problem of dualism. The compulsion to solve the religious problem of meaning through

55. Cf. "Theory," p. 328.   56. *ES*, p. 451.

more and more abstract conceptions, to order the relation of god, man, and world meaningfully, has led to two different but consistent theodicies, apart from many compromise solutions.[57] According to Weber, in India the most consistent theodicy is the doctrine of karma, which has been intimately linked with the doctrine of the migration of souls and with the ritual duties of the caste members, with samsara and dharma. The karma doctrine interprets the dualism *ontologically* as opposition of "the transitory events and actions of the world and the immobile persistence of the eternal order and what is identical with it, the motionless divinity which rests in dreamless sleep."[58] The karma doctrine also interprets the individual's religious fate as exclusive consequence of his personal merit, as a balancing of his good and bad deeds, of which an account is kept from eternity to eternity. In Christianity the most consistent theodicy is the doctrine of predestination. It interprets the dualism *ethically* as opposition of the perfect god and the creaturely, sinful world, and the individual's religious fate as exclusive consequence of divine grace, which ultimately cannot be influenced by good or bad deeds.[59] Once they have been accepted, the two solutions must not only reinforce religiously motivated world rejection, but also lead to different practical consequences. For the karma doctrine motivates the believer not to change the world but to remove himself from it in order to escape from the eternal cycle of rebirth and death.[60] By contrast, the doctrine of predestina-

57. Cf. Parsons, *loc. cit.*; *ES*, p. 506. Among the compromise solutions I count those theodicies which operate with the juxtaposition and opposition of light and darkness, good and evil, and which Weber illustrates under the heading of dualism with the example of Zoroastrianism. In this construction both god and world retain autonomy. Such an auxiliary construction is well suited to ultimately mitigate the antagonistic dualism inherent in the world image of salvation religions. In one of its variants the theodicy of dualism played a reconciling role especially in the Christian tradition. On the interpretation of the theodicy of dualism, see *ES*, p. 524, where Weber points to the relativizing character of dualism: "In practically all the religions with an ethical orientation there are unavowed limitations of divine omnipotence in the form of elements of a dualistic mode of thought."
58. *ES*, p. 526.   59. Cf. *ES*, p. 522.
60. Weber impresses upon the reader the strongly conservative effect of

tion moves the believer to master the world in the name of the
Lord in order to prove worthy of the state of grace which God
has freely granted to the sinful human creature.

Thus, as the "most rational" buttresses of the dualist theocentric world view,[61] the two theodicies reinforce the char-
acteristics to which we have called attention. The karma doctrine transforms the magic world behind the world into the
superordinate divinity of the eternal order of the world,
whereas the doctrine of predestination transforms it into the
transcendence of the eternal god. Hence, at least among the
virtuosi, the two doctrines help to intensify two kinds of practical rationalism: world rejection as world flight, on the one
hand, and world rejection as world mastery, on the other.
With regard to the ethical character of the dualist theocentric
world view, these two kinds of practical rationalism also denote possible strategies of rationalization: one that weakens
the ethical component and one that strengthens it. In its most
consistent aspects the Hinduist construction aims at weakening the ethical character of the dualism. The problem is not

---

this doctrine on the positively and negatively privileged strata. The doctrine
deprives those who are negatively privileged of a motive for collective, soli-
dary action against the caste order. For a person can improve his chance for
rebirth only by fulfilling his caste duty, and these chances are not too bad,
especially for those at the very bottom. Weber remarks: "The *Communist
Manifesto* concludes with the phrase 'they [the proletarians] have nothing to
lose but their chains, they have a world to win.' The same holds for the pious
Hindu of low castes. He too can 'win the world,' even the heavenly world; he
can become a Kshatriya, a Brahman, he can gain Heaven and become a
god—only not in this life, but in the life of the future after rebirth into the
same world pattern. Order and rank of the castes is as eternal (according to
doctrine) as the course of the stars and the difference between animal species
and the human race. To overthrow them would be senseless" (*India*, p. 121f.).
The Brahmins, who are positively privileged, lose any motive for action, for it
involves the soul time and again in the karma causality and endangers the
ultimate goal of salvation—escape from the eternal, senseless cycle of birth
and death. Hinduism fetters both the religious masses and the virtuosi to the
traditionalist social order: it is not a revolutionary religion of salvation.

61. Peter Berger and Thomas Luckmann have provided an informative
survey of the way in which orders of meaning are buttressed by various
devices. See *The Social Construction of Reality* (Garden City: Doubleday, 1966).

man's sinfulness but his mortality.[62] At the same time, the Hinduist construction, like all Asian religions of intellectuals, never abandoned the belief in the inherent "meaningfulness of the empirical world," not least because of the doctrine of compensation, and the belief in the possibility of overcoming the distance to the divine through self-deification.[63] This explains the peculiar mixture of magic, contemplation, and world-fleeing asceticism which constitutes the salvation method of Hinduism. In Weber's eyes the rationalization of salvation was not really connected with a genuine demagicalization of the means of salvation in India or elsewhere. The degree of the systematic unity of the world view and the degree of the disenchantment of the world do not correspond to each other. This is one of the reasons for the fact that in Asia the religions remain a traditionalist power. Hinduism is the ideal theory of legitimation for a status order, and for Confucianism the extant world even appears as the best of all possible worlds, just as it represents the ethic of world affirmation and world adjustment par excellence.[64] By contrast, in its most consistent parts the Christian construction aims at intensifying the ethical character of dualism: not the transitoriness of man but his sinfulness is the problem. This, however, ultimately undermines the belief in the inherent meaningfulness of the empirical world. The foundations of the Christian world view permit even the denial of any inherent value of the world. At the same time this world view suggests the abandonment of magical as well as mystical means in the search for salvation. One cannot coerce a transcendental creator god, and in the face of his omnipotence even self-deification is not a convincing solution. Hence, in the Judeo-

62. Cf. *India*, p. 167. Something similar is true of the early Buddhist construction. Cf. *ES*, p. 627.

63. Cf. *ES*, pp. 553 and 534.

64. Especially in comparison with Puritanism, Confucianism appears as a utilitarian ethic of world accommodation. Cf. *China*, pp. 226ff.; Schluchter, *Aspekte . . .* (n. 4 above), pp. 80ff. For an evaluation of Weber's analysis in the light of the recent results of sinological research, see Arnold Zingerle, *Max Weber und China* (Berlin: Duncker, 1972).

Christian tradition the degree of systematization of the world view and the degree of disenchantment of the world are linked with each other. The intellectual pursuit of salvation increasingly exacerbates the dialectic of disenchantment of the world and of consistent world interpretation. It is true that the Christian tradition, too, has time and again counteracted this tendency by making compromises, but the possibility of the total collision between religious postulate and world has always remained. It is, so to speak, programmed into the rationalization of the world view. This possible collision made Weber early aware of the significance of ascetic Protestantism for cultural history. The history of this collision can be adumbrated by reference to three events: it was conceived with the establishment of the Judaic covenant and with the community of the Eucharist in Antioch, but it was born with the Reformation.[65]

2. ETHICO-RELIGIOUS FORMS OF WORLD MASTERY: CATHOLICISM AND PROTESTANTISM

The religious ethic and rational metaphysic of the Occident are directed toward a rationalism that aims at making an impact on the world, even at dominating it. Components of this tendency can be found very early—in ancient Judaism with its component of a "Puritan religion of Yahwe."[66] There some elements important for the subsequent development of the occidental world image were fused: Yahwe's "transcendence,"[67] his ethical relationship with the Israelite oath-

---

65. Cf. *India*, p. 38; *EH*, pp. 307ff.

66. *AJ*, p. 187; Bendix, *Max Weber* (n. 8 above), pp. 200ff.

67. In Weber's view, Yahwe is, in contrast to most deities of the period of the Exodus, a sky god, who may reside on mountains and in the temple but never on earth or in the underworld. "As far as is known, Yahwe simply has never borne any features of a Chthonian deity" (*AJ*, p. 145f.). In addition, from the very beginning there is the conception of Yahwe's remoteness. It is dangerous, even fatal, to touch or even to see him. This leads to a particular notion of sacredness: God speaks through his prophet to Israel, and when he appears, he observes a distance between himself and his people (cf. *AJ*, p. 124). Moreover, the cult of Yahwe also seems to have been without images (cf. Exodus 19). Thus, Yahwe has in a sense always been the "hidden god."

bound confraternity,[68] his relative universalism,[69] his cult's anti-magical quality in competition with the cult of Baal,[70] and especially the prophets. The latter appear as Yahwe's lonely tools and as his messengers with complete "inner-worldly" autonomy and demand, with unheard-of insistence, unconditional faith in his omnipotence as well as obedience and humility in the face of his commandments.[71] However, the rationalism of world mastery cannot simply be interpreted as an extension of Jewish ethical prophecy. For many centuries its character remained, so to speak, fragmented in the different Judeo-Christian world interpretations. All of the elements

68. "The old tradition neither considered Yahwe to be the original God of Israel, nor the God of Israel alone, nor to reside in Israel" (*AJ*, p. 123). Moses appropriated "a strange and mysterious figure" (p. 124) for the Israelite confederacy for the sake of rescue from political distress (p. 126). Thus, he is foremost a god of war and natural catastrophe, whose tremendous prestige derives from the miracle of the Red Sea (cf. Exodus 15). However, according to Weber, it was very important for the course of cultural history that Yahwe was also an elected god who became the associational god of Israel through a covenant. "This contract had to be concluded, not only among confederates, but also with him, for he was no god residing in the midst of the people, a familiar god, but rather a god hitherto strange. He continued to be a "god from afar" (*AJ*, p. 130). This mutual choice mediated through Moses was a free decision for both partners. The ethical basis of this relationship between god and man could then become the subject of intellectual rationalization (cf. p. 136 and Exodus 19).

69. Yahwe's relative universalism derives from the history of his reception (cf. *AJ*, pp. 133, 135). Consistent universalist monotheism was the consequence of intellectual rationalization—Yahwe became the god of the patriarchs and of the universe.

70. The anti-magical character is also related to the absence of the cult of images. However, Weber explains the lack of images not as "the product of any ancient 'high level' speculations concerning the nature of God. Rather the reverse holds, it was the result of the primitive level of culture" (*AJ*, p. 156). On the competition between Yahwe and Baal, cf. *AJ*, pp. 155ff. and 189ff.

71. The exceptional nature of Jewish prophecy, especially in its pre-Exilic phase, consists in the appearance of the prophets as single individuals, without any ties to a school, a community, or a political group. The Torah remains the basis of their prophecy, and the "chosen people" their public. Thus, they are not founders but renewers of religion, and therein lies their instrumental quality (cf. *AJ*, pp. 297ff.). On the importance of faith, obedience, and humility, cf. *AJ*, pp. 318ff.

which can be distilled from a comparison with certain forms of Hinduism[72]—the transcendental ethical creator god, the instrumental role of man, the predominance of ascetic methods of salvation, the "world" and its orders, especially the economy as religious proving ground and the theodicy of predestination—appeared at first neither in "pure" form nor in this particular combination. Both purity and combination are conceivable as logical developments from the given origin, but they are historically unlikely.[73] It is true that the ideal-typical reconstruction of world images, "rationality in the sense of the logical and teleological consistency of an intellectual-theoretical or practical-ethical position" has always exerted fascination and power over people, especially intellectuals.[74] Wherever the intellectual stratum has a strategically important position in a social formation, the ideal-typical reconstruction of world images has been, as a rule, not only the cognitive basis but the real ground of the historical development.[75] However, the power of intellectualism has always been limited and unstable in relation to other historical forces. This is true first of all for its relationship to everyday consciousness, whose tendency toward typification, relativization, and opportunistic conformity with values is diametrically opposed to intellectualism.[76]

72. We must keep in mind that Weber uses the ideal typical approach for multi-dimensional contrasts and that he can thus mitigate the exaggerations which result from dichotomous comparisons. See, for instance, the way in which he compares the most important carriers of the great religious ideas, the Brahmins, Mandarins, Puritans, Levites, and less systematically, the Hellenist intellectuals (cf. *China,* pp. 226ff.; *India,* pp. 139ff., *AJ,* pp. 171ff.).

73. Cf. Mühlmann, *op. cit.* (n. 28 above), p. 13.

74. Cf. "Theory," p. 324; *ES,* pp. 500ff.

75. The ideal-typical approach seems to be particularly well suited for the reconstruction of ideas, since in this case the heuristic means has a basis in fact *(fundamentum in re).* This has been the basis for a phenomenological interpretation of Weber. See Mühlmann, *op. cit.,* and J. Weiss, *op. cit.* (n. 8 above).

76. Cf. Niklas Luhmann, *Zweckbegriff und Systemrationalität* (Frankfurt: Suhrkamp, 1973), pp. 33ff.

One aspect of this connection can be used as a key to Weber's analysis of the Reformation. On the level of world imagery Weber views the Reformation not least from the viewpoint of the relationship between relativization and consistency. This does not mean that he wants to deduce the Reformation solely from processes of intellectual rationalization. For him this is just as impermissible as the opposite claim—that the Reformation is solely a consequence of economic transformations. However, the significance of the Reformation, some of its causes, and especially its consequences can be fully understood only if we take into account the issues posed by the dualist theocentric world image for Judeo-Christian tradition. The Reformation not only made these problems highly visible, it radicalized them with a consistency almost never encountered before. Medieval Catholicism succeeded at first in defusing the tensions between religious postulate and "world" inherent in this world image and, so to speak, in arresting its dialectic. Lutheranism and especially Calvinism revolted against this "traditionalist" solution. They set the dialectic in motion again and thus increased the tensions. Thus, it is possible to view medieval Catholicism, Lutheranism, and Calvinism as following a kind of developmental logic which reveals not the actual causal chain but the distinctiveness particularly of the Calvinist construction of the world.

Thus, Weber interprets medieval Catholicism primarily in terms of its success in relativizing the tension and dialectic inherent in its world view. He is interested in the reasons that made this belief system ethically not only undemanding but an outright relief for the masses of salvation seekers. One reason is the idea of divinity, the fact "that the Christian trinity, with its incarnate savior and its saints, is less of a transcendental conception than the God of Judaism, especially of late Judaism, or the Allah of Islam."[77] However, not only the attenuation of the transcendental conception of god but also salvational syncretism has a relativizing effect. In

77. Cf. "Theory," p. 325.

spite of the higher prestige of asceticism, medieval Catholicism permits a juxtaposition of ascetic and contemplative-
mystic search for salvation. In addition, there is the institutional separation of monastic and mass ethic. It is true that in
contrast to the Asian religions the linkage between elite and
mass religiosity is preserved by the unity of the church. But
the "religiously most highly qualified individuals" leave the
world and retreat into special religious communities.[78] Yet
this is not all: The predominant interpretation of salvation in
medieval Catholicism is ethically mitigating because salvation
is a combination of institutional grace and account-current
bookkeeping. The ecclesiastical universalism of grace, according to which grace is granted, as it were, *ex opere operato* to all
adherents irrespective of the individual's qualification, lessens
the need "to gain *certitudo salutis* through one's own efforts."[79]
Even where this demand is made in medieval Catholicism, it is
linked with the notion of compensating sins through good
works and is thus deflected from an ethically methodical conduct of life.[80] This helps the religiously less qualified find
inner release and favors a type of person who is directed from
without rather than from within.[81] This tendency is reinforced by the impact of the confessional. For in a religion
which, in spite of all these counter-currents, claims to be a
Gesinnungsreligion, the confession is "the means for the
periodic 'abreaction' of an affect-laden sense of guilt."[82] Thus,
in Weber's eyes, medieval Catholicism is split into the virtuosi's
religiosity, with its ethical demands, and mass religiosity,
which offers ethical relief and leads to inner-worldly accommodation. Official Catholic doctrine recognizes the "ideal of
the systematic sanctification of total conduct,"[83] but this ideal
has no effect at least with regard to everyday ethics: "The
normal medieval Catholic layman lived ethically, so to speak,
from hand to mouth."[84]

The compromise character of medieval Catholicism was
undermined by the Reformation and its consequences on the
level of the world image. Interpretations less inclined toward

78. Cf. *EH*, p. 310f.   79. *ES*, p. 561.   80. Cf. *ES*, p. 532.
81. Cf. *ES*, p. 562.   82. *PE*, p. 106.   83. *PE*, p. 234.
84. *PE*, p. 116.

compromise had existed before, but the church contained them through the institutionalization of a special ethic for the orders and monasticism. Now these interpretations achieved a breakthrough and released an anti-traditionalist potential, which first affected the religious realm but later transcended it. It is true that this religious innovation, too, was ultimately subject to the dialectic, described by Weber in various contexts, between the extraordinary and its decline or its routinization (*Ausseralltäglichkeit und Veralltäglichung*).[85] But this antitraditionalism permanently changed the religious basis by eliminating the double ethic[86] and applying the idea of particularist grace to the religious layperson. Through this combination the church's monopoly over the Judeo-Christian tradition was shattered. The sect emerged next to the church. If the church is an institution (*Anstalt*) of grace, "which administers salvation like an entailed estate and makes membership obligatory (in theory) and hence the member's qualification irrelevant," the sect is "a voluntarist association of those who (in theory) are exclusively qualified and join voluntarily, as long as they are accepted by virtue of their proven religious qualification."[87] Thus, for the layperson, too, religious status results, in principle, from achievement. From now on, free will and recognized performance rather than ascription could become decisive for religious membership.[88]

This switch from ascription to achievement was prepared by the development of world imagery during the Reformation, but there was no direct relationship.[89] This development

85. This dialectic is basic to Weber's sociology of domination. The perspective is connected with the idea of a change between the opening and closure of social relationships through which the social order is dissolved and reconstructed. Constans Seyfarth has criticized Weber for treating dissolution and reconstruction in *The Protestant Ethic* as one process and has argued that the two processes must be kept apart for the sake of structural and genetic terms by recourse to the theory of Calvinist single-mindedness (*Vereinseitigungstheorie*) and the theory of institutionalization.

86. Cf. *EH*, p. 312.

87. Cf. Weber, "The Protestant Sects and the Spirit of Capitalism," *From Max Weber*, p. 305f.

88. *Ibid.*, p. 320f.

89. There is not even a one-to-one correspondence between the univer-

can be understood as a radicalization, even a totally one-sided interpretation, of dualist theocentrism along the lines of the religious virtuoso's total rejection of the world. The first step in this direction was taken by Lutheranism. Four components, in particular, deserve attention in comparison with Catholicism: (1) The double god in the form of the "revealed benign and kind father" of the New Testament and of the *deus absconditus*, the "arbitrary despot" of the Old Testament,[90] makes possible once more an orientation toward the idea of the hidden god. (2) The interpretation of salvation is shifted from merit to grace in connection with God's "secret resolution" as the source of grace, and the sanctification of life through work (*Werkheiligkeit*) in the service of divine will.[91] (3) The monastic road to salvation through ascesis is generalized to all believers.[92] (4) Generalized monastic salvation is joined with inner-worldly vocation.[93] In this way Lutheranism exacerbates not only the tension between religious postulate and "world" but imparts to world rejection, as it were, an inner-worldly turn. In clear contrast to Catholicism, Lutheranism's achievement consists primarily in "powerfully augmenting the moral value and the religious premium for inner-worldly, vocationally organized labor."[94] Nevertheless, Lutheranism, especially in its late phase, goes only half way. It is inconsistent and prone to compromise.[95] In the end, Lutheranism not only gives unambiguous precedence to the god

---

salism of grace and the church, on the one hand, and the particularism of grace and the sect, on the other. Calvinism rejected the idea of institutional grace but did not abandon the church as an organization.

90. *PE*, p. 221. Weber seems to explain the innovative potential of the Reformation and its consequences not least in terms of the restoration of the Judaic component in the Judeo-Christian tradition.

91. Cf. *PE*, p. 101f.

92. The generalization of monastic ascesis through the Reformation is illustrated by Sebastian Franck's remark: "You may believe that you have escaped from the cloister, but now everybody must be a monk all his life" (*EH*, p. 312; cf. *PE*, p. 121).

93. Cf. *PE*, p. 79ff.   94. Cf. *PE*, p. 83.

95. Weber distinguishes between Luther the author of "The Freedom of a Christian" and Luther the politically realistic churchman. Representative for the late Lutheran period are for him Praetorius, Nicolai, and Meisner (cf. *PE*, p. 229).

of the New Testament,[96] but also abandons a rigorous interpretation of the doctrine of predestination and of the ascetic path to salvation in its inner-worldly form. Grace can be lost and thus must be regained time and again through "penitential humility and trusting belief in God's word and the sacraments."[97] The notion of vocation remains tied to a traditionalist interpretation. Even more, in the late Lutheran period piety takes on again mystical features. This leads not to a quietist world flight of Pascal's kind but to an inner-directed religiosity of sentiment (*Stimmungsreligiosität*).[98] Only Calvinism and several sects[99] went all the way, without compromise, toward the one-sided articulation of dualist theocentrism. They accomplished this primarily by giving primacy to the god of the Old Testament, by radicalizing the doctrine of election through the theodicy of predestinarian determinism, and by the subsequent "degradation" of man into an exclusive tool of God. Not for his own sake but for the sake of God's majesty must man control himself and the creatural world through pursuing a vocation ascetically.[100] In addition, there is the notion of the gulf, unbridgeable for all time, between God and man. There is no *unio mystica*. In fact, ultimately every religious cultivation of sentiment (*Gefühlskultur*) is abhorred. Even more, the idea of institutional grace as a compensatory means, which Lutheranism retained at least in the form of sacramental grace, is completely abandoned. Man's salvational status cannot be changed by any sacrament, not to mention any preacher or church, and not even by

96. Cf. *PE*, p. 221.   97. Cf. *PE*, p. 102.
98. Cf. *PE*, pp. 81, 85, 112ff. Weber explicitly links the differences between the Lutheran religiosity of sentiment and the Calvinist religiosity of action with the contrast between vessel and mysticism, on the one hand, and tool and asceticism, on the other. However, this passage seems to be a later addition (cf. Arthur Mitzman, *The Iron Cage*, New York: Knopf, 1970, p. 195).
99. Apart from seventeenth-century Calvinism, Weber's "Protestant Ethic" deals with Pietism, Methodism, and the Baptist sects, partly with a view toward their relativizing of the Calvinist world view. This is particularly true of Pietism and Methodism, whereas the Baptist movement does not accept the theodicy of predestination and is an independent agent of Protestant asceticism.
100. Cf. *ES*, p. 556.

Christ himself. Man is saved or damned from eternity on the basis of God's unfathomable resolution. For Weber the Calvinist destruction of all intermediary agencies between God and man is historically decisive: "The rejection of all ecclesiastic-sacramental salvation, which Lutheranism by no means carried through to its conclusion, was the absolutely decisive difference from Catholicism. The great historical process of the disenchantment of the world, which began with the ancient Jewish prophets and, in conjunction with Hellenic scientific thinking, condemned all magical means of salvation as superstition and blasphemy, was here completed."[101]

The idea that all of God's creatures are separated from him by an unbridgeable gulf leads not only to the demagicalization of the relation between God and man but also to that between man and "world." The religious postulate erodes not only the religious but also the worldly cultivation of affectivity (*Gefühlskultur*). For the relations of the believer to the world are threatened primarily by one danger—the idolatry of the flesh. This danger can be avoided only by attaining an attitude of matter-of-factness and distance vis-à-vis the world. Religious isolation is paralleled by worldly isolation. Herein Weber perceives the "root of that pessimistically colored individualism free from all illusions as it still plays a role today in the national character and the institutions of peoples with a Puritan past."[102] This individualism is the harbinger of the "world dominion of unbrotherliness."[103]

The consistent Calvinist world view was bound to lead not

101. Cf. *PE*, p. 105.

102. Cf. *PE*, p. 105. Note also the following formulation: "Love of neighbor is practiced primarily by fulfilling the vocational tasks imposed by the *lex naturae*, since it must serve God's glory, not one's fellow man. Thus love of neighbor takes on a peculiarly impersonal character, serving the rational reconstruction of the social cosmos" (cf. p. 108f.). On these connections, see also the illuminating remarks by Abramowski, *op. cit.* (n. 7 above), pp. 34ff.

103. "Theory," p. 357. Weber perceives this pessimistic individualism and its image of man in contrast to the Enlightenment and also to more recent Catholic doctrine. However, there is a common denominator for this pessimistic individualism and the Enlightenment: Descartes' *cogito ergo sum* (cf. *PE*, p. 118).

only to the idea of an insuperable particularism of grace but also to the idea of its total uncertainty. Once God's absolute demand for submission is combined with the idea that one's fate is absolutely unchangeable and unforeseeable, an uncertainty arises which is intolerable even for the religious virtuoso. Weber remarks quite appropriately that Calvinism should logically have led to fatalism.[104] The fact that this did not happen points not only to the influence exerted by the believers' interests on the interpretation of their faith but also to a compromise that even Calvinism makes in at least one respect—it adjusts itself to the believer's need for certainty. Calvinist popular theology and pastoral care made this compromise by reinterpreting the notion of proving oneself.[105] A person's works constitute not the real but the cognitive grounds of his fate. Works are "technical means, not of purchasing salvation, but of getting rid of the fear of damnation."[106] One consequence of this auxiliary construction is that the believer continues to be under the religious compulsion to practice "a system of intensified good works," to exert "rational, methodical control over his total conduct," and to perfect "the ethical integration of his personality."[107] But the auxiliary construction also attenuates the inhuman features of this religious demand for submission and frees the individual from unbearable suffering. Moreover, it opens the gate to further reinterpretations of the Calvinist world view. The construction makes it feasible to transform the cognitive grounds into the real ones, and historically this indeed came to pass. It is well known that Weber deduced the elective affinity between the Protestant ethic and the spirit of capitalism from these two contexts, the consistency of the Calvinist world view as well as the compromise character of Calvinist praxis. He added to it a theory of the way in which the

104. Cf. *PE*, p. 232.
105. Weber mentions in particular Baxter's *Christian Directory*. No matter how suggestive Weber's reasoning is, his thesis is, of course, in the final analysis unproven and unprovable, at least on the basis of the sources cited by him.
106. *PE*, p. 115.   107. *ES*, p. 534.

idea of vocation and specialization was realized as one historical expression of human nature.[108] However, for Weber
ascetic Protestantism is only one of the formative elements
that shaped modern culture, and it is not the only basis of its
justification.[109] Other formative elements came to the fore
with the very development of the capitalist spirit and the
capitalist economic system—for instance, utilitarianism, one
product of the dissolution of religiously motivated inner-
worldly ascesis.[110] Nevertheless, the Protestant ethic in its
Calvinist form remains important to our understanding of
the origin and character of the occidental ethos. In its radical
world rejection, which expresses itself as radical world domination, it reveals preconditions and consequences of a type of
rationalism which is part of the ideational underpinnings of
modern society.

Three elements of the Calvinist world construct should be
once more emphasized: (1) The interpretation of the "world"
as a merely creaturely, religiously worthless cosmos of things
and events to which the heterogeneity of natural and ethical
causality applies; (2) the idea of this "world" as object of
fulfillment of duty through rational control; and (3) the compulsion to develop an ethically integrated personality, a compulsion that also demands an ethical commitment (*Gesinnung*). The Calvinist world view fuses all three elements into
one unified attitude: In the name of God you must control
yourself and dominate the "world" through your vocation.
However, once acted upon, this religious postulate is self-
defeating, for the religiously devalued "world" forces those
who would control it to recognize its own laws; and the more
this happens, the more independent (*versachlicht*) the "world"
becomes. This means not only that it continues to be valueless
before the religious postulate, but also that it becomes im-

108. Cf. *PE*, p. 180. Weber remarks that this means the "abandonment of
the Faustian universalism of human nature" (p. 181).
109. Weber (*PE*, p. 182f.) sketched a research program for a more comprehensive explanation of the origin and development of modern occidental
culture.
110. Cf. *PE*, p. 176f.

mune to it. At first the religious postulate devalues the "world"; now a reversal occurs. As both realms consistently rationalize themselves according to their own laws, their mutual alienation becomes obvious.[111] Witness the very capitalist ethos which for Weber was the most prominent product of a religiously buttressed, systematized inner-worldly ascesis. It fused with the capitalist economic system into an impersonal cosmos in which "the religious ethic is confronted with a world of interpersonal relations that cannot conform to its ancient norms."[112] As this paradox unfolds, not only the Calvinist world view but also the ethico-religious world view—dualist theocentrism in general—must lose plausibility. This does not mean that religion gives up its claims, but it is more and more likely that it must compete with non-religious interpretations. It is true that the ethico-religious world view continues to make itself felt in its secularized guise, for instance in the form of the three Calvinist elements which have become an integral component of the modern vocational system. But the meaning of the disenchanted world cannot be reduced to its origin: it must be able to formulate its own laws, and this requires not only a transformation (*Umsetzung*) but also a replacement (*Umbesetzung*).[113] The disenchanted world must take into account not

111. Cf. "Theory," p. 357.   112. *ES*, p. 585.

113. The question of whether secularization is an appropriate category for the description of socio-cultural developments is highly controversial in the literature. Weber used the term in several passages referring to cultural contents and institutions. One example is his study of the American sects, in which he explained the character of the American voluntary associations in polity and economy in part by recourse to the fact that at least in New England the sectarian congregation had been the first form of association ("The Protestant Sects," pp. 309ff.). There can be no doubt that Weber intended to use "secularization" neutrally as a sociological process category (cf. H. Lübbe, *Säkularisierung*, Freiburg: Albert, 1965, pp. 59ff., 68ff.). For him it could not be the dominant category for characterizing modern occidental culture. In my view this is apparent from his methodological position, which proceeds from the disjunction of genesis and validity. By contrast, Karl Loewith clearly used the theory of secularization for determining the intellectual situation of the modern world: "The modern world is equally Christian and non-Christian, since it is the result of a centuries-old secularization

only transcendental but especially immanent expectations, not only interests in salvation but, above all, interest in worldly success.[114] Thus it is likely that certain "items in the household of cognitive human needs" become obsolescent and new ones emerge.[115] This replacement does not mean that we can do without giving meaning to the world. For the disenchanted, impersonalized, rationalized "world," too, continues to pose a problem of meaning. The mind has a persistent metaphysical need to comprehend the "world" and to develop a unified attitude toward it. The disenchanted world,

---

process" (*Weltgeschichte und Heilsgeschehen*, Stuttgart: Kohlhammer, 1953, p. 183). Loewith's important interpretations of Weber derive not least from his view of Weber as diagnostician of a world that has lost God (cf. also Loewith, "Die Entzauberung der Welt durch Wissenschaft," *Merkur*, 18 (1964): 501ff.). There are some good reasons for taking this perspective, but it also reinforces the tendency to view Weber's reaction to his diagnosis as an "objectively unsupportable ideal of individual autonomy," an interpretation which permits at the least some qualification, as my further analysis will try to show. On this score, see also Lübbe, *op. cit.*, p. 71f., and "Die Freiheit der Theorie," *Archiv für Rechts-u. Sozialphilosophie*, 58 (1962): 343ff. For a critique of the various uses of "secularization" see, besides Lübbe, especially H. Blumenberg, *Säkularisierung und Selbstbehauptung* (Frankfurt: Suhrkamp, 1974). Blumenberg argues that "secularization" can explain historical events only if the common features, for instance of the systems of world interpretation, are seen not in the contents but in the functions: "What has happened in the historical process interpreted as secularization cannot be described, except in a few recognizable cases, as a transformation of authentic theological contents into their secular self-alienation, but only as the replacement of vacated answers by questions that continue to be asked" (p. 77). Only if we look at Weber's analyses of world constructs and their development with the double perspective of transformation and replacement can we elucidate his ambivalent attitude toward progress and decline vis-à-vis the problems of modern culture, an attitude decisive for his substantive analyses (cf. my *Aspekte* (n. 4 above), pp. 301ff.). Only then can we also relativize the charge of decisionism which still dominates the German Weber debate.

114. On the problem of the way in which ideas and interests change their primacy in relation to one another, see also Luhmann (1972) and especially Seyfarth (1973). Niklas Luhmann, "Religiöse Dogmatik und gesellschaftliche Evolution," in K. W. Dahm et al., *Religion–System–Sozialisation* (Neuwied: Luchterhand, 1972), and especially C. Seyfarth, "Protestantismus" (n. 7 above), pp. 358ff.

115. Blumenberg, *op. cit.*, p. 76f.

too, needs a world construct. Weber analyzed this situation especially in regard to the relation between religion and science. At the same time he discussed the meaning of the rationalism of world control under the conditions of established modern occidental culture.

3. THE DIALECTICAL DEVELOPMENT OF THE RATIONALISM OF WORLD MASTERY: RELIGION AND SCIENCE

In the monistic magical world view there seems to be much overlap between empirical knowledge and world interpretation, between magic science and magic ethics. Whatever happens in the world does not merely happen, it also has a definite meaning.[116] This near-identity between cognition and interpretation becomes problematical with the transition to the dualist theocentric world view. Now cognition and interpretation can separate in the name of the autonomy of the value spheres, and thus the relations between scientific rationalism and ethico-religious rationalism can become tense. Yet the autonomous development of scientific rationalism still encounters severe limitations. Basically, empirical knowledge and know-how remain wedded to religious premises, but these can vary considerably depending, among other reasons, on the social situation of intellectualism. Its character is influenced by whether it addresses problems of internal need or external want, whether it is supported by monks, priests, or laymen, whether these come from positively or negatively privileged strata, and whether it is politically disenfranchised or must face the competition of ethical prophets.[117] This also affects the degree of tension between the two kinds of rationalism. Thus, the social situation of intellectualism is not

116. Cf. *ES*, p. 506. At least in his treatment of Confucianism and Taoism, Weber appears to define magic science in terms of the absence of all knowledge in the realm of natural science (cf. *China*, p. 227). Weber himself employs the term "magic ethics," which is easily open to misinterpretation (cf. *ES*, p. 437).

117. Cf. *ES*, pp. 500ff.

without consequences for the disenchantment of the world. Where the tension between ethico-religious and scientific rationalism is great, empirical knowledge and know-how have a disenchanting potential of their own.[118]

This can be illustrated once more by a comparison between the Asian and the occidental developments, for in Asia this tension appears to be less important than in the Occident. The Asian religious doctrines are the creations of lay intellectuals from socially privileged strata, who are kept depoliticized and demilitarized by the patrimonial state "with its bureaucratic and military unity,"[119] and these intellectuals are not exposed to competition from ethical prophecy. The knowledge accumulated by them is primarily reflective, not productive,[120] and its relation to the world is that of the "world-ordering magician."[121] By contrast, the occidental religious doctrines are more frequently products of the perennial competition among prophets, priests, monks, and lay intellectuals, who are recruited not only from privileged ranks but also from petty-bourgeois and even quasi-proletarian strata. The knowledge gathered by them is not only reflective

118. It appears to me worthwhile to mention this, since Weber tends to explain disenchantment in terms of the paradox of consequences in relation to intention—a perspective that plays a central role in his sociology. However, disenchantment can also be promoted directly by scientific rationalism and political action, its most important agents.

119. *ES*, p. 503.

120. On this distinction, see Jürgen Habermas, "Technology and Science as Ideology," *Toward a Rational Society,* tr. J. J. Shapiro (Boston: Beacon Press, 1970), pp. 81ff. Of course, the distinction is not literally applicable here. Weber indirectly describes the type of knowledge pursued by the Indian intellectuals: "The great Indian doctrinal systems represented rational conceptions of proud and, in their own ways, consistent thinkers. The mystic nature of salvation, which affected their teachings so strongly, resulted from the internal situation of a stratum of intellectuals who as thinkers face life and ponder its meaning but do not share its practical tasks as doers" (*India*, p. 177). In another context he observes that an intellectualism of this kind tends toward illuminatory mysticism, which denigrates "the natural, corporeal and sensual" (*ES*, p. 505). Such an intellectualism cannot produce scientific rationalism.

121. *ES*, p. 512.

but also productive, and thus can serve practical concerns in the world.[122] However the difference may be weighted, it is true that in the Occident, too, the interest in empirical rationalization—in the autonomy of scientific rationalism—remained tied for a long time to dualist theocentrism. An autonomous development becomes possible only after a successful "secession"; only then can "rational empirical knowledge [accomplish] with full consistency the disenchantment of the world and its transformation into a causal mechanism."[123] However, Weber does not seem to have considered ascetic Protestantism the major promoter of this development, contrary to its role in the economic realm.[124] But we may assume that he would have analyzed this development in structural

122. Weber did not draw this conclusion in quite the same way, but his theory refers to the greater affinity to praxis and hence to the greater conflict potential of the Judeo-Christian salvation religion—his theory that Judaism was a religion of migrant traders, Christianity of itinerant journeymen, Hinduism of world-ordering magicians, and Buddhism of mendicant monks "passing through the world" (cf. *ES*, p. 512).

123. "Theory," p. 350.

124. Cf. *EH*, p. 270: "Almost all the great scientific discoveries of the 16th and even the beginning of the 17th century were made against the background of Catholicism. Copernicus was a Catholic, while Luther and Melanchthon repudiated his discoveries. Scientific progress and Protestantism must not be unquestioningly taken as identical. The Catholic church has indeed occasionally obstructed scientific progress; but the ascetic sects of Protestantism have also been disposed to have nothing to do with science, except in a situation where material requirements of everyday life were involved. On the other hand it is Protestantism's specific contribution to have placed science in the service of technology and economics." My cautious formulation takes into account that this text is based on the lecture notes of students. However, at the end of *The Protestant Ethic*, in his suggestions for further research, Weber pointed to the task of establishing the relation of ascetic Protestantism to humanist rationalism and to the rise of philosophical and scientific empiricism. Arguing against Brentano, he declared that he had never doubted the independent importance of humanist rationalism for our understanding of the genesis and development of modern culture (*PE*, p. 283). Following up Weber, Robert Merton later studied the development of science (see reissue of 1938: *Science, Technology, and Society in 17th-Century England*, New York: Fertig, 1970). See also H. Blumenberg, *Die kopernikanische Wende* (Frankfurt: Suhrkamp, 1965).

analogy to his thesis on Protestantism—as the perhaps unintended consequence of a certain solution to the problem of "psychic distress."[125] Just as in the economic realm, so in science too the rationalism of world mastery is based on "irrational" presuppositions. Only these presuppositions make possible the faith in the autonomous value of cumulative knowledge. Yet this faith does not only show an elective affinity with faith in capital accumulation, it must also turn into an opponent of the belief in God. For faith in science not only justifies the autonomy of the "world" vis-à-vis the religious postulate, but also renders possible discoveries which run counter to its content—"that the world has been ordered by God and hence must somehow be an ethically meaningful cosmos." Even more, faith in science tends to usurp the exclusive claims of faith in religion. Thus, under the conditions of a presupposed autonomy of the world, religion becomes for rational thought "*the* irrational or anti-rational superhuman power."[126] Hence, "liberated" and unfettered scientific rationalism is alien to God.[127] It forces religion to retreat into the "unassailable incommunicability of mystical experience"[128] and at the same time to concede that it can assert itself only against, not with, rational thinking. It is no accident that in the disenchanted world "liberation" from scientific rationalism becomes the "precondition of living in union with the divine."[129] After all, religion demands from every believer, in the final instance, the sacrifice of the intellect.[130]

However, in this manner religion expresses not only the resentment of the most recent loser. It bases its claims also on the psychic distress into which scientific rationalism has

---

125. Cf. especially Tenbruck, who emphasizes this viewpoint in his Weberian proposal for a sociology of science, while maintaining a critical distance from Merton. Tenbruck believes that for Weber there was a continuity between the Protestant ethic and science as a vocation. See F. H. Tenbruck, "Max Weber and the Sociology of Science: A Case Reopened," *Zeitschrift für Soziologie*, 3 (1974): 315, 320.

126. "Theory," p. 351.   127. Cf. "Science," p. 142.
128. "Theory," p. 353.   129. "Science," p. 142.
130. Cf. "Science," p. 154; "Theory," p. 352; *ES*, p. 567.

plunged the world. For scientific rationalism has established a "world domination of unbrotherliness" in alliance with other components of modern culture, and it must insist on self-sufficiency, which continuously threatens to founder because of the need to escape from its very autonomy. In spite of its exclusive claims, scientific rationalism is ultimately capable only of a partial synthesis. It can only promote the striving for inner-worldly cultivation, the "unbrotherly aristocracy of those who have acquired rational culture," a condition made ultimately meaningless by the inescapability of death, if for no other reason.[131] Thus, the religious postulate remains an irritant to an intellect that must rely on its own self-sufficiency without really being capable of it. The postulate responds to man's longing for an acosmistic brotherliness in an impersonal and unbrotherly world.[132]

Thus, in this relationship between religion and science we encounter the conflict among autonomous value spheres as it is generally found in the context of the disenchantment of the world.[133] However, Weber's analysis goes beyond this point.

131. Cf. "Theory," p. 357f.

132. Weber frequently uses this notion of acosmistic brotherliness in contrast to the objectified and ethically indifferent cosmos of the social and natural relations. Cf. Mitzman, *The Iron Cage* (n. 98 above), p. 197, who calls attention to the opposition of acosmic and cosmic and links the former notion to mystic love.

133. This formulation is imprecise insofar as for Weber this conflict among the value spheres exists in the "enchanted world" as well. However, kind and degree of this conflict differ if we compare the phase of theocentrism and of anthropocentrism in ideal-typical exaggeration. This can be illustrated with the examples of religion, politics, and economics, the spheres to which Weber pays particular attention. Under dualist theocentrism religion claims primacy, especially in relation to economics. The degree of disenchantment is low and thus the autonomy of the spheres is very limited. But the relationship of religion and politics is problematical. Here compromises must be found on the ideological and the institutional level. The prototype of the ideological compromise is the organicist theory, to which the (feudal) separation of powers between political and hierocratic rulership corresponds on the institutional level. If no compromise is found and one side prevails, caesaropapism or theocracy arises. Under dualist anthropocentrism religion has lost its primacy. The degree of disenchantment is high and thus all spheres have at-

For this conflict is also indicative of the tension "which results from the inevitable disparity of the ultimate formulations" of the religious and the purely intellectualist world view.[134] It is true that this disparity also exists under dualist theocentrism, but there it remains relative because of religion's primacy. After dualist theocentrism radicalized itself through ascetic Protestantism and thus legitimated the rationalism of world mastery, pure intellectualism was then free to make its own world view absolute. It became the proponent of the world view diametrically opposed to that of religion. Ascetic Protestantism had championed the rationalism of world mastery "in the name of God"; scientific rationalism now propagated it "in the name of man." Anthropocentrism takes the place of theocentrism, anthropodicy that of theodicy.[135]

At this point the construction of the world views seems to relapse into monism. Just as in the magical world view, phenomena in the world are again meaningful, but their control by and for man rests no longer on magical but on empirical manipulation.[136] The conflict between religion and science can now be explained in familiar terms: the opposition of monism and dualism manifests itself in the transition from salvation religion to rational science just as it had in the transition from magic to salvation religion. But for Weber the matter is more complex than that. Science which interprets itself monistically is not the antithesis of religion—it is itself a religion.[137] It not only proceeds from the conviction that scien-

---

tained autonomy. Now every sphere can advance its claims to primacy. This is especially true of economics. However, its claim never goes unchallenged. There is a continuous struggle among utility, charity, power, truth, and beauty. The relation of economics and politics is particularly problematical. Here too we have a prototypical compromise: the doctrine of pluralism and the modern separation of powers. But one side may prevail in the form of charismatic domination or bureaucracy or technocracy.

134. "Theory," p. 352.

135. Cf. Blumenberg, *Säkularisierung* (n. 113 above), p. 165.

136. Bellah, too, refers to the new monism and distinguishes it from the old (cf. "Religious Evolution" (n. 13 above), pp. 294ff.). The following remarks are meant to make this distinction more precise.

137. This is the background for Weber's polemics against monocausal

tific rationality in the disenchanted world is the "only possible form of rational world interpretation,"[138] but also presupposes that it can decipher the objective meaning of the world. On this score science as religion follows the Christian path—it continues working on the Great Illusion.[139] It contributes to the obfuscation of the tremendously difficult problems of living in the disenchanted world. The vocation of science as religion is mystification, not enlightenment.[140]

But if rational science cannot give meaning to the world, must we fall back in the end on salvation religion? Is the theocentric dualist world view the appropriate framework for understanding even the disenchanted world? Do the mystical search for salvation or the sacraments of the Christian churches provide not only acosmistic brotherliness and certainty of other-worldly salvation but also an ethical style of life adequate to the disenchanted world?[141] Weber was aware, of course, that even under the conditions of established modern occidental rationalism both religious and magical attitudes

---

theories and models of linear evolution. All these approaches transform science into theology and critique into revelation. In Hans Albert's terms, the theory of cognition based on revelation can be described in this way: acceptance of the principle of adequate justification by means of identifying a source of knowledge, striving for absolute certainty, exegetic attitude, claim of infallibility, and interpretive monopoly (cf. Albert, *Traktat über kritische Vernunft.* Tübingen: Mohr, 1969, pp. 15ff.). In Albert's eyes Weber himself remains partially tied to the classic model of rationality, but I think that this limitation applies, if at all, to his ethic rather than his methodology (cf. *ibid.,* pp. 68ff.).

138. Cf. "Theory," p. 355.

139. Cf. "Science," pp. 142f., 147f. The Great Illusion consists in nourishing the belief that "polytheism" can be overcome. For the last time this illusion was attained by ascetic Protestantism.

140. Here is one of the reasons for Weber's polemical remarks about the modern intellectuals, especially the literati, who chase after mystical experience and tend to take a feeble relativist stance. At the same time the "almost superstitious veneration of science as the possible creator or at least prophet of social revolution, violent or peaceful," inevitably leads to disappointments (*ES,* p. 515). See also Karl Popper's *The Poverty of Historicism* (London: Routledge and Kegan Paul, 1960, 2nd ed.).

141. Cf. "Science," p. 154f.; "Theory," p. 357.

persist.[142] In contrast to the magical attitude, he paid his personal respects to the religious attitude.[143] But it is obvious that for him salvation religion was at most the second-best solution in "a time without god and prophet." Salvation religion can diagnose the central problems of meaning of this time, but it does not react in an "up-to-date" manner,[144] for it flees either into the past or into the future. In both respects salvation religion does not have the same contemporary fit, so to speak, as disenchantment.[145] Not least because of the Reformation, two developments are irreversible on the level of world views: first, the change of a religious ethic of submission into a non-religious ethic of personal autonomy and personal authenticity, and second, the transformation of salvation interests in the direction of success.[146] The tension between divine will and worldly order has been transformed into the tension between human will and social order, and the primacy of transcendence has been replaced by that of this world.[147] The world view that has an elective affinity to modern society remains dualist, but it has lost its transcendental moorings—it is a world view of immanence. It is dualist because non-religious modern man, too, is confronted with the irreconcilable opposition between the "cosmos of natural causality" and the "postulated cosmos of the causality of ethical compensation";[148] it is immanent because the cosmos of ethical causality—the central values controlling and directing man—must be created and justified by man himself.

Thus, for Weber neither rational science elevated to an inclusive world view nor salvation religion provides meaning adequate to the conditions of disenchantment. The one sets

142. Cf. *China,* p. 226f.

143. Cf. "Science," p. 155; *Max Weber: Werk und Person,* ed. Eduard Baumgarten (Tübingen: Mohr, 1964), p. 670.

144. Cf. "Science," p. 153.

145. See the end of "Science as a Vocation" with its conclusion that "yearning and tarrying" won't do, that we must meet "the demands of the day" (p. 156).

146. Cf. Seyfarth, "Protestantismus" (n. 7 above), pp. 360ff.; Weiss, *op. cit.* (n. 8 above).

147. Cf. *PE,* pp. 181ff.   148. Cf. "Theory," p. 355.

technological ideals as absolutes and leads to adjustment; the other makes religious submission absolute and leads to world flight.[149] Neither a dualist theocentrism nor a monistic anthropocentrism can help us. What is needed is a dualist anthropocentrism for which self-control and world mastery are recognizable as ethical problems and moral tasks. The dualist tension cannot be resolved in one or the other direction. Rather, life must be accepted in the tension between ought and is, good intention (*Gesinnung*) and outcome, world rejection and recognition of the autonomy of the disenchanted world.

Has Weber outlined the ethical life-style adequate for a disenchanted world? Yes, if we are ready to argue in his own terms against him. And this can be done by recourse to his contrast between the ethic of conviction and the ethic of responsibility.[150] With these terms Weber described two alternatives, apart from the world views of magic, salvation religion, and "science as ideology" and the attitudes adequate to them. The two ethics are variants of the immanent world view and can therefore be examined, just like "science as an ideology," in terms of their ability to accomplish conscious world mastery under the conditions of the disenchanted world.[151] Even

149. Cf. my *Aspekte* (n. 4 above), pp. 65ff.

150. For a critique of the position I have taken in chapter two, see Wolfgang Mommsen, "Rezension," *Historische Zeitschrift,* 215 (1972): 434ff., and *Max Weber und die deutsche Politik 1890–1920,* (Tübingen: Mohr, 1974, 2nd ed.), p. 472. Mommsen maintains that for Weber the two ethics have equal rank and that science cannot influence in any way the choice of ultimate ends. This view is compatible with many passages in Weber's work, especially if we approach it from the perspective of political sociology. However, this interpretation does not provide any solution. It neither improves on Weber's own imprecise usage of the two ethics nor leads to a systematically satisfactory formulation. Thus, it is indeed a matter of whether one is ready to argue in Weber's own terms against him.

151. I make the assumption that Weber's sociology contains an explicit decision for the cultural tradition of occidental rationalism (cf. *Aspekte,* p. 305f.). If I am correct, one can argue that Weber uses at least implicitly two mediating principles in defining the ethical life-style adequate to modern society: in the face of dualism ought and is can be linked and mutually corrected through the postulate of congruence and feasibility.

more than by world flight, Weber was repelled by unconscious world control, for it inevitably results in world adjustment —the typical attitude of the man of "law and order" (*Ordnungsmensch*).[152]

For this examination we must look more closely at Weber's description of the disenchanted world. In contrast to the "world" of dualist theocentrism, the disenchanted world appears impersonalized. Its spheres operate in relative autonomy according to their own laws, satisfying man's need for calculability of the world to an historically unparalleled degree. This calculability rests on the confidence that in principle one can count on the rules of these spheres, that one can "orient one's own action according to clear expectations created by them."[153] Thus, confidence is based on "the system" and no longer on persons.[154] The everyday consciousness of modern man differs from that of his ancestors, not by having a better grasp of the conditions of his inner-worldly existence but by the kind of consensus. Everyday consciousness has reified features not least because it is oriented to "the system."[155] These features may be attenuated by reflection. But reflection cannot liberate man from the fatefulness of this impersonal cosmos for every rationalism of world mastery. Reflection not only reveals that this cosmos has been created and hence is changeable, it also shows that it has laws of its own. Within this cosmos the opposition of coercion and kindness, matter-of-factness and love, has definitely entered the world, and it fetters everybody who acts within it to the dialectic of formal and substantive rationality.[156]

---

152. See Weber's speech against bureaucratization at the meetings of the Verein für Sozialpolitik in Vienna in 1909, in Weber, *Gesammelte Aufsätze zur Soziologie und Sozialpolitik* (Tübingen, 1924), p. 413.

153. Cf. "Über einige Kategorien der verstehenden Soziologie," *WL,* pp. 452ff. (An English translation has been made by E. E. Graber, unpublished M. A. thesis, University of Oklahoma, 1970.)

154. Cf. Luhmann, *Vertrauen* (Stuttgart: Enke, 1968).

155. Cf. J. Israel, *Der Begriff der Entfremdung* (Hamburg: Rowohlt, 1972), pp. 127ff.

156. Cf. my *Aspekte,* p. 90f.

Thus, the disenchanted world with its impersonal spheres creates conditions alien to brotherliness. If you wish, this world is the quintessence of legality, not of morality. These conditions, however, lead not only to a conflict with the religious ethic of brotherliness, but also to the conflict within the ethic of the autonomous person (*Persönlichkeitsethik*). In view of the world's very autonomy, rational action must face the question "of what should determine in a given case the ethical value of action—its outcome or its intrinsic ethical value."[157] Different answers lead to different life-styles based either on an ethic of responsibility, which is guided by the outcome of an action, or on an ethic of conviction, which is concerned with an act's intrinsic value. Thus, the non-religious ethic of the autonomous personality, too, seems to be caught up in the opposition of world adjustment and world flight. The ethic of responsibility adjusts to the outcome in the disenchanted world, whereas the ethic of conviction rejects it and therefore remains ultimately "condemned to the irrationality of its effects."[158]

Thus, the ethical life-style adequate to the disenchanted world seems to lie, as it were, *between* the two ethics. Both are in tune with the times, but only if they are combined. Weber has given some hints that would seem to justify such an interpretation.[159] But I believe that this would be logically unsatisfactory, and would besides be at odds with his own premises. Weber employed both concepts in order to characterize not only two principles of realizing *any* given value position

157. Cf. "Theory," p. 339.   158. *Ibid.*

159. Cf. "Politics," p. 127: "It is immensely moving when a mature man—no matter whether old or young in years—is aware of a responsibility for the consequences of his conduct and really feels such responsibility with heart and soul. He then acts by following an ethic of responsibility and somewhere he reaches the point where he says: 'Here I stand; I can do no other.' That is something genuinely human and moving. And every one of us who is not spiritually dead must realize the possibility of finding himself at some time in that position. Insofar as this is true, an ethic of ultimate ends and an ethic of responsibility are not absolute contrasts but rather complements, which only in unison constitute a genuine man—a man who can have the 'calling for politics.' "

but also two attitudes and their corresponding value positions. In the end he preferred the ethic of responsibility to the ethic of conviction under the conditions of disenchantment, for it alone permits conscious world mastery. The ethic of responsibility is not forced into world flight, like the ethic of conviction, but it also is not compelled to world adjustment. This becomes immediately evident when we confront it not only with the ethic of conviction but also with science as ideology, the type to which Weber gave particular attention in his political sociology, if under another name—*Realpolitik*.[160]

For this comparison a systematic consideration may be useful. The opposition of world and human will, of nature and postulated ethical causality, corresponds to the world view of immanent dualism. The world must be shaped according to the postulates of human will. But this will is not completely free; it is faced with the conditions within which it can transform the world.[161] Therefore, the relation of human will to the world may have a double meaning. It may be guided by

160. Cf. H. H. Bruun, *Science, Values and Politics in Max Weber's Methodology* (Copenhagen: Munksgaard, 1972), pp. 267ff. Only if we juxtapose the positions of religion, ethic of conviction, and "science as ideology" (or *Realpolitik*) with the ethic of responsibility can we identify sufficiently the latter's particular nature. Only then can we prevent the misunderstanding that by accepting feasibility as one of its criteria the ethic of responsibility is identical with the art of the possible. This runs counter to Weber's intention, as Mommsen has correctly shown. In my first essay I have perhaps not made this point with sufficient clarity, and therefore I want to emphasize it here. However, I consider unsuitable the notion of a decisionist ethic of responsibility, as Abramowski and Mommsen have proposed it. This notion narrows the comparison of the several orientations to just that between the ethic of conviction and the ethic of responsibility, between charisma and rationalization. Bruun's notion of "responsible ethic of conviction" is better, but it is redundant insofar as for Weber ethic of responsibility always implies conviction (*Gesinnung*).

161. This is true in the sense of Marx's famous dictum in "The Eighteenth Brumaire of Louis Bonaparte," according to which "men make their own history, but they do not make it just as they please; they do not make it under circumstances chosen by themselves, but under circumstances directly encountered, given, and transmitted from the past" (*Marx/Engels, Basic Writings on Politics and Philosophy,* ed. L. Feuer [Garden City: Doubleday, 1959], p. 320).

the idea of efficiency or by the idea of moral appropriateness. There is tension between both ideas, and it can be resolved only by establishing a hierarchy and following a strategy of maximization. Exactly this is done by the ethic of conviction and the attitude of ideologized science, and of *Realpolitik*. The former maximizes moral appropriateness, the latter efficiency. Only the ethic of responsibility endeavors to keep both appropriateness and efficiency in a precarious balance by a strategy of optimization: it is the art of the possible as well as the art of accomplishing the impossible.[162]

The problems of anthropocentric dualism, then, can be confronted with the help of three non-religious attitudes, apart from the religious approach: with an ethic of conviction, which elevates the moral appropriateness of an action above its efficiency; with an ethic of adjustment, which subordinates moral appropriateness to efficiency; and with an ethic of responsibility, which attempts to balance moral appropriateness and efficiency in view of the given conditions. However, the three ethics also differ in their relation to scientific rationalism. The ethic of conviction generally tends to ignore its knowledge; the ethic of adjustment tends to overestimate it; and the ethic of responsibility tends to examine it critically, at the same time permitting scientific rationalism to examine it in turn.

Wherever the ethic of responsibility prevails, the exclusive claims of transcendental faith are definitely abandoned. At most, an inclusive sense of obligation and duty remain (*Totali-*

162. I emphasize the art of the impossible; utopian anticipations can be realistic as well as unrealistic. As early as 1943 Eduard Baumgarten made an attempt similar to mine. He tried to dissolve the opposition of ethic of conviction and ethic of responsibility by interpreting both in terms of commitment and success (cf. his "Erfolgsethik und Gesinnungsethik," *Blätter für die deutsche Philosophie*, 17 (1943): 96ff.). Baumgarten shows impressively that only an attitude which recognizes the interplay between conviction and success can protect the actor against egocentric self-indulgence and can realize truthfulness, carefulness, and sincerity as structures of psychic distance. He also points to the elements of dialogue, which have an elective affinity to reflexive thinking. Baumgarten's analysis is also a phenomenological analysis of the character and problematics of openness.

tätspflicht).[163] For in the disenchanted world you must reckon not only with the dualism between value and reality, but also with a value pluralism, with the fact that a person can find different "gods" and be obedient to them. The ethic of responsibility can effect a reconciliation neither among the various value positions and reality nor among the different values themselves. It can only establish the preconditions for facing up to the oppositions and for arranging a rational confrontation. After the breakdown of the dualist theocentric world view, backsliding into monism can be prevented only if man creates his own values that guide him and juxtaposes them responsibly to other value positions and reality. In this sense the world of religious faith has indeed turned into a world without faith, the world created by God has become the world of the autonomous person. To put it in Karl Loewith's words: "In comparison with every transcendental faith this belief in the fate of a time which must be faced and in the passions that should go into time-bound action is positive lack of faith. The positive element of this lack of faith in anything that transcends the fate of the time and the 'demands of the day' ... is the subjectivity of rational responsibility as the purely autonomous responsibility of the individual before himself."[164]

Such autonomous responsibility is not as empty as this formulation might seem to indicate. It is aware of presuppositions: the readiness to be clear-eyed and to live with dualist, pluralist tension, even affirmatively. The problems of meaning and mastery of the disenchanted world cannot be adequately handled by either world flight or world adjustment. What is needed is conscious world mastery, the subjective correlate of which is self-control vis-à-vis one's own and alien "gods."

Weber has been called a nihilist, a relativist, and a deci-

163. Cf. Blumenberg, *Säkularisierung* (n. 113 above), p. 78.
164. Cf. Karl Loewith, "Weber's Interpretation of the Bourgeois-Capitalistic World in Terms of the Guiding Principle of 'Rationalization,' " *Max Weber,* ed. Dennis Wrong (Englewood Cliffs, N.J.: Prentice-Hall, 1970), p. 119.

sionist. He is all of these things if you believe in the existence and discernibility of an objective meaning of the world. With Nietzsche, Weber believed that neither exists any more, but in contrast to Nietzsche he turned this experience into an object of empirical historical research. He objectified his experience in the thesis of disenchantment. From it follows a situational diagnosis that is bound up with two ways of gaining distance: from faith in the possibility of ultimate certainty, and in the ultimate feasibility of human happiness. Today this diagnosis regains importance in a period in which a cycle of world flight and world adjustment seems to be running its course in the disenchanted world. This diagnosis shows us the reasons for our discontent with modernity, but it also makes clear why we will do well not to give in to this discontent.

Excursus: The Selection and Dating of the Works Used

This chapter attempts to reconstruct Max Weber's analysis of modernity on the basis of his sociology of religion, to understand the character of modernity with his means, "the configuration and the cultural significance of its components in their present form, on the one hand, the reasons for their historical development on the other" (*WL,* p. 170f.; cf. E. Shils and H. Finch, eds., *Max Weber: The Methodology of the Social Sciences* (Glencoe: Free Press, 1949), p. 72). For practical reasons I have limited myself to the dimension of the construction of world images. However, I have tried to reconstruct not only Weber's diagnosis of modernity but also his own position toward it, his philosophy of life, so to speak, insofar as it has relevance beyond his own person. For this reason I have selected the following texts for analysis: "Politics as a Vocation," "Science as a Vocation," parts of the *Collected Essays in the Sociology of Religion* (especially the "Author's Introduction," and the "Introduction" and "Intermediate Reflections" from "The Economic Ethic of the World Religions"), and finally the chapter on the sociology of religion in *Economy and Society.*

The two speeches on "Politics as a Vocation" (1919) and "Science as a Vocation" (1917) will be dealt with in chapter two and can therefore remain in the background here. The connecting link between the two speeches and Weber's written work is "Intermediate Reflections: Theory of the Stages and Directions of the Religious Rejection of the

World." "Science as a Vocation," in particular, is closely related to it in time and content. In spite of the hastiness of its composition, "Intermediate Reflections" is one of the most important of Weber's writings. Eduard Baumgarten even believes that it "belongs to the most ... enduring chapters written by Weber." (Cf. *Max Weber: Werk und Person*, ed. Baumgarten. Tübingen: Mohr, 1964, p. 473; on the importance of the "Intermediate Reflections" for Weber's late work, see also Friedrich H. Tenbruck, "Das Werk Max Webers," *Kölner Zeitschrift für Soziologie*, 27 (1975): 663f., esp. 676 and 679.)

There are three versions of the "Intermediate Reflections." The first is found mainly in *ES*, VI: xii–xiv (pp. 576–606). (Some elements, such as the typology of salvation and theodicy, were first formulated in *ES*, VI: viii–xi, pp. 518–575). The second version appears under the title "Intermediate Reflections: Stages and Directions of Religious World Rejection." It was published in December 1915 in the *Archiv für Sozialwissenschaft und Sozialpolitik*, 41: 287–421, as part of the essays on the economic ethic of the world religions, together with chapters three and four of *China*. (The first two chapters appeared in October 1915.) The second version served Weber as a systematic connection between the studies on Confucianism (*China*) and the studies which by 1915 were partly drafted, partly in the planning stage: the studies on Hinduism, Buddhism, ancient and Talmudic Judaism, early Christianity, the Christian medieval orders and sects, and Islam. At that time chapter four of *China* had already established the substantive connection with "The Protestant Ethic and the Spirit of Capitalism." Subsequently the *Archiv* published the following studies: "Hinduism and Buddhism" in April 1916, in December 1916, and in May 1917; "Ancient Judaism" in October 1917, March 1918, July and Dec. 1918, June 1919, and Jan. 1920. However, the latter study only contained the pre-Exilic and Exilic phases of Judaic religious prophecy and the formation of the Jews as a pariah people. Weber needed to write a connecting chapter because of the content of the series. The study on Confucianism dealt with a religious ethic of world adjustment; the following studies turned to religious ethics of world rejection in different stages and directions. The analytical end point of the studies was the religious ethics of ascetic Protestantism, about which Weber had written first. When in 1919/20 Weber began preparing his collected studies in the sociology of religion, which were to comprise four volumes, he revised the "Intermediate Reflections" once more. Thus we have a third version with yet another title: "Intermediate Reflections. *Theory of the Stages and Directions of the Religious Rejections of the World.*" There is some evidence that Weber worked on this text until shortly before his death. Thus, the "Intermediate Reflections" is not only analytically but also biographically something like his last word. In its last formulation these "Intermediate Reflections" became part of the first volume—the only one authorized by Weber—of the *Collected Essays in the Sociology of Religion,* together with the new "Author's Introduction" and the revised version of "The Protestant Ethic and the Spirit of Capitalism" (first published in 1904/5), "The Protestant Sects and the Spirit of Capitalism" (1906), the "Introduction" (first published in 1915), and "Confucianism and Taoism" (which first appeared under the title "Confucianism" in 1915).

Thus, the third version of "Theory of the Religious Rejections of the World" was written in 1920, but we do not know for certain when the first two versions were composed. The first version presents the same unusually difficult dating problems as all of the older part of *Economy and Society.* In December 1913 Weber was ready to publish the first parts of the *Handbook of Social Economics,* which he later entitled *Outline of Social Economics.* He began planning for this handbook in 1909, and in May 1910 he distributed a first printed table of contents to the numerous collaborators. Weber himself wanted to write on economy and society in the part on "Economy, Nature and Society." His headings were "A) Economy and Law (1. Their Basic Relationship, 2. Epochs of the Development of the Present State of Affairs); B) Economy and Social Groups (Family, Community, Status Groups and Classes, State); C) Economy and Culture (Critique of Historical Materialism)." (Cf. *Handbook of Political Economy,* table of contents. Archive of the Mohr/Siebeck publishing house.)

As the preparations proceeded and encountered various difficulties, the original plan was changed, and thus also the section on "Economy and Culture." In the table of contents of the whole *Outline of Social Economics,* which appeared in all instalments from their very beginning in 1914, the following heading was announced: "5. Religious Groups. Class Conditions of the Religions; World Religions and Economic Ethics" (cf. *Economy and Society,* LX). After Weber's death, when Marianne Weber and Melchior Palyi published *Economy and Society,* they named the section "V. Types of Religious Groups (*Vergemeinschaftung*)—Sociology of Religion"; in the most recent, the fifth German edition, this has been changed once more into "V.

Sociology of Religion (Types of Religious *Vergemeinschaftung*)." Reviewing the stages of the work's composition, we can guess that the first version of the "Theory of Religious Rejections of the World" (under the title "Religious Ethics and the World") was ready by the end of 1913 or early 1914, but was probably written earlier.

The dating of the second version of the "Intermediate Reflections" is also uncertain. Tenbruck assumes that it was written in 1915, when the "Introduction" to "The Economic Ethic of the World Religions" had been typeset by the printers, because he views the "Intermediate Reflections" as a correction of the "Introduction" (cf. Tenbruck, *op. cit.*, pp. 676 and 698). The passages on the war, which are found in this version, could also point to 1915. However, according to Weber himself, the "Introduction" was ready in 1913—see his remark in "Die Wirtschaftsethik der Weltreligionen. Religionssoziologische Skizzen," *Archiv für Sozialwissenschaft*, 41 (1915): 1: "The following text is published unchanged just as it was written down two years ago and read to friends at the time." Moreover, important themes of the "Intermediate Reflections" are contained in *Economy and Society*. Thus, an earlier date of composition cannot be excluded.

The assertion that important themes of the "Intermediate Reflections" can be found in the older part of *Economy and Society* can be supported by a comparison of the three versions. The first version spells out the position to which Weber continues to adhere—the paradox of rationalization in the context of a theory of value conflicts and of a conflict model. The more religious orientations are sublimated in the direction of an ethic of conviction (*Gesinnungsethik*), the more does tension arise between the religious commitments and the state of the "world"; the more these tensions are articulated, the more are they reflected in the *Gesinnung* of the religious virtuoso. This in turn provided further motivation for another round of sublimations based on the ethic of conviction. The result is an attitude of world rejection, which is characteristic of salvation religion in contrast to magical religion and religion founded on law (*Gesetzesreligion*). Weber thus diagnoses the conflict between a religious ethic of single-minded conviction and the state of the world and then analyzes it in an ideal-typical manner in four value spheres: the economy, politics, sexuality and eroticism, and art. Before making his diagnosis, Weber distinguishes the demands of religious brotherhood toward the world from the requirements of brotherhood that are rooted in the bonds of family, clan, neighborhood, and ethnic group. Religious brotherhood based on an ethic of conviction abolishes the difference between internal and external moral rules in favor of a universalism which tends to make everybody a brother at the same time that he becomes not only an equal but also the other. (See Benjamin Nelson's Weberian study, *The Idea of Usury: From Tribal Brotherhood to Universal Otherhood.* University of Chicago Press, 1969, 2nd ed.)

If we compare this first version with the one published in 1915, we find that it too is mainly concerned with religious rationalization in the context of a conflict model. However, the text not only is freed from its original mass of details but also has a different emphasis. Now the value sphere of science is included; there are the beginnings of a distinction between a religious and a non-religious ethic of conviction and the ethic of responsibility; and more attention is given to the impact of the consistently rationalized value spheres on the religious ethic of conviction. This suggests that, beyond the intermediate function of the text, Weber now addresses himself more intensively to the origin and future of the vital problems of modern occidental rationalism. Thus, he arrives at an intellectual position which anticipates "Science as a Vocation" and "Politics as a Vocation." There are, then, important differences between the first and the second version. In my judgment Baumgarten is mistaken in asserting that the subject matter of the "Intermediate Reflections" did not change significantly "between 1911 and 1916 [it should read 1915] with the exception of one important point." (See Baumgarten, *op. cit.,* p. 473, and also Arthur Mitzman, *The Iron Cage.* New York: Knopf, 1971, p. 204.)

There are few differences between the second and the third version, apart from the methodological remarks at the beginning. The new text is only three pages longer than the old one. This is the result primarily of additions, not of revisions. This is even true for the section on sexuality and eroticism, which has been changed more than the others. However, Weber now distinguishes explicitly between a religious and a non-religious ethic of conviction—he speaks of the religious ethic of brotherhood and a priori rigorism, an obvious reference to Kant's ethic of reason (see "Theory," p. 341).

However, in the course of these remarks on dating and sequence we must not forget that the chapter on religion in *Economy and Society* and the studies on the economic ethic of the world religions do not follow so much as complement one another. As Weber wrote in 1915, with all the clarity we could wish for, the essays on the economic ethic of the world religions were meant "to appear at the same time as

Economy and Society and to interpret and supplement its chapter on religion, but also to be interpreted by it in turn" (see "Die Wirtschaftsethik der Weltreligionen. Religionssoziologische Skizzen," *Archiv,* 41 (1916): 1). When Weber revised both works in 1920, he held to the same opinion.

However the question of the dating of the various versions may be decided, it remains true that Weber presented the result of his studies in the sociology and history of religion in the "Author's Introduction," "Introduction," and "Intermediate Reflections." (See also Tenbruck, *op. cit.,* pp. 676, 679, 681.) We can go even further: the "Intermediate Reflections" provide us with an illuminating perspective on the two great speeches, especially on "Science as a Vocation," and contain Weber's diagnosis of modernity and its problems of meaning. Although his dating is wrong, Arthur Mitzman remarked correctly that "the last pages of 'Religious Rejections' (largely unchanged from the 1916 version) and the second half of 'Science as a Vocation' (1919) reveal Weber's most troubled reflections on the problem of meaninglessness in modern society" (*The Iron Cage,* p. 219).

II

VALUE-NEUTRALITY AND THE ETHIC OF RESPONSIBILITY

Wolfgang Schluchter[1]

1. The Character of "Science as a Vocation" and "Politics as a Vocation"

For the world and for Germany the period from 1917 to 1919 was a time of dramatic social and political change. Historians have rightly called 1917 an epochal year in world history. For Germany it was a year of decisions which might have helped political reason to prevail in spite of external and internal difficulties. In the realm of foreign policy the Peace Resolution was intended to make possible a negotiated peace; in domestic politics, the newly constituted Interparty Committee (Interfraktionelle Ausschuss) of the Reichstag prepared the introduction of parliamentary government and the Weimar coalition, the transition from the monarchy to the

---

1. Translated by Guenther Roth. There is no adequate rendering of *Wertfreiheit*, which I prefer to translate as "value-neutrality" because this term has been used most frequently in the general controversy about issues of scientific "objectivity" in the United States in recent years. See my essay on "Value-Neutrality in Germany and the United States," in Reinhard Bendix and G. Roth, *Scholarship and Partisanship: Essays on Max Weber* (Berkeley and Los Angeles: University of California Press, 1971), pp. 34–54. Weber always used the term in quotation marks to denote a very specific meaning, which is central to his ethical and institutional theory of modern science. René König has pointed out that a better German choice for Weber would have been *Werturteilsfreiheit*, freedom from value judgment (see "Einige Überlegungen zur Frage der 'Werturteilsfreiheit' bei Max Weber," *Kölner Zeitschrift für Soziologie*, 16 (1964): 1–27). I have sometimes used the phrase "freedom from value judgment" instead of "value-neutrality." The reader should keep in mind that science was a value for Weber and that scientific subjects were constituted by their value relevance. The main point about *Wertfreiheit* is the

republic, but in the winter of 1918/19 political reason foundered again.[2] It is true that a reorganization of Europe and a lasting peace appeared possible on the basis of Wilson's Fourteen Points, but the armistice conditions undermined the hope for a negotiated peace. In domestic politics the road to the republic and to a parliamentary system of government seemed to be open after the collapse of the monarchies, but the political left in particular suffered from internecine strife and was split over basic constitutional issues. In this dramatic period Max Weber made several speeches in Munich. He spoke up for a negotiated peace and against the danger of the Pan-German movement; he talked about science as a vocation, the political reorganization of Germany, and politics as a vocation. Two of these speeches—"Science as a Vocation" and "Politics as a Vocation"—had a more academic character than the others. They were addressed primarily to students, to a

---

scientist's freedom from having to make *practical* value judgments in his scientific work.

Edward Shils and H. Finch translated *Wertfreiheit* as "ethical neutrality" in their translation of "The Meaning of 'Ethical Neutrality' in Sociology and Economics," in *Max Weber: The Methodology of the Social Sciences,* ed. E. Shils and H. Finch (Glencoe: Free Press, 1949), pp. 1–49. H. H. Bruun, T. Parsons, and W. G. Runciman have preferred "value-freedom." For Bruun's preference, see his *Science, Values and Politics in Max Weber's Methodology* (Copenhagen: Munksgaard, 1972), p. 16; see also T. Parsons, "Value-Freedom and Objectivity," in *Max Weber and Sociology Today,* ed. Otto Stammer (New York: Harper, 1971), pp. 27–50; W. G. Runciman, *A Critique of Max Weber's Philosophy of Social Science* (London: Cambridge University Press, 1972).

"Ethic of responsibility" is a literal rendering of *Verantwortungsethik,* but there is no equally easy translation for *Gesinnungsethik,* for which I have chosen "ethic of single-minded conviction" instead of the more familiar "ethic of ultimate ends." Bruun, too, speaks of the ethic of conviction. *Gesinnungsethiker* has been rendered as "true believer." There is no concise solution for the *Verantwortungsethiker,* the "believer in an ethic of responsibility." Action based on the two ethics will be called respectively "principled action" and "responsible action."

2. On the Interparty Committee, see *Der Interfraktionelle Ausschuss 1917/18,* ed. Erich Matthias and R. Morsey (Düsseldorf: Droste, 1959), 2 vols. For a general background, see Arthur Rosenberg's pioneering study of 1928, *Die Entstehung der Weimarer Republik* (Frankfurt: Europäische Verlagsanstalt, 1961), and Erich Eyck, *A History of the Weimar Republic* (Cambridge: Harvard University Press, 1962), chap. 1.

young generation that would have to live with a new social and political order that was barely visible at the time. Both lectures were part of a series intended to orient students about "intellectual work as a vocation." The organizers chose the well-known scholar and publicist, who might also be a teacher in the future,[3] because they were interested not only in professional concerns in the narrower sense but also in the significance of intellectual work in this period of social and political revolution. However, Weber seems to have deliberately disappointed their expectations. For instance, his speech on politics as a vocation begins with the remark that nobody should expect from him a commentary on problems of the day. Even more, form and content of the speeches seem to indicate an intention to belittle the magnitude of the contemporary problems. Weber offers no dramatic show but lengthy analyses carefully formulated; he does not diagnose current political problems, but sidesteps them in favor of wide-ranging excursions into intellectual and social history. He does not encourage political activism, but spreads around him a mood of resignation.

However, we must qualify this statement. To begin with, the speeches were not identical with the printed text. Weber was particularly dissatisfied with his speech on politics as a vocation and modified and expanded his arguments considerably, as we can see from a comparison of his notes with the final printed formulation. We must also distinguish the speaker's effect from the writer's. The writer struggles to find the most responsible formulation in view of the immense complexity of reality; the speaker takes more subjective liberties. As many contemporaries have testified, Weber was a powerful speaker with demagogic talents, reminiscent of the prophets of the Old Testament, whose rhetoric he described so movingly in

3. In the spring of 1919 Weber accepted a chair of economics and sociology in the faculty of *Staatswirtschaft* at the University of Munich, the first chair he held in almost twenty years. He lectured for only two full semesters before his death on June 14, 1920. On Weber's numerous connections with political, literary, and academic life in Munich, see M. Rainer Lepsius, "Max Weber in München," *Zeitschrift für Soziologie*, 6 (1977): 103–118.

his study on ancient Judaism. This is also true of his two "academic" speeches. They were fascinating, according to Rehm, and had the effect of "an explosive improvisation of thoughts which the speaker had mulled over for a long time" (Baumgarten). Moreover, the resigned mood of the two speeches had different causes: "Science as a Vocation" provides a diagnosis of modernity, "Politics as a Vocation" applies it to the German political situation. In addition, in 1917, when Weber spoke about science as a vocation, he still expected an acceptable outcome of the war. He hoped that Germany would be able to continue, even under changing conditions at home and abroad, to play the role in world politics which it had to take on with the founding of the empire in 1871. But early in 1919 this hope was greatly dampened by the unholy alliance of intransigent right-wing chauvinism and left-wing politics of single-minded conviction (*Gesinnungspolitik*). The developments in Munich, in particular, seemed to demonstrate prototypically the direction in which the moralization of domestic and foreign politics was leading—to the brink of civil war and separatism and, in their wake, to permanent foreign control and the resurgence of reactionary forces. Kurt Eisner, journalist and litterateur, member of the Independent Socialists to the left of the Social Democrats and representative of the literary crowd, was in Weber's eyes an example of this political romanticism, similar to humanitarian anarchists and pacifists such as Toller, Mühsam, and Landauer. Eisner had proclaimed himself Provisional Bavarian Prime Minister on November 7, 1918. During the winter of 1917/18 he had actively participated in the strike movement that pushed for a quick peace even if it meant acknowledging the German responsibility for the war, and demanded the immediate establishment of the republic. He now continued in domestic politics this policy of single-minded conviction, which was unconcerned about its consequences. "Politics as a Vocation" is directed against the champions of such a policy, but also against the Communists, who were more realistic, even though they too disregarded the ethical paradoxes of politics. Even more, the speech is directed against the youthful followers of these currents, as this passage makes clear:

Now, then, ladies and gentlemen, let us debate this matter once more ten years from now. Unfortunately, for a whole series of reasons, I fear that by then the period of reaction will have long since broken over us. It is very probable that little of what many of you, and I too—as I candidly confess—have wished and hoped for will be fulfilled; little—perhaps not exactly nothing, but what to us at least seems little. This will not crush me, but surely it is an inner burden to realize it. Then, I wish I could see what has become of those of you who now feel yourselves to be genuinely "principled" politicians and share in the intoxication signified by this revolution.[4]

Thus, it seems that Weber deliberately wants to hurt this young generation's feelings about life. Those who view themselves as the children of a revolutionary time, who perceive previously undreamt-of opportunities and want to follow the maxims of an ethic of conviction he calls—with Simmel's words—persons who suffer from sterile excitation and have trouble satisfying the sober demands of the day. It is true that this is not a verdict about all of youth or all of his listeners.[5] Weber seems to follow a defensive strategy against claims that might arise from the situation in which lecturer and audience find themselves. Weber knows that a time in need of meaning demands prophet and prophecy. But he is not that prophet. He takes the role of the scientist and teacher, who has nothing to say about the events of the day.

Weber does not satisfy the great need of his audience for an

4. "Politics," p. 127.

5. Weber distinguishes between those whose intentions (*Gesinnung*) are pure and those who only imagine they have pure intentions. The test lies in the true believer's readiness to maintain his position even after the consequences resulting from the deliberate disregard of an action's outcome must be faced. Whoever wants to be a prophet but founders on the world's irrationality must be able to bear his failure without collapsing; he must be prepared for martyrdom. Weber did not think that most of the left-wing true believers had such stamina. He was willing to concede it more readily to Rosa Luxemburg and Karl Liebknecht than to others, although he sharply rejected their strategy of mass mobilization, their "politics of the street." Cf. Lepsius, *op. cit.*, pp. 106ff., esp. p. 108.

interpretation of the world.[6] This is our first impression. But in spite of their soberness the two speeches are suffused with pathos. Many passages sound like an appeal. The speaker who appeals to us does not say what must be done, but unmistakably he tries to indicate what should not be done. This negative insistence retains for both speeches the very quality which they seem to deny by their manifest stance—they are political speeches. However, they are political in a more emphatic sense than would be true of a commentary on current events. Weber turns the themes suggested to him into fundamentals; he takes them out of their momentary context and uses them for defining the intellectual situation of the present. By gaining distance from current events and making them appear alien through historical comparisons, Weber shows his intention to tackle a fundamental problem of the present from which to elucidate the import of the contemporary political troubles.

We must briefly justify this assertion. We gain a first support for it when we penetrate the external form and reach the underlying structure of Weber's reasoning. In spite of all digressions which the speaker permits himself he follows a strict

6. An example for the effect of Weber's deliberate technique of alienating his listeners by means of comparative analysis and ideal typical constructs is Max Horkheimer, who in the course of Weber's 1919 lectures on "The Most General Categories of the Science of Society" listened to his remarks on the Soviet system expecting to receive guidelines for the current situation and the political options and potentialities. "The lecture hall was overcrowded but there was deep disappointment. Instead of theoretical reflection and analysis, which would be guided by the idea of a rational construction of the future, not only in the way the tasks were posed but also in every single step, we listened for two or more hours to carefully weighed definitions of the Russian system, astutely contrived ideal types, with the help of which the Soviet order might be analyzed. Everything was so precise, so scientifically rigorous, so value-free that we went home very sad." Cf. Horkheimer in Stammer, ed., *Max Weber and Sociology Today*, p. 51. However, such an alienating procedure was part of a "heroism of objectivity" and could exert a fascination of its own, as we know from Jörg von Kapher's testimony cited in Marianne Weber, *Max Weber*, trans. Harry Zohn (New York: Wiley, 1975), p. 662f. Weber himself said about his course: "I am deliberately talking very abstractly, purely conceptually," cited in *ibid.*, p. 664.

scheme, which is the same in both speeches. First, the external conditions are taken up, the institutional constellations within which the vocations of science and politics are possible. Then the question is raised about the demands which these vocations make upon the individual. This question, which has as its subject the role of the scientist and the politician in a structurally objective sense and the problem of meaning in a subjective sense, is turned into the question of the vocation of science and politics as such. Apparently Weber wants to make this point: just as the individual cannot understand the meaning of his vocational role without thinking about the institutional context, so the meaning of the institutions cannot be understood unless their general social context is taken into account.

But that is not all. Weber not only wants to demonstrate that such themes require sociological analysis, he also wants to make it clear that determining the function of science and politics is *the* dominant issue of the present. Insofar as the most significant intellectual events of modern history have been the disenchantment, intellectualization, and rationalization of the world, the question about the role of science and politics affects the question of the modern world's meaning. For scientific knowledge has broken the monopoly of the salvation religions for providing meaning by spreading the belief that "in principle, one can master all things by calculation."[7] Science and politics seem to have displaced religion. Must they also take over its specific function? After all, a society in which the religious monopoly has been destroyed remains still in need of meaning. The disenchanted world, too, poses a problem of meaning. What is more obvious than to think of assigning its solution to these dominant powers, science and politics? Must not both become *the* vocations, especially when this disenchanted world enters a revolutionary phase, as in Germany? Is it not readily understandable that in this situation the expectations once directed toward seers and prophets—those dispensers of sacraments and revelations—

7. Weber, "Science," p. 139.

are transferred to scientists and politicians? And above all: Is it surprising if these are willing to accept such transference? In asking these questions, Weber at the same time answers the question of the meaning of the disenchanted world. This basic connection makes clear that both speeches not only are organized in the same manner, they also deal with the same subject matter. The question is whether science or politics can be a vocation, whether the unity of knowing about the world and doing something about it can be realized in either one under conditions of disenchantment. Science and politics are treated not in isolation from each other but in relation to each other. By probing into the inherent limitations of science, Weber discusses at the same time its relation to politics; and by showing the limits of political action, he relates politics and science. Doubtlessly, Weber gives more attention to the first perspective. This is one of the shortcomings, if you will, of his analysis of the relation between science and politics. But this shortcoming can be mitigated if we understand both speeches in their systematic unity.

I shall take this systematic approach in order to determine the role of science and politics on the basis of these two speeches.[8] I shall also choose another approach by distinguishing two levels of reasoning which are not kept separate in the speeches. I shall call them the methodological and ethical (*methodologischethisch*) level and the institutional level. We hardly need emphasize that Weber deals with his problem under methodological and ethical aspects. Concepts such as *Wertfreiheit*, value relation, value analysis, but also ethic of single-minded conviction and ethic of responsibility come from the arsenal of ethics and philosophy of science. But it is

8. Apart from the two speeches, we shall draw on "The Meaning of 'Ethical Neutrality' in Sociology and Economics," "Parliament and Government in a Reconstructed Germany: A Contribution to the Political Critique of Officialdom and Party Politics," Appendix II of *ES*, pp. 1381–1462, and "Wahlrecht und Demokratie in Deutschland," in Weber, *PS*, pp. 386–395. The first essay, the original version of which dates from 1913, is written on the level of methodological and ethical analysis and can be closely linked with "Science as a Vocation"; the other two essays deal with the institutional level.

less clear that Weber also argues on the institutional level. We have already pointed to his sociological analysis of the present. However, Weber is also interested from another perspective in sociological questions in the narrower sense. His attention is directed toward the relationships which do and should prevail in and between science and politics. This statement may sound surprising. For Weber does not talk of value systems and their institutionalizations, but at best of scientific and political "personality." He lists the qualities scientists and politicians must possess for their vocations. In doing this, however, he achieves more than is at first apparent. In Weber's analyses the concept of personality has a double meaning which corresponds to the different levels. First, Weber uses "personality" in an ethical sense, defining it in terms of the "consistency of its inner relationship to certain ultimate values and meanings of life, which are turned into purposes and thus into teleologically rational action."[9] Since man is thought of as a personality in this sense, interpretive sociology can understand human behavior by means of constructing instrumentally rational relations.[10] The *conceptually presumed* (*gedachte*) consistency of personality is a kind of transcendental precondition of interpretive sociology.[11] That man should achieve this consistency is the very content of the Weberian ethic. However, next to this ethical notion of personality, there is from the beginning a sociological one, which comprehends personality as the consequence of a behavioral

9. Cf. Weber, *Roscher and Knies: The Logical Problems of Historical Economics*, Guy Oakes, trans. (New York: Free Press, 1975), p. 192.

10. In the same essay Weber observes: "The possibility of interpretation implies that interpretable processes are more calculable than non-interpretable natural processes" (p. 127).

11. In the essay on "Objectivity in Social Science and Social Policy" (*Methodology*, p. 81) Weber states that "the transcendental presupposition of every cultural science lies . . . in the fact that we are cultural beings, endowed with the capacity and the will to take a deliberate attitude towards the world and to lend it significance." I believe that there is a connection between this statement and the use of the notion of personality in this particular meaning. For a similar interpretation, see Dieter Henrich, *Die Einheit der Wissenschaftslehre Max Webers* (Tübingen: Mohr, 1952), p. 82f.

typification, which results from the character of the value system and the manner in which persons are socialized. Weber takes note of the impulses that issue from value systems and become relevant for action as psychic motives.[12] Only in this way can man *empirically* achieve a consistent relationship to the values and meanings of life. Thus, when Weber speaks of the personality of the scientist and the politician, he also has in mind the institutionalized value system of science or politics. Therefore, a systematic interpretation of his ideas about their relationship in his two speeches must take into account not only the complementarity of the speeches but also the connections between the ethical and institutional levels of analysis.[13]

Before beginning our substantive analysis, we must raise the question of the frame of reference within which the results of such an interpretation can be placed. I am going to work with the classification of the most important conceptions of the relation between science and politics proposed by Jürgen Habermas, who distinguishes between a decisionist, a technocratic, and a pragmatic model.[14] In his view, the first rests on a radical division of labor between political leaders and bureaucrats. Strong-willed leaders, who are capable of making decisions on their own, use the services of the substantively informed and technically trained bureaucrats and leave the citizens only the opportunity to acclaim the leaders' subjective decisions that have been executed in a technically correct manner. By contrast, in the technocratic model the irrational decision is superfluous. Decisional premises crystallize during the decision-making; they follow from what is technically feasible (not vice versa), and leadership is reduced to administration. Political participation amounts to even less than plebiscitary acclamation; it is merely acceptance of

12. Cf. the statement by Reinhard Bendix in Stammer, *op. cit.*, p. 158.

13. This could lead to some sort of synthesis of the interpretations advanced by Henrich and Parsons at the Heidelberg Sociology Convention of 1964 (see Stammer, *op. cit.*, pp. 27ff. and 66ff.).

14. Cf. Jürgen Habermas, "The Scientization of Politics and Public Opinion," *Toward a Rational Society*, tr. J. J. Shapiro (Boston: Beacon Press, 1970), pp. 62ff.

technological necessity.[15] In the pragmatic model, the possibility of a rational discussion of the relation between technology and practical decision is not denied, and in fact the public is not prevented from rational discussion. On the contrary, the acknowledged necessity of a continuous communication between science and public opinion helps constitute a political public within which an informed confrontation can take place between technical knowledge and know-how and traditional value positions. In this way practical questions can be translated into scientific problems, and these in turn, after their resolution, can be handed back as scientific information to an informed public. According to Habermas, only this model satisfies democracy's claim to mediate knowledge, technology, and praxis in a manner promoting the welfare of the polity.

This approach is of interest in two ways. First, Weber's position is subsumed under the decisionist model. Second, in sketching his models Habermas operates on both the methodological and the institutional levels of the argument. Thus, we must examine whether he classifies Weber correctly under the methodological and the institutional aspects. With regard to the former, we must clarify whether Weber limited the function of science to the production of technically useful knowledge or whether he gave science a role in society's tradition-bound interpretation of itself "within which the needs are interpreted as goals and the goals are hypostatized as values."[16] With regard to the second aspect, we must ask whether Weber advocated a radical division of labor between science and politics or instead had in mind a structural differentiation of science and politics,[17] which can support competing value orientations and utilize them, through institutionalized communication, for the mutual correction of end

15. *Ibid.,* p. 64. Habermas mentions the variant which considers an ultimate core as not amenable to rationalization and thus as the proper subject of the decision.

16. *Ibid.,* p. 74.

17. In my view it is a shortcoming of the previous interpretations that Weber's theoretical model of the relation of theory and praxis has been translated into the institutional relation of administration and political lead-

and means. Once we have clarified these two issues we can answer the larger question as to whether Weber succeeded in his intention of providing a theoretically consistent and institutionally effective alternative to a directionless decisionism as well as a meaningless perfection of "the iron cage."[18] It is beyond doubt that Weber wanted to accomplish this. He abhorred power politics for its own sake no less than bureaucratic domination under which efficient administration and an adequate standard of living for the citizenry are made the highest and ultimate value.[19] We must try to ascertain whether Weber succeeded.

2. VALUE-NEUTRALITY AND ETHIC OF RESPONSIBILITY AS METHODOLOGICAL AND ETHICAL CATEGORIES

In order to clarify the question of whether Weber saw the calling of science fulfilled in the technical critique of practical problems, or whether he went beyond it using an ethical

---

ership. Such a view is not surprising, since Weber speaks of the scientist as well as the civil servant as an expert. I shall try to demonstrate, however, that Weber distinguished between the scientist and the civil servant with regard to the kind of expertise required and for this very reason had to define their relation to politics differentially. In this way we can also qualify Parsons' famous footnote which charged that Weber overlooked expertise as an independent source of authority, by merging technical and legal competence in the bureaucratic staff, and hence disregarded professionalism. Cf. Parsons' introduction to his translation of part I of *Economy and Society,* published as *The Theory of Social and Economic Organization* (Glencoe: Free Press, 1947), pp. 58ff. n. 4. Heinz Hartmann has elaborated Parsons' view in his reformulation of Weber's sociology of domination in his *Funktionale Autorität* (Stuttgart: Enke, 1964), pp. 7ff.

18. Henrich, in particular, has tried to show that Weber attempted to reconcile this alternative theoretically; see his remarks in Stammer, *op. cit.,* pp. 66ff. It is more commonly believed that Weber could not resolve the difficulty because of his "dichotomized concept of reason" (an expression from Habermas). This view unites authors who otherwise are antagonists, such as Leo Strauss and Herbert Marcuse. Cf. L. Strauss, *Natural Right and History* (University of Chicago Press, 1953), and H. Marcuse, "Industrialization and Capitalism," in Stammer, *op. cit.,* pp. 133–151; for a revised version, see Marcuse, *Negations* (Boston: Beacon Press, 1968), pp. 201–226.

19. Cf. Weber, "The Meaning of 'Ethical Neutrality' " (n. 1 above), p. 46, and "Parliament and Government," *ES,* p. 1402.

perspective, a concise reconstruction of his train of thought in his speech on "Science as a Vocation" will be useful.[20] After a brief description of the structural change in the German university, and after some rather aphoristic remarks about the material and intellectual risks of scholarship, Weber faces his central problem—whether science (*Wissenschaft*) finds its purpose in furthering technical progress.[21]

However, in order to examine the value of science for the "whole of mankind"[22] on the basis of this question, we must have not only a notion of this entity but also an idea about its meaning. For only when technical progress serves this meaning can the support of technical progress constitute the task of science in turn, only then can we say that "the result of scientific work is important in the sense of being worth knowing."[23]

There are two conceivable ways to ascertain the meaning of human life and make it a constituent component of science. Either science recognizes it with its own means or it is provided by another agency in a manner that will not endanger the nature of scientific knowledge. Weber declares that the first solution is no longer feasible. He adds up the disappointed expectations that once were wedded to the attempt to elevate science into an instrument giving meaning to human life. Science has been unable to show us the road to true reality, the true deity, true nature, true art, or true happi-

20. We do not want to argue that a science which provides only technical critique has no value. To the contrary, technical critique is more demanding than is commonly understood. Although technologies are, from a logical viewpoint, tautological transformations of nomological hypotheses, their discovery requires a great deal of constructive technological fantasy. This is overlooked by those who view technology and science, insofar as they give technical directions only, in their service roles. Hans Albert, in particular, has called attention to this point. See Albert, *Plädoyer für kritischen Rationalismus* (Munich: Piper, 1971), pp. 45ff., and *Marktsoziologie und Entscheidungslogik* (Neuwied: Luchterhand, 1967), pp. 157ff.

21. I deliberately use the concept of technical progress instead of rationalization. Weber conceives of different kinds of rationalization, subjectively and objectively correct ones. Technical progress means an increase of the objective correctness of action in the sense that causal relationships, nomological knowledge, are applied. Cf. Weber, "The Meaning of 'Ethical Neutrality,'" p. 516.

22. "Science," p. 140.   23. "Science," p. 143.

ness.[24] Basically, science has been successful only as an empirical enterprise, and this only by purposively abandoning the attempt to give meaning to life. Thus, science has increased its practical value at the expense of its value as a guide to life (*Gesinnungswert*).[25] That is its dilemma. Weber believes that science cannot resolve it with its own means.

This raises the question of who can provide meaning if science cannot. There has always been one agency which has offered meaning—salvation religion. But salvation religion inevitably collides with the rationality standards of modern science. Religion cannot do full justice to science in two regards: it would force it to abandon its own history and curtail its intrinsic progress. For if science were deliberately to be founded on religion, it would have to become theology, which would be limited to "an intellectual rationalization of the possession of salvation."[26] Science would have ethical but no practical value. But such a solution appears hardly feasible, especially since in the disenchanted world the unified Christian value cosmos has been dissolved into a new polytheism.[27] The value cosmos which tended to be integrated by the Christian ideal has been fragmented: now there is irreconcilable conflict among the individual value levels and the different value spheres.[28] The result is a value antagonism whose different positions are engaged in "an irreconcilable deadly struggle" as

24. *Ibid.*

25. According to Weber, every action and action system has an intrinsic and a practical value. It is a matter of one's ultimate values how one wants to determine their relation. Practical value refers to feasibility and thus must be in agreement with ascertainable nomological knowledge. By providing such knowledge, science makes it more feasible for given ends to be acted upon successfully. However, as an action system science also has a double value. To this extent science is, in Luhmann's sense, a reflective mechanism. Cf. Weber, "The Meaning of 'Ethical Neutrality,' " p. 24; Niklas Luhmann, "Reflexive Mechanismen," *Soziale Welt*, 17 (1966): 1ff.

26. "Science," p. 153.

27. Weber, "The Meaning of 'Ethical Neutrality,' " p. 17.

28. It appears useful to me to distinguish between normative order and value sphere. Normative order refers to ideology which integrates the value spheres. In Weber's sense, value spheres are ethics, politics, etc.

"between God and the Devil."[29] In such a situation the question about the meaning of science can no longer be resolved unambiguously. Where life is understood in different ways, there cannot be one obligatory meaning for science. Science may be successful, but it must remain without intrinsic value (*gesinnungslos*).

Has Weber accepted this resigned conclusion? I don't think so. Weber's famed postulate of freedom from value judgment has not only one central but also a double meaning. His demand for a value-free empirical science aims, in the first instance, at making *possible* practical empirical research under the conditions of an antagonistic universe of values,[30] but it is also meant to *make* such research *desirable*.[31] Empirical science should be protected against the irresoluble struggle of the different value systems because a science that is independent in this sense has an intrinsic value. This amounts to asserting that a "free" empirical science is a value that must be defended, that it is intrinsically valuable. Only because it is an "objectively valuable vocation" can it become "a vocation for somebody" under the given circumstances.[32]

At first sight this may appear to look like an exaggerated interpretation. For Weber emphasizes time and again that science is indeed not without presuppositions, but that presuppositions that make science valuable depend on subjective decision. Whoever affirms them has a vocation; whoever is indifferent to them has perhaps only a job, which permits its holder to live off science, if he cannot live for science.[33] This

29. Weber, "The Meaning of 'Ethical Neutrality,' " p. 17.

30. Weber himself stated most emphatically that freedom from value judgment is not identical with an inability to make an evaluation or even with the absence of values. Cf. Hans Albert, *Traktat über kritische Vernunft* (Tübingen: Mohr, 1969), pp. 62ff.

31. It has long been known that Weber's postulate of freedom from value judgment is more than a methodological principle. See especially Karl Loewith's 1932 essay, "Max Weber und Karl Marx," in his *Gesammelte Abhandlungen* (Stuttgart: Kohlhammer, 1960). More recently Ernst Topitsch, e.g., has made the same point. See his essay in Stammer, *op. cit.*, pp. 8–26.

32. "Science," p. 152.

33. Weber applies this formulation mainly to the politician, distinguishing

does not imply that the jobholder cannot be a good scientist. On the contrary, a person can be a capable scientist without attaching any "higher meaning" to science. However, we are concerned not only with vocational questions in the narrower sense but also with the meaning of intellectual work, and this question is connected with the justification of science as an institution.

Here we encounter a surprising connection. Weber attempts such a justification by means of a diagnosis of the specific course of disenchantment. He speaks of the inescapable "factualness of our historical situation which we cannot deny if we want to be true to ourselves";[34] he speaks of the "fate of our culture" that should be accepted.[35] To be sure, these are subjective positions, but they also claim to be more; they claim the character of a *well-founded* position, they are of "*informed subjectiveness,*" to use a phrase by Ralf Dahrendorf.

This reveals the previously mentioned political core of the speech. How does Weber justify this position without succumbing to "subjectively colored professorial prophecy," which he ridicules so much and which his speech, in form and content, serves to unmask?[36] Wherein lies the justification that separates Weber's position from professorial prophecy? How can Weber achieve "objectivity" if all attribution of meaning has become subjective? These questions can be clarified by analyzing more closely the relationship of salvation religion and modern science. In this way we can uncover the foundations of Weber's position.

Weber asserts that the person who is positively religious under present-day conditions must accomplish the religious virtuoso's achievement of sacrificing his intellect;[37] he is incapable of bearing "courageously the fate of our times."[38] Religion makes impossible what serving science apparently grants

---

between those who live for and those who live off politics. Cf. Weber, "Politics," p. 84.

34. Cf. "Science," p. 152.   35. Cf. "Science," p. 149.

36. Cf. Weber, "The Meaning of 'Ethical Neutrality,'" p. 4.

37. Cf. "Science," p. 154.   38. Cf. "Science," p. 155.

to us—living in concordance with the conditions of a rationalized world. This thesis is at first sight unconvincing on the basis of Weber's own assumptions about the structure of the world of values. All action, not just religious action, depends on presuppositions which must be believed in order to establish its meaning. Thus, the natural sciences, medicine, and the cultural sciences presuppose our desire to control the world, to preserve life, and to know about the origin and path of civilized man. These sciences accomplish rationalizations for certain realms of action that are "valuable" only if these presuppositions are accepted. But the very same is apparently true of religion and the discipline that rationalizes it, theology. If you accept this particular presupposition, it can lead to action whose norms clash irreconcilably with those of other realms of value and action. But we cannot derive from this the thesis that one presupposition is inferior to another. Given Weber's theoretical assumptions, whoever denigrates religious action seems to indulge in personal prejudices.[39]

However, Weber wants to prove that there are historically adequate and inadequate valuations, depending on their intellectual rationale. He considers it demonstrable that the positively religious person cannot be a "contemporary." In contrast to science, theology adds to the kind of preconditions that are always necessary "specific presuppositions for its workings and for the justification of its own existence."[40] Theology presupposes not only that the world must have a meaning but also that this meaning is revealed by certain facts of salvation. But in this case it is "not knowledge in the usual sense but a spiritual possession" that is the condition for intellectual rationalization.[41] The difference from science is not that something is believed in but that the content of the belief leads to a positive faith.

But what does this mean? Is faith not always positive in the

39. Weber esteems the religious attitude which requires the sacrifice of the intellect more highly than the compromises of relativizing habit and the professorial prophecy of his colleagues.

40. Cf. "Science," p. 153.   41. Cf. "Science," p. 154.

sense that you must affirm what you believe? If Weber means more by "positively religious" than a redundancy, then it seems to be this: There are preconditions that restrict the range of knowledge and action, and others that enlarge it, depending on whether the principle of certainty or the principle of uncertainty is dominant.[42] Every religion must limit "objectively correct" knowledge and subjective decision.[43] Knowledge is reduced to rationalization of salvation, decision is reduced to surrender. Thus, religious behavior cannot be in concordance with the conditions of a polytheistic cosmos of values and with the conditions of a society rationalized according to objectively correct criteria. Religion must turn away from the world. Weber's "rejection" of the religious attitude results from this consequence.[44]

42. Cf. also Ralf Dahrendorf, "Ungewissheit, Wissenschaft und Demokratie," *Konflikt und Freiheit* (Munich: Piper, 1972), chap. 14.

43. I am using Weber's own distinction between subjectively and objectively correct action as the basis for this statement. Every correct action presupposes a theory of information.

44. By judging a religious attitude as being incompatible with the times, Weber as a scholar is not led, of course, either to underestimate religious orientations in their social significance and impact or personally to disrespect the consistently religious person. Weber's rejection is also not simply expressive of an anti-religious or irreligious attitude, but follows from an historical diagnosis of the present. This diagnosis has consequences at the least for anybody who wants to live with full awareness in this present. A letter to Ferdinand Tönnies demonstrates how unambiguous and yet complex Weber's position is. "It goes without saying that religions must clash with scientific truth insofar as they assert empirical facts or the causal impact on them of something supernatural. However, when I studied modern Catholic literature in Rome a few years ago, I became convinced how hopeless it is to think that there are any scientific results this church cannot digest. The steady slow impact of the practical consequences of our view of nature and history may perhaps make these ecclesiastical powers wither away (unless such fools as Ernst Haeckel will spoil everything), but no anti-clericalism based on 'metaphysical' naturalism can accomplish this. I could not honestly participate in such anti-clericalism. It is true that I am absolutely unmusical in matters religious and that I have neither the need nor the ability to erect any religious edifices within me—that is simply impossible for me, and I reject it. But after examining myself carefully I must say that I am neither anti-religious nor irreligious. In this regard too I consider myself a cripple, a

But if Weber makes these valuations with regard to the religious and the scientific attitude, does he not simply substitute faith in science for faith in religion? Does the "vocation" of science not consist then in spreading a technocratic consciousness which functions as a background ideology for the progress of industrial society?[45] Weber can apparently prevent this misunderstanding only if he succeeds in making clear that the ultimate decisions about meaning are made with the help of science but not by science itself. He succeeds on this score. The meaning of science lies in making possible, and at the same time restricting, our leeway for decision-making. Science is an enabling agent insofar as it shifts the decision into the subjective sphere through the application of the principle of value-freedom. Science limits decision-making by formulating restrictive conditions which must be accepted by the decision-maker. These conditions result from the risks that are inherent in every decision made in the present. In the main, there are two risks: Every decision has consequences for the individual, for "the salvation of the soul,"[46] and it has consequences for the social surroundings. Science must make explicit both risks: it must clarify the one by the discussion of values, and the other by establishing the chances of success and the likelihood of subsidiary consequences. In this lies the meaning of science: it is "today a vocation orga-

---

stunted man whose fate it is to admit honestly that he must put up with this state of affairs (so as not to fall for some romantic swindle). I am like a tree stump from which new shoots can sometimes grow, but I must not pretend to be a grown tree. From this follows quite a bit: For you a theologian of liberal persuasion (whether Catholic or Protestant) is necessarily most abhorrent as the typical representative of a halfway position; for me he is in human terms infinitely more valuable and interesting (according to the circumstances, of course—I may find him indeed inconsistent, confused, etc.) than the intellectual (and basically cheap) pharisaism of naturalism, which is intolerably fashionable and in which there is much less life than in the religious position (again depending on the case, of course)." Quoted from E. Baumgarten, ed., *Max Weber: Werk und Person* (Tübingen: Mohr, 1964), p. 670.

45. Cf. Jürgen Habermas, "Technology and Science as 'Ideology,'" in Habermas, *op. cit.* (n. 14 above), pp. 81ff.

46. Cf. "Politics," p. 126.

nized in special disciplines, in the service of reflection and of recognizing the factual state of affairs."[47]

Science in this sense is of this world and yet retains a critical distance from it. Science is of this world by taking into account the historical process of rationalization through the separation of knowledge and action. Science retains a critical distance from the world by reattaching decision-making, which has been freed by historical rationalization, to self-clarification and knowledge of the facts. Thus, science is given a task transcending that of a pure service role in subjective decision-making. Every action, especially political action, must let itself be disturbed by science through value discussion and must let itself be corrected by inconvenient facts. The disenchanted world must at least subject itself to the principle propagated by science: The ought depends on know-how.[48]

A good deal of Weber's line of reasoning seems to contradict this assertion. Not only did he maintain time and again that feasibility was irrelevant for the quality of a decision,[49] he also spoke of the opposition between the ethic of single-

47. "Science," p. 152.

48. Cf. Hans Albert, *Traktat* (n. 30 above), p. 76, who comes to this conclusion in his critical Weber reception. For Weber value analysis was not an esoteric, purely academic matter removed from praxis. This is shown by a passage in a letter which reads: "After long experience and as a matter of principle I take the position that the individual can gain clarity about what he stands for only by testing his own presumably 'ultimate' convictions through his reaction in the face of sharply delineated, critical issues." Cited from Eduard Baumgarten, ed., *Max Weber,* p. 535f. Thus, value analysis moves us closer to reality, not further away from it. Incidentally, Baumgarten has used this passage for comparing the different intellectual interests of Weber and Jaspers in a subtle examination which demonstrates the method of value analysis. Cf. Baumgarten, "Für und wider das radikale Böse," in Paul A. Schilp, ed., "Karl Jaspers," *Philosophen des 20. Jahrhunderts.*

49. Weber explicitly rejects the view that politics should be understood only as the art of the possible; cf. "The Meaning of 'Ethical Neutrality,'" p. 24. On the same page he adds: "It was, after all, not the truly consistent ethic of adaptation to what is possible—represented by the bureaucratic morality of Confucianism—that has created our own culture's qualities, which probably are (subjectively) appreciated by all of us more or less positively in spite of all other differences."

minded conviction and the ethic of responsibility in his essay
on freedom from value judgment and in his speech on "Politics as a Vocation." The two ethics, he argued, differed exactly
in the manner in which they evaluated know-how and feasibility.[50] Whereas the believer in an ethic of responsibility considers the instrumental value (*Erfolgswert*) and hence the chances
for success as well as the consequences, the believer in an ethic
of conviction is concerned with commitment for its own sake,
independent of any calculation of success. The true believer
wants to rekindle over and over again "the flame of pure
intention," and he seeks out "irrational deeds which can and
should have only exemplary value."[51] Even more, Weber goes
so far as to assert that only a person who observes both
maxims can pursue "politics as a vocation." Even though the
maxims contradict each other, no politician can act solely according to the dictates of the ethic of responsibility, even if he
claims he does. There are situations in which he, too, must
stick to his ultimate commitments and leave the consequences
to God.[52] If one wants to support the interpretation suggested
here, he must apparently doubt Weber's statement.

We can now establish the connection with the second
speech. In "Politics as a Vocation," too, Weber leads us to his
central question after first considering the external conditions
under which politics can be a vocation and after discussing the
qualities of political leadership. The central question concerns
the role which politics can nowadays play "within the total
moral economy of conduct."[53] Weber's answer is given in
terms of a (secular) theory of value, which has already been
sketched. In the course of disenchantment, politics has
emerged as a sphere with values of its own. Politics has attained relative autonomy vis-à-vis religion and science. The
relationship between politics and ethics, in particular, has become problematic. Two aspects are involved: First, politics
today can no longer be understood simply as the application

50. "Politics," p. 120f.; "Science," p. 148.
51. Weber, "Politics," p. 121.
52. Cf. "Politics," p. 127.
53. Cf. "Politics," p. 117.

of ethical principles. There are alternative solutions which are indifferent to ethical principles. The most diverse institutional arrangements can be reconciled with the postulate of justice.[54] Second, there are those two antagonistic ethical maxims to which political action can be oriented. We cannot derive an answer from the presuppositions of ethics as such as to whether political action should realize a value position without regard to consequences or whether it should be guided by a sense of responsibility for them. Political action today is faced with an ethical alternative. It remains tied to ethics, but seems free to choose its ethical limitation.

What does this mean? By granting this choice to political action, Weber also concedes to it the decision as to whether or not it is willing to accept the restrictive conditions formulated by science. The believer in an ethic of responsibility submits to them, the believer in an ethic of conviction does not. For it is distinctive of the ethic of conviction that the ought must not depend on feasibility. Hence the true believer stands outside a cultural tradition of which science has been one carrier. He breaks out of the disenchanted world, not in the sense that he disregards the "demand of consistency" (*Gebot zur Persönlichkeit*),[55] which prevails in this world, but in the sense that he wants to achieve self-clarification and self-determination in opposition to, and no longer within, the iron constraints of this society.[56] Whoever believes that political action should only be founded on single-minded resolution seems indeed very close to the decisionist model. The interpretation of Weber's "confession" proposed here is tenable only if we can

54. Cf. "The Meaning of 'Ethical Neutrality,' " p. 13f.

55. Cf. Dieter Henrich, *op. cit.* (n. 11 above), p. 122, who discovers in Weber's theory of value the idea of personality as the guiding principle of an objective ethics and who relativizes from this perspective the current notions about Weber's decisionism. The content of a decision can be only that which is compatible with the highest moral obligation—to be a personality.

56. This is the way Loewith, in particular, has characterized Weber's position. According to him, Weber's grand design culminates in finding a foundation for freedom within, not from, the rationalized society. Cf. Karl Loewith, *op. cit.* (n. 31 above), p. 30.

demonstrate that he "devalues" the ethic of conviction in addition to religion.

In my view Weber indeed "devalues" the ethic of conviction.[57] This is not contradicted by his remark mentioned above that in certain situations the believer in an ethic of responsibility must be capable of acting according to the ethic of conviction. His remark is first of all indicative of the ambivalence with which Weber uses both terms. On the one hand, he tends to distinguish the ethic of responsibility as an ethic of means-ends relations from the ethic of conviction as a goal-oriented ethic; on the other, both relate ethics and politics in a manner that provides purely formal directives for the realization of values. In the first case the two ethics complement each other in the sense that an ethic of means-ends relations is meaningful only if certain goals are envisaged; in the second case both ethics exclude each other, since in a concrete instance of social action only one principle can be followed. In my view only the second interpretation is convincing, for the fact that a believer in the ethic of responsibility demonstrates his own ultimate values in a certain situation can be interpreted as a consistent application of the maxims of this ethic. It is exactly the weighing of consequences that can lead one to say in Weber's sense: "Here I stand. I cannot do otherwise."[58] This would be impossible only if the believer in an ethic of responsibility did not have any ultimate value,[59]

---

57. Cf. Hans Henrik Bruun, *Science, Values and Politics in Max Weber's Methodology* (n. 1 above), pp. 267ff. The point we made in connection with the "devaluation" of the religious attitude is also pertinent here. The "devaluation" does not amount to a disregard of the historical importance of true believers or a lack of respect for their consistency. Rather, we try to establish Weber's own evaluations and their rationale and to suggest that his "confession" derives from a reasoned position which has general applicability beyond his own case. For another analysis that qualifies the charge of Weber's alleged decisionism, see Gerhard Hufnagel, *Kritik als Beruf: Der kritische Gehalt im Werk Max Webers* (Frankfurt: Propyläen, 1971), pp. 215ff., 253ff., 293ff.

58. "Politics," p. 127.

59. Cf. "Politics," p. 120, where Weber emphasizes that the ethic of ultimate ends is not identical with irresponsibility and the ethic of responsibility is not identical with lack of commitment.

if the ethic of responsibility would, for instance, be identical with *Realpolitik.*

This alone should make it clear that on the basis of Weber's own theoretical premises there is no complementariness between the two ethics. Moreover, his own line of reasoning in "Politics as a Vocation" shows that he does not even personally accept their equality. Ultimately, for Weber the two ethics do not represent two principles of realizing any value position or an ethic of goals versus an ethic of means-ends relations so much as two kinds of commitment (*Gesinnungsstrukturen*) and the corresponding value positions. In spite of some remarks to the contrary, the two concepts denote in the final analysis two diametrically opposed political ethics between which he chooses with regard to their appropriateness for the present time. I should like to call these two ethics the absolute and the critical political ethic.[60] As a political ethic, the ethic of conviction is absolute, in the first instance, insofar as it finds intolerable "the ethical irrationality of the world."[61] The ethic of conviction cannot recognize that in politics, in particular, which employs force as its specific means, good can create evil and vice versa. In a specific sense this ethic is blind to reality. As a political ethic the ethic of responsibility is, in the first instance, critical insofar as it not only takes account of the ethical irrationality of the world but also recognizes that the peculiar dilemma of realizing values in politics consists in using power and force as means and therefore in leading to "a pact with diabolical powers."[62] In a specific sense the ethic of responsibility is realistic.[63] Thus, because of their basic struc-

60. Weber himself speaks of an "absolute ethic." Cf. "Politics," p. 119f.
61. Cf. "Politics," p. 122.   62. Cf. "Politics," p. 123.
63. Reality-oriented politics must not be equated with *Realpolitik* in the traditional sense of the word. Since Weber interprets the ethic of responsibility as a value position, it follows that action in accord with its maxims is not the same as action on the basis of *Realpolitik.* Cf., "The Meaning of 'Ethical Neutrality,'" p. 23, where Weber remarks: "By and large men have a strong tendency to go along with success or with whatever promises to be successful, not only—and this stands to reason—in the choice of their means and in their desire to realize their ultimate values, but in the sense of giving them up. In Germany the name *Realpolitik* has been draped around this surrender."

ture the two ethics are obviously not equally capable of taking into account the conditions of disenchantment. After the disintegration of the Christian illusion we must face the inescapability of value conflict and the permanent ethical problem of how to act upon values. Now, if we relate the two ethics to these conditions, then their difference becomes especially clear in terms of presupposition and effect. The true believer is a rationalist in terms of a cosmic ethic.[64] He seeks to base his value position on an objectively given or intelligible principle that makes possible a permanent hierarchical order of values and at the same time ethically neutralizes the paradox of consequences vis-à-vis the act's intention. He tends toward principled action which is in the nature of a monologue, and either flees from the world or tries to revolutionize it. He sanctifies either the retreat to inwardness or the charismatic new beginning. His political maxim is "all or nothing." By contrast, the believer in an ethic of responsibility is a rationalist in terms of a critical ethic. He seeks to base his value position subjectively on a dialectic of contradictory im-

64. Cf. "Politics," p. 122. The analysis of the relationship between the ethic of conviction and the ethic of responsibility in Weber's writings is unnecessarily complicated by the fact that in many passages he identifies the ethic of conviction with the religious ethic, the postulate of brotherliness. This creates the impression that the contrast between the two ethics is one between the religious and the secular, especially the political, ethic. Weber reinforces this impression by illustrating, in "Politics as a Vocation," the ethic of conviction with the Sermon on the Mount. This insufficient differentiation between a religious and a non-religious ethic of conviction is, of course, related to Weber's research interests: He is, after all, interested in establishing the conditions under which religion becomes a religion of ultimate ends and the consequences which this development has for man's relation to the world. However, in "The Religious Rejections of the World and Their Directions" (1920) Weber himself points to the difference between a religious and a non-religious ethic of conviction, when he speaks of the ethic of religious brotherhood in distinction from a priori rigorism (cf. "Theory," p. 341), presumably a reference to the Kantian ethic and thus to the ethic of reason. Only through this reference does it become clear that Weber's notion of the ethic of responsibility can serve to clarify the ethical problem in Kant's sense. However, this is possible only if we distinguish between religious and non-religious ethic of conviction and put both, together with the ethic of responsibility, in an historical model of development.

peratives, the impossibility as well as the compulsion of mediating among them. This makes possible at best momentary and changing hierarchies and ethically dramatizes the paradox of consequences vis-à-vis the act's intention. He tends toward action that is organized in terms of the situation and a dialogue. Such action aims at controlling the world by foregoing an ultimate harmonization and by ethically liberating the choice of means. It builds on what is given and proceeds with the knowledge that, though everything can be changed, not everything can be changed simultaneously and without contradictory consequences. Its political maxim is "in spite of."[65]

We can discover still another difference. A cosmic-ethic rationalist will either overestimate or underestimate what modern science can do for the rationalization of action. He will overestimate it on the assumption that science can recognize ultimate values. In this case science will serve him "to comprehend the universe somehow as a cosmos with a meaningful order."[66] Scientific concepts must have a normative and descriptive double function, which Weber exemplifies by the concept of progress.[67] The cosmic-ethic rationalist will underestimate what science can accomplish by taking it for granted that it cannot discover the grounds of being. For the consequences that science can discover, the identification of the personal and social costs of realizing monistic values, are irrelevant to the warrior of the faith. They belong to the irrationalities of the world, and their recognition would spoil

---

65. The similarities of these views to the position of critical rationalism are striking. See especially the works of Karl Popper and Hans Albert. For English translations of Albert, see his "The Myth of Total Reason," in Anthony Giddens, ed., *Positivism and Sociology* (London: Heinemann, 1974), pp. 157–195; also "Behind Positivism's Back?" in T. W. Adorno et al., *The Positivist Dispute in German Sociology*, trans. G. Adey and D. Frisby (New York: Harper, 1976), pp. 226–257.

66. Ernst Topitsch in Stammer, ed., *op. cit.* (n. 1 above), p. 12.

67. Cf. Weber, "The Meaning of 'Ethical Neutrality,'" pp. 25ff., 35ff. See also *Roscher and Knies* (n. 9 above), p. 229; "The concept of 'progress' is required only when the religious significance of the human condition is destroyed and the need arises to ascribe to it a 'meaning' which is not only this-worldly, but also objective."

the purity of the ethic of conviction. By contrast, the believer in an ethic of responsibility is not only dependent on modern science but also forced to assess its possibilities and limitations correctly. He needs a relatively autonomous and "value-free" science, which can create the presuppositions for his action on the basis of the empirical analyses of means-ends chains and of the logical and cognitive (*sinnhafte*) analysis of maxims of action. In a society in which there is no objective knowledge about causal and value relations it is impossible, strictly speaking, to act "responsibly." Value-free but value-relational knowledge creates the very facts which can then be "responsibly" evaluated. In this way modern science has not only a necessary but a critical relationship to "responsible" action. Under the conditions of disenchantment value-neutrality and ethic of responsibility belong together.[68]

All of this does not mean that Weber considers "principled" action impossible in the present. To the contrary, he sees the danger of an ethical eruption in the present in general and in Germany since 1917 in particular. It is the very purpose of Weber's speeches to make visible the motivations of such an eruption through an analysis of the social and value structure of modernity and at the same time to explain why such an eruption is undesirable. It is not desirable because the principled deed, whether it be justified with religious or secular arguments, ultimately leads to the closure of social relationships and to the destruction of structural pluralism and value antagonism. Significantly, Weber speaks of the prophet who alone could overcome the inherent dualism (*Zwiespalt*) of the disenchanted world, and even in the definition of charismatic leadership there is an undertone of this prophetic element.[69]

---

68. On the relationship between freedom from value judgment and the ethic of responsibility, see also René König, "Einige Überlegungen zur Frage der 'Werturteilsfreiheit' bei Max Weber" (n. 1 above), pp. 1ff. and 22; see also Hans Albert, "Wissenschaft und Verantwortung. Max Webers Idee rationaler Praxis und die totale Vernunft der politischen Theologie," in Albert, *Plädoyer* (n. 20 above), pp. 76–105.

69. I purposely use the term "charismatic leadership," in contrast to "charismatic domination," as it has been proposed by Reinhard Bendix, *Max*

Whatever may be the justification and the content of principled action in politics, it detracts from the conditions of the present; it requires the sacrifice of the intellect or of empirical lessons or of both. The principled deed polarizes: it turns the political follower into a disciple and the political opponent into an enemy. The principled deed cannot tolerate a critical empirical science as an independent agency. It must disregard the very cultural tradition in which value-free science alone can have a vocation. This, then, is Weber's diagnosis of the present situation, and it is also a political confession—it is a fact that man's "fate today is to live in a time without god and prophet."[70]

Scientific reflection which can judge the religious as well as the secular variant of the ethic of conviction as being politically out of step with the times is a practical science. However, it becomes practical, not in Marx's sense, by striving to transcend (aufheben) itself, but by maintaining itself, not by growing into a philosophy of totality, but by limiting itself to specialized disciplines. It is only through standing its ground and knowing its limits that scientific reflection becomes a practical science. It opposes not "the totality of existence and analysis but the possible congealment of a particularity into a whole, thus a certain kind of pseudo-totality."[71] Science struggles against its own potentially total claims and those of other realms. Therefore it is dependent on a society whose institutional structure corresponds to this basic pluralist conception.

3. VALUE-NEUTRALITY AND ETHIC OF RESPONSIBILITY AS INSTITUTIONALIZED VALUE SYSTEMS

This conclusion leads us to the institutional level of analysis. If from the ethical perspective Weber's views on the relation of science and politics can be fitted into Habermas's

---

Weber (Berkeley and Los Angeles: University of California Press, 1977), pp. 298ff. See also Wolfgang J. Mommsen, *Max Weber: Gesellschaft, Politik und Geschichte* (Frankfurt: Suhrkamp, 1974), pp. 97ff.

70. Cf. "Science," p. 153.   71. Loewith, *op. cit.* (n. 31 above), p. 65.

decisionist model only through a distortion, his ideas about the institutional isolation and connection of both realms, about the autonomy and reciprocity of the scientific and political subsystem,[72] could still justify Habermas's classification. Even though Weber's political confession demonstrates his desire for science to have a practical influence on politics, his views about the structure of a society codetermined by science could turn into a bad utopia, for this society has also developed the coercive association "state" and, after the political expropriation of the traditional powers, has tied the monopoly of legitimate force to elections.[73] In analyzing Weber's views on the relation of science and politics we must not rest content with the methodological and ethical level, but must also identify the institutional arrangements which Weber may have had in mind.

Our analysis up to now has yielded two points from which we can proceed further. First, we have found that Weber interprets freedom from value judgment and ethic of responsibility not only as methodological principles but also as values which one must consciously embrace. Second, we have shown that Weber recognizes different value spheres which are separate from one another and which for this very reason make different demands upon individuals. If we link the first idea with the second, it is easy to interpret science and politics as

72. On these concepts and their possible relationships, see especially Alvin W. Gouldner, "Reciprocity and Autonomy in Functional Theory," in *Symposium on Sociological Theory,* ed. L. Gross (Evanston: Row, Peterson, 1959), pp. 241ff.

73. "Politics," p. 82f. On Weber's use of the concept of the state, especially on his sociological transposition of the old dualism of state and society, see Johannes Winckelmann, "Max Weber: Das soziologische Werk," *Kölner Zeitschrift für Soziologie,* 17 (1965): 761ff., and *Gesellschaft und Staat in der verstehenden Soziologie Max Webers* (Berlin: Duncker, 1957), pp. 38ff.; Reinhard Bendix, *Max Weber,* chap. 15, sections B and E. The social relationships ordered by the modern state are characterized especially by the existence of positions from which decisions for the whole society can be made. If politics is primarily action in such positions, if the sociologist is confronted by the governmental leader with his great powers, then the influence of science appears restricted from the very beginning.

two value spheres to which correspond certain institutional
structures as well as attitudinal expectations. Both science and
politics are realms (*Ordnungen*) which strive to make a certain
"human type" dominant by means of "external and internal
(motivational) selection";[74] both are social powers which have
a political relationship with each other.[75] Weber speaks literally of "the ethos of politics as cause (*Sache*)."[76] In the terminology of modern sociology this refers to the cultural subsystem "politics." On the attitudinal side this ethos implies
"that each man's participation in his society involves a personal commitment both to the behavior patterns and to the
material and ideal interests of a particular status group."[77]
This leads us to expect that we will also find in Weber's
speeches references to role expectations among scientists and
politicians and to the mode of their social mediation.[78]

This is indeed the case. The speech on "Science as a Vocation" is not only a political speech but also a speech on political
education. This is apparent even from a purely external aspect. Even though Weber begins his speech by treating the
scientist in his double role as researcher and teacher, the focal
point of his argument is the teaching role. Even though he
declares at the outset that the classical German university is
dead,[79] he tries to explain how the idealist notion of the practical character of science as *Bildung* through teaching can be
realized under the conditions of specialization.[80] Weber no
longer shares the idealist belief in the unity of specialized

74. Cf. "The Meaning of 'Ethical Neutrality,'"p. 27.

75. Remember that the title of the second part (and the original beginning)
of *Economy and Society* is "The Economy and the Arena of Normative and de
facto Powers."

76. "Politics," p. 117.   77. Bendix, *Max Weber,* p. 260.

78. Along such lines Parsons has analyzed the scientific order that follows
from Weber's methodology. Cf. Parsons, "Value-Freedom and Objectivity," in
Stammer, ed., *op. cit.* (n. 1 above), pp. 27ff. However, we do not want to imply
that Weber was a reductionist sociologist. See J. Winckelmann's objection to
such a view in "Max Weber: Das soziologische Werk," p. 755f.

79. See "Science," p. 131: "Inwardly as well as externally, the old university
constitution has become fictitious."

80. This position has been formulated most clearly by Fichte. According to
him, the scientist can, just because he is educated (*gebildet*), "apply the ac-

training and general education (*Bildung*), but in his eyes a teacher who prevails upon his students to "account to themselves for the ultimate meaning of their action" serves "moral powers."[81] It is true that Weber relativizes his own statement by noting that it is a matter of "practical academic politics" whether a teacher even wants to aim at a general education within the constraints of the empirical disciplines. However, for him specialized training can be undertaken not only in a spirit of modest claims but also in a "rather exuberant" fashion.[82] If a teacher decides to pursue the latter path, then the goal of teaching is not the mere specialist but a person who knows that the ultimate problems of life cannot be solved by the expert's mind. It is possible to provide this understanding on the basis of value-free empirical science. However, it is incompatible with such science to aim at "shaping minds, in the sense of propagating political, ethical, artistic, cultural or whatever world views (*Gesinnung*)."[83] Today, genuine education (*Bildung*) through science can only amount to making explicit the very limitations of science. Science demands of the teacher that he forego propaganda.[84]

Education so understood is politically relevant in two respects. It saves science from political importunities, and it promotes qualities that are of fundamental importance for consciously coping with all vital problems, especially in the political realm. For Weber a person who claims the right "to grip the spokes of the wheel of history"[85] must today have

---

quired knowledge to concrete cases and so transform it into works. He can succeed not merely in reproducing knowledge but in accomplishing something new. Thus, here too the ultimate purpose is not just knowledge but the art of applying what has been learned." Quoted in Ernst Anrich, *Die Idee der deutschen Universität* (Darmstadt: 1959), p. 130.

81. Cf. "Science," p. 152.

82. Cf. "The Meaning of 'Ethical Neutrality,'" p. 3.   83. *Ibid.*

84. Cf. *ibid.*, p. 5. Using Hermann Heller as an example, I have tried to show that the notion of self-restraint can be an essential element of a political philosophy appropriate to the times. See W. Schluchter, *Entscheidung für den sozialen Rechtsstaat.* (Cologne: Kiepenheuer & Witsch, 1968).

85. "Politics," p. 115.

three qualities, apart from a sense for power: passionate commitment, a sense of responsibility, and a sense of proportion. Passionate commitment means dedication to a cause, sense of responsibility means sensibly pursuing this cause, and sense of proportion means being able "to face the realities with concentration and calm—thus, to maintain inner *distance* from issues and men."[86] Although every politician should have these qualities, it cannot be doubted, after the analysis provided so far, that true believers and believers in an ethic of responsibility possess these qualities in different degrees. Sense of proportion, in particular, is a quality which prominently characterizes only the believer in an ethic of responsibility. It is buttressed especially by science properly pursued.[87] If we want to put it in present-day terminology, we could say that value-free science furthers the value orientations that must be possessed by the professional politician who is guided by an ethic of responsibility.

Since Weber believes that science can be helpful for sorting out one's values in the political realm, somebody might want to conclude that the scientist is the ideal politician. But this was not in Weber's mind. He lists other occupations as stepping-stones for a political career, especially that of lawyer and, with some qualifications, that of journalist.[88] However, he explains this preparation not in terms of value orientations

86. *Ibid.*

87. This argument seems to contradict Weber's statement that scientists tend to lack distance, that vanity is their professional disease (see "Politics," p. 115). If this is so, then the politician for whom vanity is a deadly sin cannot learn his sense of proportion in the university. True as this may be, it would be an objection not against the argument advanced here but against the manner in which teachers play their roles. According to Weber, the university fails in its task of providing a political education exactly because many of its members, in their vain overestimation of themselves, pretend that in his role the professor "carries the marshal's baton of the statesman (or the cultural reformer) in his knapsack" ("The Meaning of 'Ethical Neutrality,'" p. 5). Yet wherever the scientist acts upon the role which alone is in accordance with value-free science, he is also a political educator.

88. Cf. "Wahlrecht und Demokratie in Deutschland," *PS*, p. 285; "Politics," pp. 523, 525.

but in terms of the skills demanded by these occupations—the ability to use the spoken and written words combatively for the advancement of one's own position. For today no politician can succeed without "demagoguery," no matter how much he adheres to an ethic of responsibility. Irrespective of the intellectual and emotional self-discipline which contemporary politics demands, politics remains "partisanship, struggle, passion."[89] In science you cannot learn how to assert yourself in politics. The roles of the scientist and politician correspond to each other only partially insofar as the performance standards are concerned as well as the institutional arrangements within which they can be learned.

Whenever Weber sketches the portrait of the professional politician in some detail, he contrasts it not with that of the scientist but with that of the civil servant. This is not accidental. Weber's treatment is influenced by his assessment of the development of a rationalized society based on the capitalist mode of production as well as by his evaluation of Germany's situation since Bismarck's resignation in 1890. The trend toward the rationalized society has turned the civil servant into a politically important type. For Weber, "every domination functions through administration."[90] In a compulsory association that aims at realizing the idea of the "objectively correct" rationalization of men's relation to nature and to one another, domination functions primarily as bureaucratic administration. This type of administration is best suited to a social and economic system oriented toward instrumental rationality and to a rules-oriented legal system.[91] It necessitates the civil

89. Cf. "Politics," p. 95.

90. *ES*, p. 948. Johannes Winckelmann, in particular, has called attention to the connection between domination and administration. See his "Max Webers historische und soziologische Verwaltungsforschung," *Annali della Fondazioni italiana per la storia administrativa*, 1 (1964): 27ff., 49, 56. On Weber's combination of organizational and ideological analysis in the sociology of domination, see Bendix, *Max Weber*, p. 290.

91. Cf. *ES*, p. 975. Weber's organizational analyses in the narrower sense of the word, especially his statements about the efficiency of bureaucratic administration, invite misinterpretation if their conceptual framework is not

servant who with expertise and impartiality transforms the ruler's commands into routine applications; the civil servant is prepared for this task through "rational specialization and training"[92] and kept under control through the separation from the means of administration.[93] But the development of rationalized society in Germany made the civil servant the *dominant* political type. Bismarck left behind "a nation without any political education" and "without any political will of its own."[94] Thus, Germany ended up not with domination employing a bureaucratic staff but with domination *by* a bureaucratic staff. In Weber's eyes Germany was subjected to rule by bureaucrats.[95]

---

clearly kept in mind. In his analysis of bureaucracy Weber employs three perspectives: (1) the global perspective of universal history (patrimonial bureaucracy versus modern civil service), (2) the perspective of the sociology of domination (political versus bureaucratic domination), and (3) the perspective of internal organization (the bureaucratic-hierarchical principle versus the democratic-avocational principle). The evaluation of bureaucratic efficiency varies with the perspective taken. This conceptual manifold has frequently been overlooked, especially in the United States. Some aspects of the "creative misinterpretation" of Weber's analysis of bureaucracy are examined in Renate Mayntz, "Max Webers Idealtypus der Bürokratie und die Organisationssoziologie," in R. Mayntz, ed., *Bürokratische Organisation* (Cologne: Kiepenheuer & Witsch, 1969), pp. 27ff.

92. Weber, "Parliament and Government," *ES*, p. 1401.

93. Cf. *ES*, p. 980. The distinction between the personal and the impersonal, just like the one between routine and non-routine, instability and stability, openness and closure, interest constellation and authority, is one of those paired opposites with which Weber analyzes the structure of authority relations. In contrast to what has sometimes been done, the distinction must not be set parallel to that between the psychological and the sociological. The paired opposites indicate dimensions along which a concrete structure of domination can be examined.

94. "Parliament and Government," *ES*, p. 1392.

95. Weber distinguishes three kinds of bureaucratic domination: domination with the help of a bureaucratic staff, domination by a bureaucratic staff, by virtue either of monopoly (official information) or of autonomy, and finally domination by leaders who have a civil service mentality. Since Bismarck's resignation German politics suffers from the fact that policy is made by men who are recruited from the bureaucracy and have its mentality. This shows up most clearly in foreign politics, where Germany's position as a world power has been put in jeopardy: "In decisive moments the conservative

According to Weber, there are fateful consequences for a polity when persons "with a bureaucratic mentality"[96] take over. Public discourse is abandoned and nobody takes responsibility for political decisions, for the civil servant in his official role has not been trained to hold a politically independent conviction and publicly to stand up for it. His supreme virtue is obedience to the institution, subordination of his own person to his task, in the sense that he must adhere, at least up to a point, to the principle of official loyalty, even if an order runs counter to his own conviction.[97] The civil servant is unsuited for politics not so much because of the skills he must master but rather because of the very value orientations indispensable for effective bureaucratic administration—the ability to administer impartially. The civil servant can achieve this only if he manages "to be 'above partisanship'—in truth, to remain outside the realm of the struggle for power."[98] Thus, bureaucracy finds its limits at the very point where the real political challenge begins—to provide leadership and to take personal responsibility for its underlying principles. This can be accomplished only by "men experienced in weighing the effects of public statements, men with the politician's sense of responsibility, not the bureaucrat's sense of duty and subordination that is proper in its place but pernicious in political respects."[99] The crucial difference between the civil servant and the politician is that the former learns to serve what is in

---

bureaucracy put bureaucrats into the top positions of government which instead should have been manned by *politicians*" (*ibid.*, p. 1438). On the basis of these considerations Weber's plea for introducing parliamentary government, which was supposed to guarantee the selection of competent political leaders, has been interpreted, not surprisingly, as a project for the promotion of German imperialism. See especially Wolfgang J. Mommsen, *Max Weber und die deutsche Politik, 1890–1920* (Tübingen: Mohr, 1974, 2nd ed.), pp. 204, 422.

96. Cf. "Parliament and Government," *ES,* p. 1438.

97. Cf. *ES,* p. 959, and "Parliament and Government": "The civil servant must sacrifice his convictions to the demands of obedience" (p. 1438).

98. "Parliament and Government," *ES,* p. 1404.

99. "Parliament and Government," *ES,* p. 1438. See also Weber's memorandum on changing Article 9 of the Reich constitution, reprinted in Mommsen, *op. cit.,* first edition (1959), appendix III, p. 425f.

the most unfavorable case an alien cause, whereas the politician must learn to make completely his own a cause which he recognizes as morally binding and to stand up for it.

At this point we must draw a careful distinction. What does it mean to say that the civil servant serves an alien, the politician his own, cause? Let us first be clear about one point: According to Weber, only he has a vocation who serves a cause and makes the cause he serves his own, who finds it personally meaningful and is passionately devoted to it.[100] In this respect there is no difference between politician and civil servant. Wherein, then, lies the difference? Apparently, it lies only in the fact that the civil servant must find personal meaning in a socially recognized purpose, whereas the politician must find social acceptance for what is personally meaningful to him. The civil servant accepts a publicly recognized purpose, the politician tries to turn his own into a social cause. He can do this only if he fights for recognition and if he takes public responsibility for what he champions. "This struggle for personal power, and the resulting personal responsibility, is the lifeblood of the politician."[101] If he succeeds in winning recognition, his cause will also become the civil servant's, who must serve the alien cause.[102]

100. This distinguishes the person who has a vocation from the one who merely has a job. Weber contrasts vocation in an external and an internal sense. As Henrich has put it, the concept of passionate commitment to a cause fuses reason and experience (*Erleben*). Cf. Dieter Henrich, *op. cit.* (n. 11 above), p. 127.

101. "Parliament and Government," *ES,* p. 1404.

102. This is one line of reasoning upon which Weber rests the superiority of politics over administration. Only the politician who, by virtue of his institutional position, succeeds in gaining a following for his ideas through free competition is allowed to determine the content of authority. However, there is another line of reasoning: in contrast to the civil servant the politician alone is "free," and this only puts him in the position to make a decision. He alone follows his demon and submits his decision to the acclamation by which he stands or falls. Thus, the politician is the person who comes closest to the ethical postulate that one must become a "personality." In this way the institutional and ethical levels of the argument are related. This leads to an idealization of the politician, which was not without consequences for Weber's constitutional reform proposals.

Does the politician's cause also become the scientist's? This is certainly not what Weber had in mind. There are some similarities in the relation of civil servant and scientist to politics, but there are also important differences. Both take a "value-free" position toward a political stand, but in the official's case the political evaluation is accepted in a "value-neutral" manner, whereas in the scientist's case it becomes the subject of study. Both serve a given policy, but in the one case a policy is carried out, whereas in the other it is criticized and the responsibility involved is clarified. The professional ethic of the civil servant finds its fulfillment in making the dominant ideals effective. By contrast, the scientist must strive "to keep a cool head vis-à-vis the dominant ideals of the time, even the most majestic ones, in the sense of having to preserve his ability, if need be, 'to swim against the stream.' "[103] It is true that civil servant and scientist need similar skills for playing their roles,[104] but the value orientations are clearly different. The scientist's virtues are not loyalty toward the master, but intellectual integrity, not subordination to a given goal, but distance and clarity. All three vocational models—of the politician, the scientist, and the civil servant—overlap and yet are sharply delineated from one another. Therefore, they can be learned not in one and the same but only in different institutional settings.

One point now emerges clearly: Although Weber analyzes on the institutional level primarily the relation of politician and bureaucrat and defines it as subjective decision and professional execution, it would be wrong to perceive the relationship, which he considers theoretically correct, between practical evaluation and value-free cognition institutionally realized only through this very relationship. For Weber the scientist's role is not identical with the civil servant's, nor is the

---

103. Cf. "The Meaning of 'Ethical Neutrality,'" p. 47.

104. Civil servants and scientists both use scientific methods, for instance, but they employ them differently because of their divergent value organizations. Science seeks the progress of knowledge, administration its application. For this reason administration also develops a special technical expertise (*Kunstlehre*). Cf. *ES*, p. 958.

function of science the same as that of administration. It is true that, especially in his political statements toward the end of the First World War, Weber was mainly concerned with opening the road to domination for the professional politician, and he demanded the introduction of parliamentary government and plebiscitary selection of leaders largely in order to tear down the barriers which until then had prevented domination by politicians in Germany.[105] But it did not occur to him to assign to science a service role, not to speak of an apologetic one. As the features of the three models show, the scientist, in contrast to the civil servant, was supposed to remain autonomous from the politician.

Autonomy means more than differentiation. After all, there is role differentiation, too, between the civil servant

105. A shadow has been cast on Weber's proposals for organizing politics in a mass democracy, especially on his plea for plebiscitary leadership democracy, because of the fate of the Weimar Republic and the Nazi seizure of power. In Germany, in particular, the critical reception of Weber's work after the Second World War developed into a political critique. Cf. Guenther Roth, "Political Critiques of Max Weber: Some Implications for Political Sociology," *American Sociological Review*, 30, no. 2 (April 1965): 213-222, reprinted in R. Bendix and G. Roth, *Scholarship and Partisanship* (n. 1 above), chap. 8. As early as 1952 Johannes Winckelmann endeavored, through a systematic analysis and further development of the Sociology of Domination, to demonstrate the difference between Weber's conception of democracy and that of Carl Schmitt. See his *Legitimität und Legalität in Max Webers Herrschaftssoziologie* (Tübingen: Mohr, 1952), esp. pp. 60ff., 79ff. Later Wolfgang J. Mommsen, *op. cit.* (n. 95 above), took up this issue again. We owe to Mommsen an analysis which brings out Weber's militant National-Liberal position, of which his "ideal of the powerful nation state was a part," but those passages appear to me vulnerable to critique in which the historical argumentation is fused with the systematic one (cf., e.g., pp. 46ff., 64ff., 420ff.). A carefully balanced critique of Mommsen's book, on the occasion of its second edition, was provided by Jürgen Kocka, "Kontroversen über Max Weber," *Neue politische Literatur*, 21 (1976): 296. Something of an alternative to Mommsen's approach is provided by Karl Loewenstein, *Max Weber's Political Ideas in the Perspective of Our Time* (University of Massachusetts Press, 1966). We can only refer in passing to the problem posed by Mommsen. In our analysis we are concerned not so much with Weber's vassalic loyalty toward his own country as—from a systematic perspective—with the way in which he managed "to keep his head clear vis-à-vis his own country," as Eduard Baumgarten put it in Otto Stammer, ed., *op. cit.* (n. 1 above), p. 126.

and the politician. Autonomy means first of all the scientist's *freedom from* political interference. In his interpretation of Weber's methodology from the perspective of the sociology of knowledge, Talcott Parsons was quite right in understanding value-neutrality as the scientist's freedom "to follow the values of science within relevant limits, without having them overthrown by other values which contradict those of scholarly research or are irrelevant to them."[106] However, autonomy also means the scientist's *freedom to relate to* politics in a double sense: The scientist, like every citizen, can play several roles, which he tries to integrate, but he also confronts politics with the value position of science. Freedom from practical value judgment defines not only the limits of science but also its cultural claim. This freedom constitutes the basis from which the scientist can take his stand for the value of science.[107] This value is a component of that particular cultural tradition of which modern science is a constitutive part, and it becomes the foundation of the "value universalism"[108] which guarantees to science a critical distance vis-à-vis the culture-at-large and yet leaves it embedded within it. Freedom from practical value judgment defines programmatically the commonality and isolation of culture-at-large and the culture of science. This freedom does not transform science into the politically dominant power of the disenchanted society, but it does turn it into a politically relevant power. This program can be realized only if science has a maximal degree of institutional independence.

Weber left largely unanalyzed the internal and external organization of scientific autonomy.[109] He paid much attention

106. Talcott Parsons, "Value-Freedom and Objectivity," in Stammer, *op. cit.*, p. 33.

107. Parsons prefers to derive this double aspect not from the concept of value-neutrality itself but from its opposition to the concept of value relationship. In my judgment this makes transparent neither the particular basis on which the universal character of the values of science rests nor the political relevance of this value system.

108. Parsons, *op. cit.*, p. 38.

109. There are only two passages in Weber's *Economy and Society* in which Weber deals with organizational aspects of science. The third passage is

to the way in which the professional role of the civil servant is embedded in the bureaucratic apparatus, and that of the politician in the party and the politically effective parliament,[110] and he dealt extensively with the relationship between the two realms.[111] However, there are no comparable analyses for the scientist and science. There can be no doubt that the university was for Weber the most important vehicle of the autonomy of science, but he did not examine this institution from the perspective of organizational sociology. It is true that Weber applied his thesis of the universal tendency toward bureaucratization also to the German university and that he spoke of the Americanization which was making fictitious the old German university constitution,[112] but these are not much more than casual remarks. Hence we must venture a reconstruction of his views. In relation to the outside world, Weber seems to have viewed science as the organization of an occupational status group, in which equals, who have been homogenized by virtue of their formal education, life-style, and vocational prestige, offer advice on the basis of their professional authority.[113] Professional organizations of this kind appeared to Weber particularly well suited "for providing expert opinions or purely routine administrative services."[114] Internally, Weber seems to have considered the collegiate principle operative, as is shown by his remarks about faculties,[115] both as a kind of division of power among them and as a governing principle within them.[116] Professional representation and collegial organization may be thought of as being buttressed by the far-reaching autocephaly of the

found in Johannes Winckelmann's reconstruction of Weber's unwritten *Sociology of the State*. See Weber, *Wirtschaft und Gesellschaft* (Tübingen: Mohr, 1976), Part II, chap. 8.

110. On the notion of the politically effective parliament, see Weber, "Parliament and Government," *ES*, p. 1414.

111. Cf. *ibid.*, pp. 1381ff.   112. "Science," p. 130ff.

113. Cf. Weber, *ES*, p. 305f. The concept of professional authority does not originate with Weber, but it can be linked with his analysis of occupational status groups.

114. *PS*, p. 261.   115. Cf., e.g., "Science," p. 134f.

116. Cf. Weber, *ES*, pp. 271ff.

scientific association.[117] But both forms put science into diametric opposition to the voluntarist political association, which is purely an enterprise of political interests and oriented to political market opportunities.[118] This contrast also explains why Weber emphasized time and again that politics does not belong on the rostrum. The lecture hall is part of an institutional setting which is organized, so to speak, in opposition to the domination of the market principle. In science, statements that can ultimately prove their correctness only through the mobilization of a following are as out of place as is basing the correctness of scientific theory on majority agreement. Weber's statements against professional prophecy are statements for the protection of scientific autonomy. He did not want the university to be misused either as a church or as a sect, nor as a state-supportive institution.[119]

Bureaucratic organization with monocratic leadership, voluntaristic organization with democratic leadership, and professional organization with collegial leadership[120]—these

117. Cf. *ES*, p. 49f.   118. Cf. *ES*, p. 284f.

119. Cf. Weber, "The Meaning of 'Ethical Neutrality,'" p. 9. See also the passages quoted by Käthe Leichter on Weber's assessment of freedom of teaching, "Max Weber als Lehrer und Politiker," *Max Weber zum Gedächtnis*, ed. R. König and J. Winckelmann (Cologne: Westdeutscher Verlag, 1963), pp. 125ff.

120. In my view these three models can be distilled from Weber's sociology of domination and from his political writings as organizational alternatives within the framework of legal domination. This procedure allows us also to demonstrate that the charge of one-sidedness that has sometimes been leveled against Weber's sociology of organization is not always justified. However, it is true that Weber gave only passing attention to the professional principle as a principle of organization. For an analysis of the autonomy of science along the lines of the idea of profession, see M. Rainer Lepsius, "Die Autonomie der Universität in der Krise," in Gerhard Schulz, ed., *Was wird aus der Universität? Standpunkte zur Hochschulreform* (Tübingen: Mohr, 1969), pp. 179ff. Such an analysis is complicated particularly by the fact that research and teaching cannot be subsumed equally well under the principle of profession and that the "clients" are members of the organization. On the first issue, see Harold L. Wilensky, "The Professionalization of Everyone?" *American Journal of Sociology,* 70 (1964): pp. 137ff., esp. p. 141; on the second issue, see especially Talcott Parsons, "Some Ingredients of a General Theory of Formal Organization," in T. Parsons, *Structure and Process in Modern Societies* (New

seem to be the three models with which Weber interprets the institutional anchorage of administration, politics, and science. The three institutions complement one another according to their specific competencies relating to execution, decision, and advice. They compete by means of their specific authority—political, administrative, and professional. Administrative and professional authority are directed equally against political authority in that they favor a strategy that endeavors to make the politician a dilettante, a layman. The politician can cope with this strategy only by gaining a basis of legitimation outside of science and by learning to counteract administrative information through his participation in an effective parliament. However, politics can achieve this freedom from science and administration only if the demand for limiting oneself to one's legitimate competence follows from the values that are institutionalized in the two realms. This is particularly difficult in the case of science, which in a time bereft of objective meaning—an age of which science itself is the crucial propellant—is encouraged from the most diverse sides to transgress its boundaries. For this reason science requires a special institutional protection—against itself as well as others.

4. ADVANTAGES AND LIMITS OF THE WEBERIAN MODEL

We are now at the point where we can answer the two questions about whether Weber limits, on the theoretical level,

---

York: Free Press, 1967), pp. 59ff., esp. p. 71. The general problem is further complicated by the difference between the old and the new professions. See Albert L. Mok, "Alte und neue Professionen," in *Kölner Zeitschrift für Soziologie und Sozialpsychologie*, 21 (1969): pp. 770ff. An examination of the university, which takes off from Weber and analyzes its organizational problem on the basis of the countervailing tendencies of bureaucratization and professionalization, is provided by Burton R. Clark, "Organizational Adaptations of Professionals," in Howard M. Vollmer and Donald L. Mills, eds., *Professionalization* (Englewood Cliffs, N.J.: Prentice-Hall, 1966), pp. 283ff. See also Wolfgang Schluchter, "Auf der Suche nach der verlorenen Einheit. Anmerkungen zum Strukturwandel der deutschen Universität," in Hans Albert, ed., *Soziale Theorie und Soziale Praxis* (Meisenheim: Hain, 1971), pp. 267ff.

the contribution of theory to praxis to the production of useful knowledge, and whether he favors, on the institutional level, a radical separation of decision and competent execution. Our analysis has shown that we must answer both questions more subtly than is usually done. For Weber asks more of science than merely technical critique and does not perceive in the relation of politics and administration the full institutional realization of his theoretical idea about the relation of cognition and decision. Weber's position involves more than the theory that the sciences can critically examine the practical evaluations of politicians by means of rational and empirical procedures,[121] and can help them and the public realize what is concretely at stake in a political decision. His theory also implies that the sciences contribute to the mediation of the value orientations without which politics can no longer be carried on under conditions of disenchantment. But this is not all. The sciences participate in spreading an ethic of responsibility. Unless the citizens and especially the politicians accept it, the sciences cannot fulfill their tasks for politics. Thus, the sciences can instill a social consciousness which counters decisionist as well as technocratic interpretations of politics. It does not envisage the total independence or dependence of political decision-making with regard to science; rather, this consciousness consists in the idea of a specific relationship to science. Politics must face up to scientific considerations without being fully determined by them. The relationship between the two is not merely technical and one-sided. The scientific critique of practical positions also includes the interpretation of our cultural self-image, and this in turn stimulates science to ask new questions, including politically relevant ones. The social sciences, in particular, which derive their subject matter from cultural values and value relations,[122] are part of this dialectical process. For them value analysis serves the "development of *possible* value po-

121. For a detailed summary of the ways in which science can be helpful in the discussion of practical issues, see Weber, "The Meaning of 'Ethical Neutrality,'" p. 20f.

122. On the methodological significance of the value relationship, see especially Dieter Henrich, *op. cit.* (n. 11 above), pp. 16ff.; from the viewpoint of the

sitions towards a given phenomenon."[123] Looking at it now
from the institutional perspective, we can say that for this
reason science must remain relatively autonomous as an institution. Administration can exist for politics only if it lives
from it, but science must remain independent from politics in
order to be able to live for it. This isolation is necessary not for
the sake of scientific contemplation from the ivory tower and
for the sake of "immaculate conception"—to use a formulation of Parsons—but for the reason that the communication
between science and politics, the paradigm of which is value
analysis, can be mutually fruitful only if it is free from domination. From both an ethical and an institutional perspective
Weber's model of the relation between science and politics can
be fitted only with great difficulty into the decisionist scheme.
It has pragmatic features, although it is not completely identical with the pragmatic model.

This is so for two reasons: From a theoretical perspective
Weber underestimated the degree to which practical considerations can be rationally criticized, and from an institutional
perspective he overestimated the significance of individual
action for the web of collective action. Both tendencies are
rooted in the same weakness—Weber's fixation on a classical
model of rationality. Hans Albert and Niklas Luhmann have
exposed this shortcoming and have tried to remedy it in their
analyses, respectively, of value analysis and of the bureaucratic model.[124] If we integrate their reasoning into Weber's
conception, we can further reduce its decisionist features.

---

sociology of knowledge, see especially Talcott Parsons, "Value-Freedom and
Objectivity," in Stammer, *op. cit.*, p. 34.

123. Cf. "The Meaning of 'Ethical Neutrality,'" p. 22, n. 5.

124. Cf. Hans Albert, *Fraktat* (n. 30 above). According to Albert, the
classical model of rationality rests on the principle of sufficient justification
(*principium rationis sufficientis*) and of theoretical monism: in a given case
there is always only one true or correct theory; there cannot be alternative
theories. Albert criticizes the dogmatic character of the classical model of
rationality by pointing out "that the dogmatization of intuitive insights and of
evident empirical observations which we find in classical epistemology limits
knowledge to the status quo and screens it from basic new insights" (p. 30).
Albert criticizes Weber for assuming that the ultimate value commitments of a
person are not subject to the principle of critical analysis, that "the limit of

Albert elaborated Weber's ideas on value analysis within a framework that replaces the principle of sufficient justification with the principle of critical analysis.[125] If we assess Weber's views on the possibilities and limits of value analysis within this frame of reference, it becomes clear that he championed an existential rationalism, which "combines ethical fundamentalism and pluralism" in a peculiar way.[126] Weber's rationalism is fundamentalist insofar as it recognizes in all basic beliefs a dogmatic core that is impervious to criticism. It is pluralist insofar as it presumes a multiplicity of factually existent and theoretically possible basic positions among which rational discussion is supposed to be feasible. According to Albert, the recognition that value positions can be criticized at the same time that there are intrinsic limits to a critique in view of their dogmatic core is not a tenable distinction. It is undeniable that human beings refuse to have their basic beliefs critically examined, but this indicates limits to the human readiness to accept criticism; it does not denote the limit of the critical method. If we want to make Weber's view consistent, we must abandon his fundamentalism in favor of his pluralism. Then all aspects of a given value position become accessible to critical examination, which focuses especially on the feasibility of practical lines of action. The postulate of feasibility is one of several facilitating principles which help overcome the "distance between normative prescriptions and statements of fact and thus between ethics and science."[127] Critique cannot free us from the need to make decisions, but it can rationalize them.

---

critical argumentation is reached once we have identified the consistency of the various possible positions" (p. 70). If, according to the canons of critical analysis, "ethical statements and systems are treated not as dogmas but as hypotheses, then it must in principle be permissible to consider alternatives and to sketch new perspectives that can provide different solutions for ethical problems from the customary ones" (p. 75). See also Niklas Luhmann, "Zweck-Herrschaft-System," in *Bürokratische Organisation,* ed. Renate Mayntz (Cologne: Kiepenheuer, 1968), pp. 36ff., and *Zweckbegriff und System-rationalität* (Frankfurt: Suhrkamp, 1973), chap. 1.

125. Albert, *Traktat,* pp. 29ff. 126. *Ibid.,* p. 70.

127. *Ibid.,* p. 76. However, Marianne Weber cites a passage from a letter

This critical reception of Weber's view supports a central idea of our analysis—the superiority of the ethic of responsibility over the ethic of ultimate ends. If we assume that Weber did indeed put the ethic of responsibility over the ethic of single-minded conviction, Albert's reasoning fits easily into Weber's. For the ethic of responsibility formulates the same postulate as does critical rationalism: Thou shalt expose even thy most profound convictions to critique and have them examined for their feasibility.[128] There can be no final solutions.[129] Thus, although Weber's view about the relation of cognition and decisions contains fundamentalist and hence decisionist elements, the critical component predominates. From a theoretical perspective Weber's model can easily be transformed into that of critical rationalism.

On the institutional level matters are less simple. Weber doubtlessly gave greater weight to the decisionist components than appears justified from his theoretical basis when he addressed himself to the institutional translation of his position. One indication for this is his very emphasis on the relation between the politician and bureaucracy. Moreover, his analysis proceeds under the flag of cultural criticism. He is concerned with the ways in which individualist freedom can be rescued in the face of bureaucratic might.[130] In Weber's essays rationalization had led to "subsystems of instrumentally rational

---

which indicates that Weber set a limit not so much to discussion as to confession. Only the prophet, the saint, or the artist is free to disregard that limit, and Weber emphatically did not see himself as any one of them. Marianne Weber, *op. cit.* (n. 6 above), p. 599.

128. Cf. the formulation by Hans Albert, *Traktat,* p. 73: "The closure of belief systems is therefore not a dictate of logic or of any objective agency, but a dictate of the will and the interests and needs behind it. We might say that the openness of belief systems is itself a moral issue."

129. This means that the search for certainty and the search for truth are not identical. It is true that the principle of uncertainty presupposes the principle of truth as a regulative idea, but cognition does not result in ultimate certainty. For this very reason certainty as a principle of action and uncertainty as a principle of cognition must be attuned to each other.

130. Weber, "Parliament and Government," *ES,* p. 1403.

action,"[131] which have become autonomous and thus have cut themselves loose from human needs. In his view these subsystems can be put to the right use only by the "guiding spirit," the outstanding personality. The commando posts in state and economy must be manned by these personalities. By virtue of their moral qualification, it is up to politicians and entrepreneurs to set the goals in a society hamstrung by systemic constraints and to have them pursued by virtue of their control over the subsystems of instrumentally rational action. As Niklas Luhmann has shown, Weber interprets the relation of the politician to the bureaucracy, and of the entrepreneur to the enterprise, on the basis of a means-ends scheme conceived on the level of individual action and translated into a command model (*Befehlsmodell*).[132] This explains why in many passages of Weber's analyses the rationality of "the system" is tied,

131. On this terminology, cf. Jürgen Habermas, *op. cit.* (n. 14 above), p. 65. Habermas distinguishes between systems of instrumentally rational action and the institutional framework, a distinction derived from the Marxian paired concepts "productive forces" and "productive relations" and put in parallel to the distinction between instrumental and communicative action. Habermas employs these distinctions in order to integrate Weber's analysis of the rationalized society in an enlarged and revised Marxian framework and to push Weber beyond himself. In this manner Habermas tries to resolve certain obvious difficulties of both the Marxian and the Weberian theory and to make these theories useful for the analysis of the technocratic basis of "late capitalist" societies. I have the impression that this rather increases the difficulties. For one, the concrete mediation of action and system levels, on the one hand, and of kinds of action and system, on the other, remains relatively arbitrary. It is no accident that Habermas's analysis leads to an exceedingly vague practical program. The formula of reestablishing the difference between technology and praxis through a politicization of the public by means of free (*herrschaftsfrei*) debate at best adumbrates a pragmatic model; it does not make it concrete.

132. Cf. Luhmann, "Zweck-Herrschaft-System" (n. 124 above), p. 42: "The unquestioning acceptance of ends determined by the ruler takes the place of substantively determined directives. A concept of purpose generalized in this fashion (and thereby freed from problematic aspects) is combined with the concept of command. Thus, a social system becomes rational if there is assurance that the ruler's purposes are realized within certain limits determined by the suitability of the system. The means are no longer linked to the ends by logical deduction, but by an order."

under the conditions of disenchantment, to the rationality of the politician and the entrepreneur. This also explains why in his own time Weber considered only outstanding personalities capable of eliciting and stabilizing the citizens' trust in "the system."[133] On the institutional level, then, Weber's model remains ambivalent. To a degree he polarized the individual's and the system's rationality, trust in the person and trust in the system, in such a way as to put voluntarism above structural determination and the discretion of the individual above institutional constraint.[134] However, while this is one basic feature of Weber's institutional model, we must not overlook another one which fits into the matrix of critical rationalism. This latter feature can be concretely demonstrated with the example of value analysis as an institution. If we want to accentuate this feature as against the decisionist one, we must extract Weber's model from the contemporary context in which it remains inevitably embedded, and must give precedence to the structuralist over the voluntarist analysis, to the sociological perspective over the perspective of cultural critique. If we do this, we can bring Weber's model closer to the pragmatic one even on the institutional level.

Weber's model of the relation of science and politics is ambivalent and incomplete. This forces us not only to uncover its fundamental features but also to elaborate it. However, this model sketched very broadly in two speeches more than half a century ago retains relevance for us today. It formulates in paradigmatic fashion—the paradigm of critical rationalism—the relation of science and politics. Thus, it is more than a mere relic of a scientific tradition. The problems with which it tries to come to terms remain tasks for our scientific reflection and political praxis.

133. On the concept of trust, see the investigations by Niklas Luhmann, *Vertrauen. Ein Mechanismus der Reduktion sozialer Komplexität* (Stuttgart: Enke, 1968), pp. 45ff. With the help of the concept of trust it might be possible to reformulate the concept of belief in legitimacy, which lacks clarity in certain respects.

134. On this basic issue in macrosociological analysis, see M. Rainer Lepsius, "Demokratie in Deutschland als historisch-soziologisches Problem," in T. W. Adorno, ed., *Spätkapitalismus oder Industriegesellschaft?* (Stuttgart: Enke, 1969), pp. 197ff., esp. p. 202.

EXCURSUS: THE QUESTION OF THE DATING OF
"SCIENCE AS A VOCATION" AND "POLITICS AS A
VOCATION"

There is much confusion in the literature on the dating of
Weber's two speeches. According to Marianne Weber, both were
given in 1918 and published in 1919 (cf. Marianne Weber, *Max Weber,*
trans. Harry Zohn, New York: Wiley, 1975, p. 664). Johannes
Winckelmann proceeds from the dates of publication, "Science as a
Vocation" in 1919, "Politics as a Vocation" in October 1919, and
guesses that both speeches were given in the winter of 1918/19 (cf.
Weber, *Gesammelte Aufsätze zur Wissenschaftslehre,* ed. J. Winckelmann,
Tübingen: Mohr, 1968, 3rd ed., p. 582); and Weber, *Gesammelte
Politische Schriften,* ed. J. Winckelmann, Tübingen: Mohr, 1958, 3rd
ed., p. 493). On the basis of his familiarity with Weber's correspon-
dence, Eduard Baumgarten suggests that both speeches were given
within the span of a few weeks, "Science as a Vocation" probably on
January 16, 1919, "Politics as a Vocation" with certainty on January
28, 1919 (cf. E. Baumgarten, "On the Question of Dating Weber's
Speeches," manuscript in the office of the Max Weber Edition,
Bavarian Academy of Science, Munich). Immanuel Birnbaum, who
was one of the organizers of the series on "Intellectual Work as a
Vocation" for the Bavarian branch of the Freistudentische Bund,
recalls that he persuaded Weber to participate with two speeches.
First he recruited him for "Science as a Vocation," an easy undertaking in view of Weber's own interest in the subject matter. However,
Weber did not want to talk about "politics as a vocation" in the wake
of the November revolution of 1918, because he faced a situation in
which he doubted his qualification for a political career. Weber suggested Friedrich Naumann, whom he had considered "for a long
time as the right man to lead Germany toward democracy." Only
after Naumann declined because of illness and radical students
moved to invite Kurt Eisner could Weber be persuaded to take on
the topic. (On Eisner, see Allan Mitchell, *Revolution in Bavaria 1918-
1919: The Eisner Regime and the Soviet Republic,* Princeton University
Press, 1965. Weber cites Eisner as the prototype of the charismatic
demagogue in *ES,* pp. 242, 300.) According to Birnbaum's account,
there must have been several months between the delivery of the two
speeches (cf. I. Birnbaum, "Erinnerungen an Max Weber," in *Max
Weber zum Gedächtnis,* ed. R. König and J. Winckelmann, Cologne:
Westdeutscher Verlag, 1963, pp. 19ff.; and his letter to Johannes
Winckelmann, July 15, 1970, office of the Max Weber Edition).
Wolfgang J. Mommsen penetrated beyond this farrago of memories

and speculations by demonstrating with the help of a newspaper article in the Munich *Neueste Nachrichten* of November 9, 1917, that "Science as a Vocation" was delivered in early November 1917 before the Bavarian branch of the Freistudentische Bund in the Kunstsaal Steinicke in Munich. However, since Weber wrote early in 1919 to Mina Tobler about two speeches which he had to postpone several times, Mommsen conjectured that "Science as a Vocation" was given twice, once in connection with "Politics as a Vocation," possibly in the second week of March 1919 (cf. W. J. Mommsen, *Max Weber und die deutsche Politik 1890-1920*, Tübingen: Mohr, 1974, 2nd ed., pp. 289, 345).

Even this dating is inaccurate. Martin Riesebrodt (Office of the Max Weber Edition) ascertained that "Science as a Vocation" was given on November 7, 1917, not on November 8, as Mommsen had presumed. (See *Münchener Neueste Nachrichten,* evening ed., November 7, 1917, p. 2, col. 4, and morning ed., November 9, 1917, p. 3, col. 1.) "Politics as a Vocation" was given on January 28, 1919, as Baumgarten had correctly established. (See *Münchener Neueste Nachrichten,* morning ed., January 25, 1919, p. 2, col. 5: "Prof. Max Weber (Heidelberg) will speak on "Politics as a Vocation" on Tuesday, January 28, 7:30 P.M., in the Kunstsaal Steinicke.") It is not impossible that Weber could not make it on January 28; no newspaper account has been found yet. But the dates mentioned by Mommsen must be excluded, since Weber talked about two other themes. On March 12, 1919, he lectured on "Occidental Bourgeoisie" (*Bürgertum*) before the Social Science Association at the University of Munich; on March 13, 1919, he talked about "Student and Politics" before the Political Association of German Students (also called Bund deutschnationaler Studenten). (See *Münchener Neueste Nachrichten,* morning ed., March 10, 1919, p. 3, col. 3, and evening ed., p. 2, col. 4.)

It is most unlikely that Weber presented "Science as a Vocation" twice. He would have had to do this within the same lecture series before the same group and at the same location. The presumption arose because of the two speeches in Munich at the beginning of 1919, which Baumgarten and Mommsen cited from Weber's correspondence. These two speeches, which had to be postponed several times, are obviously the two just mentioned.

Our dating is also supported by a letter from Frithjof Noack to Marianne Weber (October 25, 1924). Apparently in preparation of her biography, Marianne Weber asked Noack, who belonged to the Freistudentische Jugend, to make inquiries about "Science as a Vocation," "Politics as a Vocation," and the speech on the reconstruction of Germany of November 4, 1918. Noack's letter reports his findings, which also include a lengthy statement by Birnbaum. Noack notes that "Science as a Vocation" was given in early November 1917, "Politics as a Vocation" one and one-half years later in February or March 1919. The two speeches were revised and prepared for print by Weber on the basis of a stenographic protocol. "Science as a Vocation" seems to have been in print by early 1919. "Politics as a Vocation" was probably not ready for the printer until March 1919.

The lecture series was organized by the Freistudentische Bund in Bavaria, a left-leaning liberal student group, which stood, as Marianne Weber put it, "at the crossroads of the revolutionary and the patriotic movement" (*Max Weber,* p. 628). The series was prompted by an essay by Alexander Schwab, a pupil of Alfred Weber's, on "Vocation and Youth." Schwab took a dim view of taking up a profession insofar as it seemed to be incompatible with living in accordance with the spirit of science. The series was intended to discuss the pros and cons of this view. As Immanuel Birnbaum put it in the postscript to the first edition of "Science as a Vocation," the lectures were supposed to be "expert opinions." On the basis of four vocations—science, education, art, and politics—the same question was to be answered: How is vocation in the proper sense of the term—as *geistiger Beruf*—possible today without flight from the world or accommodation to it?

Apart from Weber, Kerschensteiner, Hausenstein, and Naumann were supposed to speak. (Noack maintains that the third speaker was Schäfer; Birnbaum seems to remember that the third theme was theology and the intended speaker Lippert.) Presumably Weber knew this student group from the meeting on Castle Lauenstein late in September 1917, where he also met Ernst Toller. On September 29, 1917, Weber talked at this meeting about "Personality and the Social Order" (*Lebensordnungen*), which was perhaps a first version of "Science as a Vocation" on the basis of "Religious Rejections of the World and Their Directions" (cf. "Theory," pp. 323-362, and Marianne Weber, *Max Weber,* p. 600). From then on members of the Freistudentische Bund seem to have belonged to Weber's audience for his numerous Munich speeches—his great speech for a negotiated peace and against the Pan-German danger on November 5, 1917; "Science as a Vocation" on November 7, 1917; the speech on Germany's political reorganization on November 4, 1918, and the subsequent meeting in the home of Erich Katzenstein, who played an important role during the revolution; "Politics as a Vocation" on January 28, 1919; and finally the memorable discussion between Weber and Oswald Spengler during the winter semester 1919/20. Through these speeches Weber also maintained public contact with sections of the revolutionary Munich Bohemia. In Noack's report to Marianne Weber we read: "It was very important to Weber that among his listeners were members of the Freistudentische Bund and a group of young literary revolutionaries (Trummler, Roth, and others), with whom he also debated privately. A good deal of the two speeches ['Science as a Vocation' and 'Politics as a Vocation'] was addressed to these groups. The second speech was probably also addressed to Ernst Toller, whom Weber, in the company of Immanuel Birnbaum, sometimes visited in the Hotel Grünwald. How strongly Weber was interested in debating revolutionaries can also be gleaned from his desire to meet Levien; he remarked that he had had no contact with Russian Bolsheviks for quite some time." (On the Munich Bohemia see Martin Green, *The von Richthofen Sisters.* New York: Basic Books, 1974, pp. 85ff., a book that suffers from a lack of sociological conceptualization.)

Weber's relationship to the Freistudentische Bund had also another, deeper significance for him. In such associations he recognized a certain opportunity for the rise of a new political culture after the phase of psychological collapse, of "detestable exhibitionism," of the loss of all upright bearing. This culture would be oriented toward matter-of-factness and discreetness; it would not continually mix up private and public matters and individual and collective problems of existence. Weber believed that Germany was finished not only militarily but also psychologically: "At the moment we have lost face as no people in a similar situation has ever lost face, neither Athens after Aigospotamoi [405 B.C.] and Chaironaia [338 B.C.], nor for that matter France in 1871." In Weber's eyes, reconstruction could be accomplished not by churches but only by sects, not by compulsory but only by voluntary associations—his model was the American club with its principle of voluntary membership and exclusiveness. Weber saw the beginnings of such a development in the Freistudentische Bund, with which he sympathized not only politically but also, so to speak, sociologically. (See Weber's letter to the classical philologist Friedrich Crusius in Munich, November 24, 1918, cited in Marianne Weber, *Max Weber,* p. 636. However, the content of the letter is apparently rendered inaccurately. Cf. Wolfgang Mommsen, *Max Weber,* p. 347. I did not have access to the original.)

Part II

III

CHARISMA AND THE COUNTERCULTURE

Guenther Roth

1. History and Sociology

Max Weber began his academic career as an historian and ended it as a sociologist, but intellectually this move meant for him a division of labor, not an antagonistic relationship between the roles of historian and sociologist. His methodological position is not well suited for the defense of vested interests in disciplinary boundaries or for the preference of one academic field over the other. I believe that the reexamination of Weber's thought is useful primarily for the sake of understanding some of the ways in which important questions about past and present can be dealt with irrespective of the narrow survival interests of the two disciplines.

In the course of his career Weber gradually came to champion a new sociology which differed from the old evolutionary sociology against detractors among historians and economists who failed to comprehend the difference. He expected to be recognized as "a partisan in methodological matters, something I want to be," as he wrote to Heinrich Herkner in 1909. One important aspect of his partisanship involved the struggle against organicist and other reified concepts of social life, which had been basic to the old sociology and its followers among evolutionary historians.[1] When

1. See my essay on "Value-Neutrality in Germany and the United States," in Reinhard Bendix and G. Roth, *Scholarship and Partisanship* (Berkeley and Los Angeles: University of California Press, 1971), pp. 37–42.

Weber took one of the first German chairs combining economics and sociology at the University of Munich after the end of the First World War, he wrote (on March 9, 1920) to the economist Robert Liefmann, who had attacked sociology: "I do understand your battle against sociology. But let me tell you: If I now happen to be a sociologist according to my appointment papers, then I became one in order to put an end to the mischievous enterprise which still operates with collectivist notions (*Kollektivbegriffe*). In other words, sociology, too, can only be practiced by proceeding from the action of one or more, few or many, individuals, that means, by employing a strictly 'individualist' method."[2] This remark anticipated Weber's position in the first chapter of *Economy and Society*, which was about to be published, albeit after his sudden death. In his introductory methodological observations he made it plain that, with regard to this "individualist" method, which only through a "tremendous misunderstanding" could be equated with "an individualist system of values," there was no difference between sociology and history, since "both for sociology in the present sense and for history the object of cognition is the subjective meaning (*Sinnzusammenhang*) of action."[3] This was meant to be true in the sense of an ultimate referent. Of course, it did not force Weber, as it has sometimes been asserted mistakenly, to limit himself to what was in the minds of individual actors. Individuals, whether "great men" or multitudes acting out "collective behavior," play almost no role in Weber's research. Instead we find an overriding concern with the dominant economic, political, legal, and religious structures of Western history and of China and India as main comparisons. All of these structures were full of internal contradictions, and in all of them people suffered the fact of unanticipated consequences. Weber did not differ from Marx in believing that human beings make their own history, though under iron constraints.

2. Cited in H. H. Bruun, *Science, Value and Politics in Max Weber's Methodology* (Copenhagen: Munksgaard, 1972), p. 38.

3. *ES*, pp. 18 and 13.

If there was no difference between sociology and history in one regard, there could be a division of labor in another:

As we have taken for granted throughout this presentation, sociology formulates type concepts and searches for general uniformities (*Regeln*) within the stream of events, in contrast to history, which aims at the causal analysis and causal attribution of individual actions, structures, and personalities that have cultural significance. Sociological concept formation takes its materials, as paradigms, essentially albeit not exclusively, from the realities of action that are also relevant from the perspectives of history. In particular, sociology proceeds according to considerations of the service it can render through its concept formation to the historically causal attribution of culturally significant phenomena.[4]

In 1920 statements such as these could be helpful in answering the often-asked skeptical question as to the academic rationale of sociology, although they were unlikely to convince the determined doubters. In his brief distinction Weber did not go all the way in reducing sociology to Clio's handmaiden, but the formulation of "type concepts and general uniformities" in *Economy and Society* was indeed primarily an auxiliary operation for historical analysis proper. Sociology in this sense was part of the "methodology" of history, basically a comparative and typological procedure, a logical precondition for causal analysis. Before the First World War, when he considered publishing *Economy and Society* in an earlier form, Weber wrote to the medievalist Georg von Below, who remained one of the most vociferous opponents of sociology as an academic discipline in the 1920s:

We are absolutely in accord that history should establish what is specific to, say, the medieval city; but this is possible only if we first find what is missing in other cities (ancient, Chinese, Islamic). And so it is with everything else. It is the subsequent task of history to find a causal explanation for these specific traits. . . . Sociology, as I understand it, can perform this very modest preparatory work.[5]

If this distinction could legitimate an academic division of

4. *ES*, p. 19.   5. Cited in *ES*, p. LVIII.

labor, it certainly did not prescribe that the individual researcher be either an historian or a sociologist. Methodologically, the important point was the recognition of the difference in levels of analysis irrespective of the labels given to them. In fact, in his earliest general methodological statement, Weber wrote about these two levels as aspects of the work carried on in one and the same discipline. When he took over the *Archiv für Sozialwissenschaft und Sozialpolitik* in 1904 with Edgar Jaffé and Werner Sombart, a major event in the history of German social science and of the methodological controversies of the time, he made a programmatic statement about what he then called "social economics" and not yet "sociology":

To the extent that our discipline (*Wissenschaft*) attempts to explain particular cultural phenomena of an economic nature by showing, through causal regress, that they originated in individual causes, be they economic or not, it seeks "historical" knowledge. Insofar as it traces a particular element of cultural life, namely the economic one, through the most diverse cultural contexts, it aims at an historical *interpretation* from a specific point of view [i.e., the problematical relationship between economic and non-economic factors] and offers a partial picture, a *preliminary* step toward a complete historical understanding of culture (*volle historische Kulturerkenntnis*).[6]

Of course, Weber did not believe in the existence of society as a quasi-organic entity, an objectively delimited structure, which would allow a complete analysis of culture and in this sense the discovery of "the truth" as it was postulated by organicist theories but also by Marxism with its correspondence theory of object and concept. Weber rejected the empirical relevance of the notion of the social totality and historical teleology—as all empirical social scientists must do. Rather, for him a complete analysis of culture meant investigating the manifold relationships among the major areas of social life, and for this reason *Economy and Society* elaborates sociologies of the "particular elements of cultural life"—economy, religion, law, domination, and "culture" (in the narrower sense of

6. *WL*, p. 163f.; cf. *The Methodology of the Social Sciences*, ed. E. Shils and H. Finch (Glencoe: Free Press, 1949), p. 66. (Weber's emphasis.)

the term), especially music. Recently Wolfgang Mommsen
pointed out, quite correctly, that Weber "remained faithful
throughout his life to the methodological position which he
had taken up between 1903 and 1907. . . . It may well be said
that [his] later work was essentially an elaborate attempt to
knit a variety of 'partial pictures' of culture into a general
framework of 'ideal types' in order to get as close as possible"
to what I prefer to call here that "complete historical understanding of culture" (rather than what he translates as "a
comprehensive perception of culture").[7]

In his methodological writings Weber took his stand on the
scholarly disputes of his time among students of history,
economics, and jurisprudence, from the aftermath of the
Methodenstreit of the 1880s to the later controversies in the
Verein für Sozialpolitik. These writings, most of which are now
available in English (in sometimes unsatisfactory translation),
are polemical or programmatic.[8] They either address themselves to the work of other scholars or deal broadly with pro-

7. Wolfgang Mommsen, *The Age of Bureaucracy: Perspectives on the Political
Sociology of Max Weber* (Oxford: Blackwell, 1974), p. 10f. It needs scarcely to
be pointed out that constructing "partial pictures" is the teaching practice of
academic sociology, which presents its subject matter in segmentalized
courses on stratification, organization, politics, religion, etc. No department
attempts that "complete analysis of culture" that Weber envisaged as an ongoing effort at synthesis. Marxist-oriented courses present a total theory of
society, but frequently this boils down to little more than summaries of the
theories of capitalism and imperialism, which put a premium on intellectual
simplification rather than on the study of the complex relationships among
the "partial pictures."

8. The oldest translation is *The Methodology of the Social Sciences*, containing
"The Meaning of 'Ethical Neutrality' in Sociology and Economics," " 'Objectivity' in Social Science and Social Policy," and "Critical Studies in the Logic of
the Cultural Sciences." See also "Marginal Utility Theory and the So-called
Fundamental Law of Psychophysics," tr. and ed. Louis Schneider, *Social Science Quarterly*, 56, no. 1 (1975): 21–36; "Some Categories of Interpretive
Sociology," tr. and ed. Edith Graber, unpubl. M. A. thesis, University of Oklahoma, 1970; *Roscher and Knies: The Logical Problems of Historical Economics*,
tr. and ed. Guy Oakes (New York: Free Press, 1975); *Critique of Stammler*, tr.
and ed. Guy Oakes (New York: Free Press, 1977). The only essay presently
unavailable is the critique of Wilhelm Ostwald, "'Energetische' Kulturtheo-
rien" (1909), but the reader should keep in mind that Weber made many
methodological remarks in a large number of his writings.

cedures which scholars use irrespective of their own methodological awareness and sophistication. They do not spell out the ways in which he himself proceeded in his own empirical studies, although they do not conflict with his general position. It is true that Weber has occasionally been criticized for forgetting to practice his own methods, most recently by Bryan S. Turner, who has charged that Weber failed to apply the method of *Verstehen* in studying Islamic saints—mistakenly, in my opinion.[9] But while I perceive no basic inconsistencies, I do consider Weber's methodological practice in need of explication. This should help us to perceive more clearly his research strategy, beyond his general remarks and scattered pointers, and thus to get a better grasp of the relationship between history and sociology in his work.

2. Socio-historical Model and Secular Theory

In approaching Weber's writings, the reader must carefully distinguish between sociological generalization and historical explanation, since Weber himself moves back and forth between them without warning. *Economy and Society* is not only a systematic presentation of sociological generalizations and typologies, it is also crammed with historical explanations. It is true that these are mainly asserted rather than elaborated and documented, but they are meant to be taken as informed judgments. After all, within *Economy and Society*, it was impossible for Weber to provide the kind of detailed exposition found in the *Protestant Ethic and the Spirit of Capitalism*, which was to him, significantly, not a sociological exercise but an "essay in cultural history," as he put it to Heinrich Rickert in a letter of April 2, 1905.

In his methodological writings, Weber did not intend to introduce any innovations; rather, he meant to clarify the manner in which many researchers proceed. Similarly, my methodological purpose here is to state as simply as possible a

9. See Bryan S. Turner, *Weber and Islam* (London: Routledge and Kegan Paul, 1974), and my critique in *Contemporary Sociology*, 4, no. 4 (1975): 368.

basic conceptual distinction in Weber's work and that of many historically or comparatively oriented scholars, whether they call themselves sociologists or historians—the distinction between socio-historical model and secular theory. Apart from psychological and sociological universals, historical analysis involves three logical steps: configurational, developmental, situational. Weber deals mainly with (1) the level of socio-historical concepts, that is, concepts with a specifically historical content in contrast to universals such as the categories of social action and the properties of social groups; and with (2) the level of secular theories. The first step consists in the construction of historically grounded sociological typologies or models—the terms are used here interchangeably; the second, in the formulation of secular theories, that is, the description of the course and explanation of the genesis and consequences of particular historical phenomena.[10] The third step, which Weber usually leaves to the historical specialist, consists in analyzing a given situation in terms of its causes and consequences, actual or potential.

The methodology of typologies has usually been discussed on the level of the so-called philosophy of science—how ideal or real, static or dynamic, types are. Here I am dealing with the applied aspect of socio-historical typologies and their substantive content, not with their epistemological status. Socio-historical models (such as bureaucracy, patrimonialism, feudalism, or the charismatic community) are useful to us

10. Secular theories deal with long-range phenomena that have emerged over decades and generations, and could also be called "developmental" theories if the term did not evoke evolutionary associations. I prefer "secular" over "developmental" since Weber opposed the evolutionary fashions of his time in favor of a specifically historical explanation of the unique Western development. Weber did not deny that there was a "general development of culture" (*allgemeine Kulturentwicklung*), involving structural differentiation and rationalization on various levels, but it was neither a necessary unfolding according to some law nor an inexorable teleological process. Finally, while Weber rejected master keys to history, he was interested in a "master theory" of Western history, of which the various secular theories constituted so many building blocks—in principle, a never-ending task of construction.

insofar as they organize historical knowledge in a specifically sociological way, that is, in the form of generalizations that emphasize the general and repetitive side of history without assuming the existence of laws in any strict sense. Such models summarize empirically similar cases and extract typical features without presuming that any one type can in turn exhaustively describe an historical phenomenon. These models are neither static nor dynamic in the scientific sense, but they can spell out a range of variation and possible tendencies toward stability, disintegration, or transformation. For instance, Weber's explanation of the inevitable routinization of persistent charisma is part of the model, whereas his secular theory about the course of charisma is part of the history of Western rationalization. Likewise, the inherent instability of political patrimonialism, on account of its decentralization, is part of the model, whereas the transition from predominantly patrimonial to bureaucratic administration is part of the secular theory of the modern state. The models, then, provide us with generalized experience for the study of past, present, and future, while secular theory attempts the explanation of the rise and fall of major historical configurations.

In general, the first step in applying a model is to look for obviously fitting features in a case; the second is to search for less visible ones, which we know from the model might exist; the third step is to draw up a kind of balance sheet of existing and missing features and thus to establish the particular configuration in terms of the model. However, all concrete cases are typological mixtures, and therefore a comprehensive typological analysis, although it cannot be attempted here, should employ a battery of types. The choice of models and the inclusiveness of the typology depend on pragmatic considerations. Models cannot genetically explain a case, but they can indicate its configurational character as it makes sense to us on the basis of historical experience. Like all theoretical constructs, models constitute a way of seeing things; they reduce the complexity of the world, with all the advantages and disadvantages of structuring our perception. If handled inadequately, their application does not go much beyond labeling and may make it appear that there is nothing new under the sun. However, we must remember with Georg Jellinek that "only because similar events repeat themselves under similiar conditions can history become our schoolmistress."[11] An adequate application will balance the return of the same against the distinctiveness of the new and identify the particular combination of features and factors making up a new situation.

In a given case the boundary between model and secular theory may be hard to draw, especially when the theory encompasses more than one state or economy. In general, a statement is part of a model when it refers to geographically and temporally separate cases. However, the construction of models and of secular theories is closely related. Models are assembled because of certain historical issues, but once formulated they can be applied to various historical constellations. For instance, Weber introduced the distinction between ethical and exemplary prophecy (which will be used below) because he wanted to understand the peculiarity of the Judeo-Christian development in contrast to other world religions. However, once certain typical attitudes and behavior patterns have been identified, they can be recognized in contexts other than the original one. The models must then be linked to other secular theories.

A familiar example of a secular theory is Tocqueville's *The Old Régime and the French Revolution,* which is concerned with the long-range causation of the revolution rather than with the particular circumstances that led to its outbreak at an unpredictable point. Secular theories, then, cannot explain (let alone predict) the point in time at which a phenomenon emerges or disappears. The secular theories of industrial or post-industrial society, for instance, cannot tell us why "the end of ideology" seemed near in the 1950s, only to be displaced by its rebirth in the sixties, which was succeeded in turn by "the cooling of America"—for an uncertain time—in the early seventies. Therefore, a third step, *situational analysis,*

11. Georg Jellinek, *Allgemeine Staatslehre* (Berlin: Häring, 1905), p. 40.

is necessary for explaining an historical constellation, as it has come about not only by virtue of freely willed actions, organizational imperatives, the logic of a system, and a plethora of social trends, but also because of historical accidents. However, situational analysis, too, can only make a specific historical explanation more plausible, not definitive, since it is impossible to weigh the factors aggregated in a given situation.

With this general scheme in mind, we can now turn to two neglected aspects of Weber's treatment of charisma, first the model of the charismatic community, and then the secular theory of the charisma of reason and natural rights.

3. A Model: The Charismatic Community of Ideological Virtuosi

No other part of Max Weber's sociology of domination in *Economy and Society* has proven so troublesome and yet so provocative as the sections on charisma. In popular usage, "charisma" has lost any distinctive meaning and merely denotes a personal *attribute,* the glamor and attractiveness of persons and objects. In contrast to this diffuseness, there has been a strong tendency in academic usage to reduce charisma to a *relationship* between national leaders and manipulated and organized masses. Declaring a moratorium on the uses of the term, as Andrew Greeley suggested some time ago for the similarly troubled concept of the Protestant ethic, would be a convenient way out, but it would also exacerbate the scholarly discontinuities that plague our efforts at cumulative scholarship.

Any attempt at viewing the counterculture in charismatic terms may appear at first sight as another step in overextending the range of their applicability. I should like to suggest, however, that on closer inspection there are two neglected aspects of Weber's analysis that warrant greater attention in view of their contemporary relevance: (1) the charismatic community of ideological virtuosi and (2) the charisma of reason as a revolutionary legitimation founded on natural rights. The youth and student rebellions of the 1960s can be viewed as the charismatic eruption of an ethic of single-minded conviction, reviving the charisma of reason, whereas the peaceful communes and the guerrilla groups that persist in the middle of the "calmer" seventies, after the charismatic mass excitement has died down, can be understood as pacifist and militant charismatic communities which exert a significant cultural and political influence far beyond their numerical size.

Although charisma has become such a widely used and misused term, it is noticeable that the literature on the countercultural movement has rarely employed charismatic categories. Even S. M. Lipset and E. Shils, who previously dealt with charismatic leadership and the charisma of institutions and later gave much attention to the nature and causes of the rebellions, have not seen the latter explicitly as charismatic challenges in spite of recognizing the great importance of the new "ethic of ultimate ends" and of the new "moral mood."[12] However, if we want to draw on Weber's analysis of charisma for an interpretation of countercultural phenomena, we must be clearly aware of the substantive and logical differences between its sociological and its historical dimension. Apart from these two levels of analysis in Weber's work there is also a substantive divergence in his writings on charisma: the model of the charismatic community is not directly related to the secular theory of charisma, especially of its course as a force of self-legitimation in modern history. Because of its trans-epochal and trans-cultural quality, the model cannot be falsified; it can only be judged to be more or less useful in a given case. The secular theory of the charisma of reason and natural rights, however, can be falsified, at least insofar as the historical impact of the phenomenon is concerned.

Weber's sociology of domination deals with legitimation and administration in the triangle of ruler, staff, and population-

12. See Seymour M. Lipset, "The Possible Effect of Student Activism on International Politics," in *Students in Revolt,* ed. S. Lipset and P. Altbach (Boston: Beacon, 1970), p. 512; Edward Shils, "Dreams of Plentitude, Nightmares of Scarcity," in *ibid.,* p. 12.

at-large, but the greatest amount of attention is given the administration. This view contrasts with the critique sometimes encountered that the types of legitimate domination deal with the problem of legitimation in a purely subjective sense. In fact, however, the bulk of Weber's sociology of domination deals with structural sources of conflict between rulers, staffs, and subjects, with the struggle over the control of the means of administration and production, and always also with the economic presuppositions and consequences of a given kind of rulership.

It is an empirical question whether charismatic groups have a strong or a weak authority structure. But they invariably require extraordinary qualifications, which set the members apart from the population-at-large, the "charismatic subjects." It is well known that Weber moved from the nascent usage of "charisma" in the chapter on religious groups in *Economy and Society* to its systematic usage in the chapters on the sociology of domination; it is less well understood that he also transferred the concept of the congregation or community (*Gemeinde*) from the religious to the political sphere and came to define *Gemeinde* as the typical charismatic association.[13] This religious provenance makes it easier to focus here on groups with ideological inspiration. After the general decline of magical and hereditary charisma, and apart from charismatic gangs concerned with violence and booty, the most prominent variant of charisma today is an ideological and acquired one, although in recent years there has been some reassertion of magical charisma.

What are some major features of the ideological charismatic community? Formally, it is an emotional consociation, which may range from an amorphous group of charismatic equals in which domination is minimized, to a well-developed "ruling organization" with a strong leader and a dedicated staff; its members, not just the leaders, are charismatics or virtuosi; whether militant or pacifist, they adhere to an ethic of single-minded conviction and tend toward ethical or

13. See *ES*, pp. 452, 243, 1119.

exemplary prophecy (or charisma); they satisfy their wants through a consumption-oriented communism either of love or of war, through gifts or spoils, which contrasts with traditionalist or rational economic activities. Lest the term "prophecy" be misunderstood, it should be clear that in our secularized world, in which religious prophecy is indeed no longer predominant, "semi-prophetic social reformers" have great appeal.[14] Since Weber's broadest definition of prophecy is a sense of mission and the proclamation of a doctrine, and since he spoke of the "prophets of revolution" in a secular sense, we can feel free to apply the term to present times. Ethical prophecy applies politically transcendent standards to the powers-that-be, which thus appear sinful and depraved and destined to ultimate destruction, while exemplary prophecy endeavors to achieve its impact not by preaching but by exemplary conduct. Exemplary prophets try to win adherents and followers by elevating their own conduct above the ordinary. Both ethical and exemplary prophets view the world as a meaningful totality and offer an integrated *Weltanschauung*, whether logically coherent or not, which requires an extraordinary correspondence between belief and action.

The notion of an ideological virtuoso, which I am introducing here, is a terminological extension of Weber's "religious virtuoso" who adheres to an ethic of single-minded conviction.[15] "Virtuosity" is one of Weber's many nominalist ironies. Colloquially, the term connotes technical brilliance or excellence, but since its root is "virtue," it is applicable to true believers. There is a double meaning here: the virtuosi are "men of virtue," but they are, so to speak, highly accomplished technicians in matters moral. Insofar as their concerns are purely religious, they are often without direct political effectiveness, as has been true of many recent American sects. However, in the realm of politics, the ideological virtuosi constitute that minority of persons whose spiritual needs and passionate commitments cannot be satisfied by piecemeal social amelioration or political compromise, in contrast to the

14. *ES*, p. 441.   15. See *ES*, p. 539f.

majority who accept the routines and rules of politics out of habit, opportunism, or affirmation. Both the pacifist and the militant virtuosi embrace a moralistic absolutism that rejects established authority, whether religious or political, and the social status quo. These persons are charismatic not only because they claim a legitimacy of their own but also because they endeavor to form their own groups. In times of relative political stability, routine politics, and even at the beginning of a crisis, the charismatics are relatively isolated. But when long-range structural changes and historical accidents lead to a crisis of legitimacy, the virtuosi will become important, whether or not they ultimately succeed in seizing power. In times of trouble, many ordinary men can be swept along by a charismatic movement, and sometimes this leads to a political revolution.

4. A Secular Theory: The Charisma of Reason and the Impact of Marxism

Weber perceived a long-range, secular decline of historically effective charismatic communities, although charismatic leadership and bureaucratized mass parties sometimes seemed to be compatible.[16] On the contemporary scene of western and central Europe there seemed to be nothing comparable to Protestant ascetics, French Jacobins, or Russian populist revolutionaries. In *Economy and Society* we find ironic references to unsuccessful revolutionary *littérateurs* such as Kurt Eisner (1867–1919), or to the anti-political circle around the poet Stefan George (1868–1933), which Weber considered a charismatic congregation of capitalist rentiers. What had happened to bring about the decline of ideological charismatic communities? For an answer, we must turn to Weber's secular theory of charisma, which concerns the revolutionary impact of natural law and the anti-revolutionary role of Marxism.

Today the anti-revolutionary impact of Marxism, whether

16. See *ES*, p. 1133.

that of the German Social Democrats in Imperial Germany or that of the present-day Communist parties in France and Italy, is general knowledge among students of the socialist labor movements. Seven decades ago Weber was one of the first to recognize this anti-revolutionary effect. The explanation for this seeming historical paradox lies in the way in which Marxism, a self-professed science of revolution, disrupted revolutionary voluntarism as it was upheld by charismatic communities. Marxism entered the historical stage with a sweeping attack on ethical socialism and its natural law foundation.

Historically, natural law became effective for the first time with the victory of Congregationalism—that is, of charismatic sects—and the triumph of the American Revolution, as Georg Jellinek showed in *The Declaration of the Rights of Man and of Citizens,* which was the immediate precursor of *The Protestant Ethic and the Spirit of Capitalism.*[17] Rationalist sects successfully fought for individualistic freedom of conscience, which Jellinek called the oldest right of man.[18] The postulates of legal equality and economic mobility were joined to this right. French intellectuals and revolutionaries in turn adopted some of these doctrines, which gave the French Revolution "all the aspects of a religious revival," as Tocqueville wrote in 1856; he also noticed the crucial importance of the ideological virtuosi: "men of letters, men without wealth, social eminence, responsibilities or official status, [who] became in practice the leading politicians of the age" and who wanted to "replace the complex of traditional customs governing the

17. Georg Jellinek, *The Declaration of the Rights of Man and Citizens,* trans. Max Farrand (New York: Holt, 1901). First German edition 1895. I am concerned here not with the tenability of Jellinek's theory, only with its influence on Weber. For an inconclusive critique of Jellinek, see Otto Vossler's 1930 essay "Studien zur Erklärung der Menschenrechte," in his *Geist und Geschichte* (Munich: Piper, 1964), pp. 100–117. For a recent treatment of the American history of natural law, see Paul K. Conkin, *Self-Evident Truths: Being a Discourse on the Origins and Development of the First Principles of American Government* (Bloomington: Indiana University Press, 1974), Part I.

18. Cf. chap. 4 below, p. 148.

social order of the day by simple, elementary rules deriving from the exercise of human reason and natural law."[19]

In Weber's terms, the passionate espousal and propagation of the natural rights depicted by Jellinek and Tocqueville signified the rise of the charisma of reason, which gave the individual a revolutionary legitimation for the enlightened pursuit of his own interests vis-à-vis the patrimonial and feudal constraints of the *ancien régime*: "This charismatic glorification of Reason, which found a characteristic expression in its apotheosis by Robespierre, is the last form charisma has adopted in its fateful historical course."[20] Thus, in the course of the historical rationalization and disenchantment of the world, charismatic legitimation comes to depend more on ideas and less on the perceived magical or hereditary qualities of its personal carriers. There is an historical movement from revolutionary challenges inherent in the personal charisma of men with magical powers, such as Jesus (ca. 6 B.C.–ca. 29 A.D.) or Thomas Münzer (ca. 1490–1525), to a charisma of self-evident rights that no longer needs a charismatic personification. The charisma of reason is an historical *impersonalization,* differing from the depersonalization of charisma along the lines of family, clan, ethnic group, or institution (which we find in many historical instances and which is part of the charismatic model).

Of course, the charisma of reason, too, was subject to routinization, and in Weber's eyes the French Revolution was the last charismatic eruption of major structural significance for western Europe. The Revolution institutionalized charismatic legitimation, which previously had been limited to the personal charisma of one or another kind of virtuoso and to lineage and office charisma, in the novel way—by "nationalizing" it. Now it was postulated that the enlightened citizens of an all-inclusive charismatic community, *la grande nation,* legitimate their leaders.[21] From the perspective of class inter-

---

19. Alexis de Tocqueville, *The Old Regime and the French Revolution* (Garden City: Doubleday, 1955), pp. 13, 139.

20. *ES,* p. 1209.

21. Here is the empirical starting point for the widespread theoretical narrowing of charisma into a relationship of national leaders and a mass

ests, the charisma of reason was institutionalized by the liberal bourgeoisie in the form of enacted natural rights in order to secure its own historical gains. Yet, because of its very abstractness, as expressed in its universalist ideals, the charisma of reason retained an inherently revolutionary potential.

Thus, in the decades of the restorative Holy Alliance, a new charisma of reason arose in opposition to the formal natural law espoused by political liberalism as well as to the legal positivism of the resurrected "old order." Ethical socialism, asserting a substantive natural law, became the new revolutionary faith in the 1830s and '40s and spread in two kinds of charismatic communities: militant secret societies and pacifist "utopian" communes. However, ethical socialism did not manage to grow into a large-scale political movement, partly because of the prevailing distribution of power, and partly because of ideological competition from scientism and evolutionism. The main competitor turned out to be Marxist anti-metaphysical radicalism, which not only denounced formal natural law as a weapon of the bourgeoisie, but also rejected ethical socialism as a petty-bourgeois concoction: "Hence in the domain of the revolutionary theories of law, natural law doctrine was destroyed by the evolutionary dogmatism of Marxism."[22] Marxism, understanding itself as the only true—since "scientific"—theory of revolution, thus undermined revolutionary voluntarism in the name of an evolutionary and deterministic interpretation of history. For the rising socialist labor movement, which grew from small charismatic communities into bureaucratized mass organizations, Marxism came to function as a defensive ideology in the face of a powerful political establishment, which negatively integrated and neutralized the movement.[23]

---

following, whereby "demagogues" must legitimate themselves by appeal to the citizens, each of whom, as Shils has pointed out, has his own quantum of charismatic legitimating power. See Edward Shils, "Charisma, Order, and Status," *American Sociological Review,* 30 (1965): 199–213. Reprinted in Shils, *Center and Periphery* (University of Chicago Press, 1975), pp. 256–275.

22. *ES,* p. 874.

23. Cf. Dieter Groh, *Negative Integration und revolutionärer Attentismus*

Historically, however, ethical postulates of social justice and equity have been the normal ideational bases for revolutionary voluntarism and have impelled action irrespective of the "objective conditions" which the *Communist Manifesto* pits against ethical socialism. Marxism could succeed in displacing ethical postulates only in a situation in which there had developed "an almost superstitious veneration of science as the possible creator or at least prophet of social revolution" and in which "scientific" prophecies, such as the prediction of the inevitable collapse of capitalism, replaced postulates within the "eschatological expectations of the masses."[24] Thus did the charisma of reason lose its historical effectiveness and a long period of charismatic silence occur.

Today, more than a century after the victory of scientism and determinism, we encounter a radical change in ideological climate: instead of a belief in continuous and irreversible progress, we face a profound crisis of faith in science as well as in orthodox "scientific" socialism. Moreover, in recent years we have had ample opportunity to notice demonstrations of the historical rule of experience (which is part of the charismatic model) that institutionalized charisma and other forms of routinization will sooner or later be challenged by personal charismatics who endeavor to form communities of their own.

Within the theoretical framework presented here, our task is now twofold: first, to look at the extent to which there are charismatic groups in the counterculture; this requires an application of the model of the charismatic community. Second, to inquire into the manner in which a resurgence of the charisma of reason may have occurred; this requires an extension of Weber's secular theory.

5. APPLICATION: CHARISMA IN THE COUNTERCULTURE

Research into both pacifist and warlike charismatic groups has encountered considerable difficulties of a practical

(Frankfurt: Ullstein, 1973); G. Roth, *The Social Democrats in Imperial Germany* (Totowa, N.J.: Bedminster, 1963).

24. *ES*, pp. 515, 874.

and ideological nature. Conventional research instruments such as the impersonal interview, the questionnaire, the field study, or documentary analysis frequently cannot be employed because the "subjects" are distrustful of scientific manipulation. This in itself is an indication of a new moral mood, of an insistence on being different from the usual respondents, who appear to be mere objects. In addition, conventional research is handicapped because groups have dissolved or moved on or because nobody kept records. This, too, is an indication of an ideological change.[25] Finally, in the case of warlike groups the researcher has normally no access to the underground, and much information useful to him is not obtainable, because it would also be evidence for the public prosecutor. Still, beyond the predominantly journalistic information at our disposal we must make an effort to improve our conceptual grasp of these groups.

By drawing on our historical knowledge, as distilled in the model of the charismatic community and exemplified by many historical cases, diverse features of contemporary groups fall into place and become recognizable as variations on historically familiar themes. Of course, this does not deny the historical individuality of these groups or denigrate their political importance. Within an inclusive model such as the charismatic community, the analyst can compare contemporary sects and communes with medieval or early modern sects or nineteenth-century utopian communities; and the present terrorist groups can be compared with, for instance, anarchist and nihilist terrorism between 1870 and 1914. The typical features of terrorist virtuosi can be traced back to the original Arab "assassins" in the age of the Crusades.

In the following, I shall identify briefly what I consider to be charismatic features in the counterculture. This is a procedure of subsumption, whereby the model permits us to see

25. For a field study of peaceful communes which resolved many of these practical difficulties, see John Hall, *The Ways Out: Utopian Communal Groups in an Age of Babylon* (London: Routledge and Kegan Paul, 1978). Apart from the phenomenology of Alfred Schutz, Hall uses some of Weber's concepts as outlined in this essay.

ideology, internal structure, and want satisfaction of various groups in terms of one configuration. There are several kinds of associations in the counterculture. They run the gamut from political clubs uneasily affiliated with the established parties as a semi-loyal opposition, single-issue associations (such as ecology groups), radical reading circles, and utilitarian living groups of radical professionals, all the way to incipient sects, urban and rural communes, and terrorist *groupuscules*. It is the relatively pacifist sects and communes and the warlike groups that come closest to fitting the model of the charismatic community. The recognition that the same basic phenomenon appears in a dualistic form is familiar to the literature on the youth rebellions, but the dualism of pacifism and militancy has been described only with the help of ad hoc typologies. For instance, S. M. Lipset has suggested a distinction between the "renunciators" and the "radicals."[26] In the broader, and historically more saturated, typology employed here, the renunciators appear as pacifist virtuosi, the radicals as militant charismatics. This wider terminology has the advantage that, as virtuosi, the renunciators can be understood equally well as "affirmators" of an ethic of their own, and both groups as radicals by virtue of their charismatic qualities.

The members of the two kinds of groups become charismatic by embracing an ethic of sheer commitment to an ethical or exemplary way of life and by adopting a distinctive mode of want satisfaction, thus forming an emotional consociation, or an "emotional form of communal relationship."[27] Both kinds of groups respond to the preaching—no matter how secularized—against the sinfulness and depravity of the political and social order. The militant groups remain more ethical in the specific historical sense of making moral demands upon the world and of trying to control the behavior of ordinary men. The pacifists tend to refrain from political

---

26. Cf. Seymour M. Lipset, "Youth and Politics," *Contemporary Social Problems,* ed. R. Merton and R. Nisbet. (New York: Harcourt, Brace, 1971), p. 761.
27. *ES,* p. 243.

activism and to subscribe to an apolitical ethos of brotherhood, to an ideology of "make love, not war." The life style of
many communes approximates exemplary prophecy (or
charisma) to the extent that it is self-consciously set off against
the "American way of life." An outward sign of the complete
break with the past and of the intended or accomplished
metanoia (transformation of self) is the change of names.
Many communards choose non-European names for themselves and their children; and the militants adopt a nom de
guerre from the history or mythology of insurgency.

It is known that religious groups with a hierarchical structure have tended to survive longer than relatively unstruc-
tured and non-religious groups. However, longevity is not the
decisive criterion for the success of a charismatic community,
especially in view of the pressures toward routinization;
rather, it is consistency with the original goals and aspirations.
Many contemporary charismatic communities are distrustful
of formal voting, the majority principle, and elected leaders;
they seem to owe their emergence to a pervasive hostility to
any kind of authority. Political pragmatism and institutional
imperatives are rejected in favor of a highly personalistic
orientation. All human beings (or at least one's peers) are
considered solely "brothers and sisters." Such a personalistic
attitude can be quite compatible with an authoritarian structure; but where anti-authoritarianism prevails in many communities, it is charismatic to the extent that members wait for
the *pneuma,* for the spirit that will overcome everybody and
create a universal consensus. This may involve continuous
communication, interminable discussion, and endless meetings. Many communes did not survive for more than a few
weeks or months because of the absence of any kind of agreed
order or authority. However, the quick demise of so many
communes does not prove the failure of the movement.
There seems to be a charismatic pool in that many communards return time and again to new attempts at building
viable communities.

There is a significant difference in the charismatic rebirth
required of militants and pacifists, although the transforma-

tion may be far-reaching for both kinds. Indeed, since a charismatic way of life is a matter of extraordinary behavior, reversal from a pacifist to a militant stance and vice versa is more consistent than a "return to normalcy." But in addition to becoming "new men," the militants must turn themselves into "warriors of the faith" and acquire the "charisma of fighting frenzy."[28] Of course, those who try to live the communism of love most of the time can at times participate in *ephemeral* communities of war and become momentary berserks during street fighting. However, the solidarity of large numbers of people in the streets is not the same as a *continuous* community, although it too can lead to formative generational experiences and give rise to small groups united by shared memories ("communities of fate"). The militants endeavor to become instruments of revolution, which they hope to lead by exemplary heroism. They are expected not only to risk their own lives, but to be ready to harm and destroy other people. "Bourgeois" inhibitions and humanitarian sentimentalism, from sexual scruples and private ties to tolerance and humor, must be overcome. Self-criticism and group-criticism of the individual are practiced relentlessly. Monogamous relations between married and unmarried couples may be forbidden. Sleep may be rationed for disciplinary reasons, and all kinds of acts of obedience and submission may be demanded.[29]

We know from historical experience that charismatic communities must either have independent economic resources or depend on various forms of subsidy. Members of a charismatic group may be capitalist rentiers, operate at the margins of the market economy, or depend on charity and outright solicitation, like mendicant monks. Of course, living on unearned income is not in itself a charismatic feature; capitalist rentiers or patrimonial benefice-holders are usually very far from being charismatics. However, many communards live either from their dividend checks or from scholarships and

---

28. *ES,* p. 242.
29. For illustrations in the case of the Weather Underground, see Thomas Powers, *Diana: The Making of a Terrorist* (New York: Bantam, 1971).

stipends, which they consider as little more than sinecures. Typically, the land for a commune is bought by a well-to-do member, who has inherited or sometimes earned money, or it is made available as a gift from a wealthy patron.[30] Frequently, no outright legal transfer can take place, since the group either refuses to incorporate, has much turnover, or simply melts away. However, once an inheritance is eaten up, or parents cut off an allowance, or sinecures are terminated, the only alternatives are charismatic solicitation or economic self-help of one kind or another, from drug-dealing to economic autarky. Thus, even street-begging, an ancient device of charismatic want satisfaction, was revived for a time by the adolescent offspring of proper middle-class families. Even those communes that make strong efforts to produce their own food or sell their craft products remain, in almost all cases, heavily dependent on outside support—allowances, alimony, welfare payments, food stamps. "Working the system" (welfare chiseling, in establishmentarian language) can be explained as a revolutionary act of expropriation, as can "ripping off" (petty thievery, in legal terms), another important source of unearned income. The militants also resort to kidnapping and highjacking for the sake of ransom, and to extortion and robbery, apart from relying on clandestine support from sympathizers.

This application of the model of the pacifist and militant charismatic community has aimed at identifying charismatic configurations in the counterculture. For some research, the model may be too simple and may need to be differentiated into subtypologies or hyphenated types. But any elaboration or modification of the model should be linked to substantive explanatory interests involving one or the other of the secular theories of contemporary polity and society. Within the present confines, I can only sketch an extension of Weber's secular theory of charisma and touch upon certain ideological changes that may justify the appellation of a renewed charisma of reason.

30. Cf. Robert Houriet, *Getting Back Together* (New York: Avon, 1971).

Whatever structural determinants were involved in the rebellion of the sixties and early seventies and the charismatic
communities in their wake—there is profound disagreement
about which objective conditions led to which outcomes—
there is general consensus that a new moral mood crystallized.
Significantly, there has been an ethical rejuvenation of Marxism, after scientific socialism had been discredited in the East
and West by Stalinism. Since the sixties, many young people
have been powerfully attracted by the ethical core of Marxian
philosophical anthropology or have harked back to the American traditions of political moralism and missionary fervor to
turn "the system's" own professed values, with their natural
rights legacies, against the prevailing way of conducting politics. Most important, there has been a strong ideological
movement from equality of opportunity—a legacy of American constitutionalism and still the dominant demand in the
early stages of the civil rights movement—toward various notions of equity, including the demands for minority quotas.
There has been a veritable inflation of rights, a "revolution of
entitlements," as Daniel Bell has phrased it.[31] The demands
addressed to state and society range from family income
maintenance and academically unregulated, publicly financed
education to the right of living one's own life without any
restrictions. Backed by non-charismatic pressure groups,
some of these rights have been legislated into positive law, but
all of them are ultimately justified by recourse to basic principles of individual rights and social justice. In a secularized
and rationalized society in which faith in revelation has little
direct political impact, this ultimate justification cannot be
anything but some notion of self-evident rights—the charisma of reason.

However, this formulation does not discriminate sufficiently between claims advanced within the routines of reform politics and those directed against the status quo from
groups outside the dominant liberal tradition. Today the as-

31. Daniel Bell, *The Cultural Contradictions of Capitalism* (New York: Basic
Books, 1976), pp. 232ff.

sertion of inherent rights is charismatic insofar as it provides a revolutionary legitimation vis-à-vis the bureaucratic constraints of industrial society—Weber's "iron cage." These revolutionary demands are thus part of the general disjunction between social structure and culture observed by Daniel Bell, between the vocational and professional specialization required by industrial society and the postulates of total freedom in the cultural sphere.[32] Carried to logical and psychological extremes, the insistence on maximum freedom tends to transcend the historical boundaries of the charisma of reason and to turn into a charisma of unreason, a new irrationalism that justifies the widespread antinomian and nihilist currents in the counterculture. Whereas the militant virtuosi must maintain some notion of a rational public order for the sake of social justice, many pacific "hippies" have gone a long way toward the new irrationalism that is totally unconcerned with the organization of society-at-large, as long as they can "do their own thing." Somewhere along this road, we encounter a renewed magical charisma, from guru worship to devil cults and other preoccupations with the occult—a mythic landscape in which the historical charisma of reason and timeless magical charisma can no longer be distinguished.

32. Cf. Daniel Bell, *The Coming of Post-industrial Society* (New York: Basic Books, 1973).

IV

RELIGION AND REVOLUTIONARY BELIEFS

Guenther Roth

1. THE ISSUE OF RELIGIOUS SECULARIZATION

The sociology of religion is one aspect of that many-faceted historical process called "secularization." Without the decline of traditionalist understandings of the world, segmental analytical approaches such as science and critical scholarship could not have come into their own. But secularization has also meant the rise of beliefs competing with revealed religions and metaphysical rationalism on their own grounds —as comprehensive world views providing meaning for one's life and and legitimation for one's actions. Within the sociology of religion there are basically two modes of comprehending these competing beliefs: the functionalist and the historical. From the functionalist viewpoint every organized group requires a belief system. Whether people consider themselves religious or not matters less than the fact that they all need a world view—divergences are mainly a matter of functional equivalents or evolutionary transformation. The logic of functionalism minimizes the historically significant difference between religious and secular world views by playing down the qualitative distinction between salvation religion and "disenchanted" beliefs. But from the historical viewpoint, which I shall adopt here, this difference remains important just because it is part of disenchantment and secularization. We must strike a balance between the identification of distinctive differences and the existence of broad similarities among religious and secular world views.

144

The historically oriented sociology of religion—such as Max Weber's—has been concerned with the character and the vicissitudes of the major religions. Strictly speaking, it is more a sociology of the revealed and ethical religions than of religion per se, which was the object of Durkheim's functionalist analysis.[1] The historical sociology of religion aims at a series of historical generalizations about the major religions and through them at contributing to explanations of specific historical constellations in terms of causality or affinity. Sociology in this Weberian sense is a part of what is sometimes called, somewhat misleadingly, the "methodology" of historical scholarship—that part dealing with the construction of types or models and the formulation of rules of historical experience. Actually, this "methodology" is a fund of generalized historical knowledge, which helps us answer questions by recourse to generalizations about—in our case—religious leadership, the religious propensities of major social strata, processes of instutionalization and routinization, and what Werner Stark has called the "heterogony of purposes."[2] As we have seen in chapter three, Weber's distinction between sociology and history in terms of the contrast between historical generalization and causal analysis appears as the juxtaposition of socio-historical models or typologies and secular theory ("secular," of course, in the sense of long-range rather than temporal or non-spiritual). In the usual historiographic practice these two analytical dimensions are interwoven irrespective of the degree to which the researcher is aware of their distinctiveness.

In this chapter I propose to examine some conceptual and historical issues resulting from the rise of secular belief systems with which Weber dealt in the chapter on sociology of religion in *Economy and Society*, a chapter written shortly be-

1. For a comparison of Durkheim and Weber along these lines, see Reinhard Bendix, "Two Sociological Traditions," in R. Bendix and G. Roth, *Scholarship and Partisanship* (Berkeley and Los Angeles: University of California Press, 1971), chap. 15.
2. See Werner Stark, "Max Weber and the Heterogony of Purposes," *Social Research*, 34, no. 2 (1967): 249–264.

fore the First World War. Confronted with such secular beliefs, the historically oriented sociology of religion must face
the question of the applicability and adaptability of its historically derived conceptual apparatus. In a highly secularized
world, in which the traditional religions have lost much of
their former scope of influence, such a sociology may find
that its subject matter recedes and its own perspective is sub-
merged within a more encompassing political sociology, in
general, and a sociology of the intelligentsia in particular, yet
without arriving at a purely functionalist scheme devoid of
historical categories. In fact, Weber himself linked his sociology of religion to his sociology of law and domination and
endeavored to adapt his religious terminology to some major
phenomena of secularization. I shall try to show that for these
reasons Weber's approach retains a considerable degree of
conceptual adequacy in the face of new historical developments.

Weber's sociology of religion in *Economy and Society* is
primarily concerned with constructing models of religious
leadership and organization and with formulating generalizations about religion and social stratification. A series of
generalizations about the creators and perpetuators of
religions—prophets, priests, and their congregations and
churches—is juxtaposed to summary statements about the
affinities between certain religious beliefs and positively or
negatively privileged status groups, from aristocratic warriors
and patrimonial bureaucrats, through manifold intermediate
layers of merchants and craftsmen, down to slaves and
pariahs. However, Weber's sociology of religion is ultimately
meant to serve the historical explanation of the course of
Western rationalism and therefore contains, in however
sketchy a form, secular theories, although their elaboration
lies beyond the scope of *Economy and Society* and constitutes a
long-range program of research for generations of historians.

The secular belief systems which make part of history
"modern" arose as revolutionary challenges to the received
and established religions, although some Protestant and even
some Catholic lines of religious thought retained a revolu-

tionary potential of their own. Later the secular world views challenged one another in the passage from revolutionary to conservative roles. The rise of new beliefs manufactured by intellectuals is always in some sense revolutionary because it disturbs the status quo. Insofar as Weber's own work on the world religions is concerned with the impact of intellectual creativity and innovation—and this is a very important dimension—it is also a sociology of the rise and spread of innovative beliefs. Indeed, his work contributes to a sociology of the intellectuals in their revolutionary as well as conservative roles. Insofar as it provides a theory of the course of modern revolutionary beliefs, it also supplies a basis for at least attempting an extrapolation to the present time.

I propose to deal first with Weber's secular theory of modern revolutionary beliefs (sec. 2), then with his sociology of ideological virtuosi and of socially marginal groups (sec. 3). The model of revolutionary religious virtuosity will be applied to the Catholic opposition against church and state in the United States (sec. 4). I shall conclude with some observations on the counterculture in the light of Weber's theory and model. This chapter, then, will follow up the preceding one in the specific context of the contemporary applicability of Weber's concepts in his sociology of religion.

Finally, I should like it to be understood that in dealing with anti-establishmentarian secular and transcendental beliefs and their immediate consequences for the believers, I am not concerned with revolution as the successful usurpation of authority and the establishment of a new ruling apparatus—that is a different issue in Weber's sociology of legitimation and domination.

2. A Secular Theory of Modern Revolutionary Beliefs

Weber's account of the course of revolutionary beliefs is a secular theory, in the sense understood here, in that it causally relates a series of events over approximately two centuries. A continuous causal regress is conceivable, but it would extend secular theory into a total evolutionary scheme devoid of specifically historical explanatory value. ("Specifically historical" here refers to explanations of the recorded actions of one or several generations without recourse to evolutionary stage theories.) Moreover, Weber's secular theories are intentionally segmental and do not construe a total theory of given historical society; herein lies a crucial difference from the Marxist method. Other theories of the same subject matter are feasible, depending on the researcher's analytical focus. Finally, such theories are "theoretical" also in the literal sense of being "ways of seeing" a subject matter (and thus of not seeing it in other respects) and in the colloquial sense of not being amenable to unambiguous, scientific proof.

Modern revolutionary beliefs originated in certain sectors of ascetic Protestantism and in philosophical rationalism. They postulated inherent rights of the individual against traditionalist authority. Ascetic Protestantism and Deist Enlightenment propagated religious and metaphysical notions of natural law that amounted to what Weber calls the "charismatic glorification of Reason"—that means, Reason became charismatic by providing a revolutionary legitimation for "natural," self-evident rights against the status quo. Here, in the most succinct form, is Weber's account of the origins and revolutionary consequences of this natual law:

The elaboration of natural law in modern times was in part based on the religious motivation provided by the rationalistic sects. . . . The transition to the conception that every human being as such has certain rights was mainly completed through the rationalistic Enlightenment of the seventeenth and eighteenth centuries with the aid, at certain periods, of powerful religious, particularly Anabaptist, influences. . . . The consistent sect gives rise to an inalienable personal right of the governed as against any power, whether political, hierocratic or patriarchal. Such freedom of conscience may be the oldest Right of Man—as Jellinek has argued convincingly; at any rate, it is the most basic Right of Man because it comprises all ethically conditioned action and guarantees freedom from compulsion, especially from the power of the state. In this sense the concept was as unknown to Antiquity and the Middle Ages as it was to Rousseau's social contract with its power of religious compulsion. The other

Rights of Man or civil rights were joined to this basic right, especially the right to pursue one's own economic interests, which includes the inviolability of individual property, the freedom of contract, and vocational choice. This economic right exists within the limits of a system of guaranteed abstract rules that apply to everybody alike. . . . It is clear that these postulates of formal legal equality and economic mobility paved the way for the destruction of all patrimonial and feudal law in favor of abstract norms and hence indirectly of bureaucratization. It is also clear that they facilitated the expansion of capitalism.[3]

The tremendous charismatic eruption that we call the French Revolution succeeded to the extent that it institutionalized part of the formal natural law of the Enlightenment. However, since formal natural law facilitated bureaucratization and industrialization and augmented their perceived evils, it provoked a critique from inside and outside its basic presuppositions—at any given point there did not appear to be enough formal equality nor enough substantive equity. Ethical socialism arose: "The decisive turn toward substantive natural law [was] connected primarily with socialist theories of the exclusive legitimacy of the acquisition of wealth by one's own labor."[4] This was the second historical stage of modern revolutionary beliefs, since it challenged liberal individualism with schemes of radical social transformation that continued to postulate individual rights but did so in the context of collectivist solutions. However, as we have seen, ethical socialism was in turn attacked and defeated by Marxism, which became the third stage:

The rise of socialism at first meant the growing dominance of substantive natural law doctrines in the minds of the masses and even more in the minds of their theorists from among the intelligentsia. These substantive natural law doctrines could not, however, achieve practical influence over the administration of justice, simply because before they had achieved a position to do so, they were already being disintegrated by the rapidly growing positivistic and relativistic-evolutionistic skepticism of the very same intellectual strata.[5]

3. *ES*, pp. 868, 1209. 4. *ES*, p. 871.
5. *ES*, p. 873.

Here too, as on many other occasions, Weber contrasts the intellectuals and the masses—part of his model of the world religions. The underlying generalization is that mass suffering leads to eschatological expectations and that intellectuals proffer various solutions. In our period of secularization they came up first with notions of formal, then of substantive natural law, but soon went on to positivism and scientism, offering prophecies instead of postulates. The third stage was characterized by the belief that capitalism's demise was inevitable, although revolutionary voluntarism, which was driven by natural law postulates, seemed destined to failure. In a sense, Marx himself became an empirical sociologist through his recognition of the importance of social structural ("objective") conditions, but in his eager polemicism and trusting scientism he developed a blind spot when it came to acknowledging the power of sheer conviction and personal determination on the part of revolutionary virtuosi.

After positivism and relativistic skepticism had become an integral part of bourgeois rationalism, Marxism provided a transition to proletarian rationalism. Both processes were accompanied by the decline of ethical and emotional religiosity, and especially of the kind of revolutionary fervor that in earlier eras had usually appeared in a religious guise. For this reason Weber thought it unlikely that the modern proletariat was going to produce a new congregational religion.

Insofar as the modern proletariat has a distinctive religious position, it is characterized by indifference to or rejection of religion, as is true of broad strata of the modern bourgeoisie. For the modern proletariat the sense of dependence on one's own achievements is supplanted by a consciousness of dependence on purely social factors, market conditions, and power relationships guaranteed by law.... The rationalism of the proletariat, like that of the bourgeoisie of developed capitalism ... cannot in the nature of the case easily possess a religious character and certainly cannot easily generate a religion.[6]

Thus, secularization seemed to run its inexorable course,

6. *ES*, p. 486.

weakening the received religions and making the rise of new religions unlikely. However, not all sections of the proletariat were "modern" (nor all lower-class groups proletarian), and proletarian rationalism displaced older beliefs only partially. Masses of German workers, for instance, were indeed largely alienated from established religion, but for many their estrangement from the benevolent god of Christianity seems to have been founded on their perception of the obvious injustice of the world—hence on a moral feeling rather than on mere positivist belief. Weber referred to one of the earliest working-class surveys undertaken by Adolf Lebenstein, a self-taught worker: "A recent questionnaire submitted to thousands of German workers disclosed the fact that their rejection of the idea of god was motivated, not by scientific arguments, but by their difficulty in reconciling the idea of providence with the injustice and imperfection of the social order."[7] Many workers, then, were converted to socialism primarily by their more or less articulate conviction of the injustice of the social order rather than by any faith in a science of society. On the grass-roots level ethical socialism remained strong, while "scientific" socialism became the official creed of the Social Democratic labor movement.

Although Weber thought it unlikely that the modern proletariat was going to produce a new religion, the labor movement was an ambiguous phenomenon from the viewpoint of his sociology of religion. After all, there were striking ideational and organizational analogies, especially when form and content were viewed separately. By ethical religion Weber meant primarily congregational religion, in which an ethical prophecy imposed a unified meaning on the world and demanded from the believer self-discipline in all realms of life. Christianity had begun as such a congregational religion, and in reaction to its transformation into a universal church, con-

7. *ES*, p. 519. See Adolf Levenstein, *Die Arbeiterfrage* (Munich: Reinhardt, 1912); Weber, "Zur Methodik sozialpsychologischer Enqueten und ihrer Bearbeitung," *Archiv für Sozialwissenschaft*, 29 (1909): 949–958; Anthony Oberschall, *Empirical Social Research in Germany, 1848–1914* (The Hague: Mouton, 1965), pp. 94ff.

gregationalism emerged time and again, reaching a high point with the rationalist Protestant sects and their inner-worldly asceticism. In its early phase the labor movement resembled Christian sects in the high degree of personal commitment and discipline which its members accepted voluntarily. It is true that socialism was not a revealed religion—this is the most obvious difference, if we leave aside variants of Christian socialism—but secular socialism was anchored in convictions about natural law, whether in the ethical sense of the "utopian" socialists or in the "scientific" sense of historical materialism. In both cases it was a matter of belief, since workers tended to accept "scientific" socialism too as an act of faith.

Weber tried to deal with these similarities by resorting to qualifying phrases, such as "quasi-religious," "equivalent to religious faith" or "approximating" a religion, or by using adjectival modifiers which, so to speak, secularized a religious term, such as "this-worldly salvation" or "economic eschatology." Thus, socialism appeared as an "economically eschatological faith" promising "salvation from class rule."[8] Proletarian rationalism tended to supplant the contents of congregational religion with "ideological surrogates."[9] Organizationally, socialism arose in the form of "anti-religious sects," which had a "stratum of declassed intellectuals who were able to sustain a quasi-religious faith in the socialist eschatology at least for a while."[10]

Potentially, the intellectuals were the religious or ethical core of the movement, but their increasingly positivistic ideology militated against whatever charismatic force in terms of ethical self-legitimation they might have constituted. Finally, as the socialist labor movement established itself, organizational concerns and the material interests of the workers gained ascendancy over the ideological predilections of its intellectuals; the socialist leaders used the intellectuals' revolutionary rhetoric, but they were basically pragmatists.

At the time of his writing—about 1910—Weber quite cor-

8. *ES*, p. 515.   9. *ES*, p. 486.   10. *ES*, p. 515.

rectly perceived an anti-charismatic, anti-revolutionary, and religiously uncreative situation in central Europe, although less than a decade later the Russian and German upheavals of 1917–1919 occurred. Over a period of decades religious and revolutionary impulses had greatly diminished in most of Europe. The ebbing of the revolutionary tide accounted in good measure for Weber's fears of impending universal bureaucratization and what he called, in analogy to ancient history, "Egyptianization"—cultural immobility through religious and political traditionalism. When the "guns of August" opened up in 1914, this immobility was disrupted by a mass enthusiasm reminiscent of a great religious revival. An orgy of self-sacrifice engulfed Europe at war, but not many months thereafter a profound disillusionment set in. Mass despair spread, undermining legitimacy, and pacifist as well as revolutionary currents resurfaced. Yet when the three great monarchies came tumbling down, this appeared to Weber more a self-inflicted collapse than the accomplishment of determined revolutionary minorities or of a revolt of the masses—of either charismatic virtuosi or charismatically excited majorities. External military pressures and the authorities' failure of nerve led to a domestic power vacuum, opening up unanticipated opportunities for the surprised and unprepared representatives of "scientific socialism." Therefore Weber refused, with considerable conceptual consistency, to recognize the German and even the Russian upheavals as great charismatic eruptions and denounced the German goings-on as revolutionary sham and bloody carnival, while suspecting, with less familiarity, the Russian events of being a military dictatorship in socialist guise.

Up to now I have proceeded primarily on the historical plane, the level of secular theory. I have sketched the manner in which the socialist labor movement was inimical to received religion at the same time that it exhibited some typical religious features. Crucial to Weber's assessment of the decades before the First World War was his conclusion that the revolutionary potential inherent in the charisma of reason with its appeal to natural rights had been dissipated by the advance of positivist Marxism and the workers' own economic rationalism. Revolutionary voluntarism alone was indeed not strong enough to overthrow established governments, but the deterministic rhetoric and strategic opportunism of the self-professed Marxist labor movement weakened the revolutionary temper that is a precondition of sustained radical action. Such an historical explanation on the level of secular theory presupposes historical rules of experience about the innovative role of intellectuals, the religious propensities of groups with and without direct economic interests, as well as the religious affinities of large social strata.

3. The Model of Ideological Virtuosi and Social Marginality

An ethically disciplined way of life has always been the accomplishment of small numbers of men and women— virtuosi with their special gifts for single-mindedness in thought and action. Moreover, the religious person par excellence has always been an intellectual, irrespective of whether in a given case he himself was anti-rationalist or even anti-intellectual. The ethical religions were created by such virtuosi, although their historical success depended on affinities with the interests of larger strata. In the past the intellectuals were mostly religious in the transcendental sense; in modern times the secular intellectuals have outnumbered the religious ones, but this has not basically changed the dual political role of intellectuals as legitimators or challengers of the powers-that-be, as mouthpieces of conservation or harbingers of revolution.

One historical rule of experience, which has become a sociological generalization, is this very difference between the ideological virtuosi and common men as it relates to economic organization. Throughout the ages most individuals have been preoccupied with the exigencies of living; material interests have strongly counteracted ethical and religious sentiments. The great majority of men have always been forced to pursue material interests in order to make a living. The capitalist market economy, which has been an overwhelmingly powerful force of secularization, has militated against religious preoccupations among businessmen, workers, and farmers by enforcing impersonal rules that have nothing to do with ethical considerations. Instead, religious and ethical creativity has typically been found among what Weber calls groups without direct economic interests—rentiers of various kinds and marginal groups of intellectuals outside the dominant status groups, whether they were declassed, petty-bourgeois, quasi-proletarian, or pariah.

To the extent that men without direct economic interests have adhered to strict status conventions—think of Confucian scholar-administrators, Prussian or English civil servants, or professors at established universities—they have been unlikely to be innovative in ethical and religious matters, although declining political fortunes at times made a difference; high-status intellectuals have in the past turned to speculation on salvation when the stratum to which they belonged went into decline. By contrast, the lowest and least rational strata have tended to be ethically unproductive because of their hankering for magical salvation. Typically, they are "susceptible to being influenced by religious missionary enterprise," desirous of "substitutes for magical-orgiastic supervention of grace," and therefore amenable, for instance, to the "soteriological orgies of the Methodist type, such as engaged in by the Salvation Army."[11] However, analogous to the way in which ancient Israel and Greece, which were peripheral to the centers of civilization in the Near East, became the world-historical locus of religious and philosophical innovations that made the West possible, so socially and economically marginal groups can have a creative potential if they move outside the status hierarchy:

Groups which are at the lower end of, or altogether outside of, the social hierarchy stand to a certain extent on the point of Archimedes in relation to social conventions, both in respect to the external order and in respect to common opinions. Since these groups are not

11. *ES*, p. 486.

bound by the social conventions, they are capable of an original attitude toward the meaning of the cosmos; and since they are not impeded by any material considerations, they are capable of intense ethical and religious sentiment.[12]

On the contemporary scene Weber recognized the innovative and revolutionary role of marginal intellectuals in Syndicalism and the Russian intelligentsia. In Latin countries no uniform socialist movement arose controlled by a disciplined working-class apparatus, and intellectuals retained greater influence on the various competing groups. Therefore, Syndicalism appeared to Weber as "the only remaining variant of socialism in western Europe *equivalent* to a religious faith," but he also noticed its tendency to "turn easily into a romantic game played by circles without direct economic interests."[13] The Russian intelligentsia, in spite of its social and ideological diversity, came closest to creating a religious movement by virtue of its commitment to natural law, admixture of traditionalist and emotionalist religiosity, and readiness to self-sacrifice.

The last great movement of intellectuals which, though not sustained by a uniform faith, shared enough basic elements to approximate a religion was the Russian revolutionary intelligentsia, in which patrician, academic and aristocratic intellectuals stood next to plebeian ones. Plebeian intellectualism was represented by the quasi-proletarian minor officialdom, which was highly sophisticated in its sociological thinking and broad cultural interests; it was composed especially of the *zemstvo* officials (the so-called "third element"). Moreover, this kind of intellectualism was advanced by journalists, elementary school teachers, revolutionary apostles and a peasant intelligentsia that arose out of the Russian social conditions. In the 1870s, this movement culminated in an appeal to a theory of natural rights oriented primarily toward agricultural communism, the so-called *narodnichestvo* (populism). In the nineties, this movement clashed sharply with Marxist dogmatics, but in part also aligned itself with it. Moreover, attempts were made to relate it, usually in an obscure manner, first to Slavophile romantic, then mystical, religiosity or, at least, religious emotionalism. Under the influence of Dos-

12. *ES*, p. 507.   13. *ES*, p. 515.

toevsky and Tolstoy, an ascetic and acosmistic patterning of personal life was created among some relatively large groups of these Russian intellectuals. We shall leave untouched here the question as to what extent this movement, so strongly infused with the influence of Jewish proletarian intellectuals who were ready for any sacrifice, can continue after the catastrophe of the Russian Revolution [in 1906]."[14]

If the Syndicalist and Russian intellectuals fitted the historical generalizations about religious virtuosi at least to some extent, the same was no longer true of many western and central European intellectuals, who had secularized themselves by abandoning religious and metaphysical value absolutism. By promoting positivism, evolutionism, and relativism, they made themselves, so to speak, atypical in the historical balance of things. They were no longer religious virtuosi but merely the creators and followers of intellectual fashions without ultimate ethical commitment, irrespective of the degree of intolerance or fanaticism that might accompany them. With the rise of neo-romanticism, which Weber greatly disliked, some of these fashions appeared in religious guise, often revolving around "the wisdom of the East." But Weber did not expect any genuine religious contribution from the "literary, academic or café-society intellectuals" of his time. In a scathing passage he observed that their

need ... to include "religious" feelings in the inventory of their sources of impressions and sensations, and among their topics for discussions, has never yet given rise to a new religion. Nor can a religious renascence be generated by the need of authors to compose books on such interesting topics or by the far more effective need of clever publishers to sell such books. No matter how much the appearance of a widespread religious interest may be simulated, no new religion has ever resulted from such needs of intellectuals or their chatter.[15]

Such intellectuals are not capable of following either an ethic of single-minded conviction or an ethic of responsibility. It is true that most human beings are not capable of strenuous ethical conduct, and in this sense the two ethics are guideposts

14. *ES*, p. 516.   15. *ES*, p. 517.

for minorities; but the ethic of single-minded conviction is distinctively a matter of spiritual virtuosity, of making maximum demands upon the true believer, while its opposite accepts the fallibility of man. There are two logical extremes within the ethic of sheer commitment: a consistently militant and a consistently pacifist position. Weber again uses religious terminology to describe adherents to the militant version as "revolutionary apostles,"[16] "revolutionary crusaders," and "prophets of revolution,"[17] who protest against the injustice of the social order. In a basically non-revolutionary situation, as it prevails most of the time—and today also in the United States—only an acute sense of elitist superiority and moral righteousness can sustain these "warriors of the faith." Just as they are unswervingly committed to their ethic of single-minded conviction, so their opponents fight them according to the maxim that "it is impossible to make peace with warriors of the faith."[18] The pacifist position is the acosmistic love ethic typified by the Sermon on the Mount, which implies

a natural law of absolute imperatives based upon religion. These absolute imperatives retained their revolutionizing force during almost all periods of social upheaval. They produced especially the radical pacifist sects, one of which in Pennsylvania experimented in establishing a polity that renounced violence toward the outside.[19]

Christian pacifism can be illustrated by its revolutionary revival in the 1960s on the part of the Catholic opposition against church and state in the United States. This phenomenon demonstrates the possibility of a religious revival carried on by religious virtuosi. To many contemporaries its appearance came as unexpectedly as the new youth movement of the 1960s, and was propelled by events that could hardly have been foreseen in the 1950s, such as the historical accident of Roncalli's papacy, although the general reform movement in

16. *ES*, p. 516.   17. "Politics," p. 125.
18. Weber, *Socialism*, trans. H. F. Dickie-Clark (Durban: University of Natal Press, 1967), p. 45.
19. "Politics," p. 124.

the wake of Vatican II must be distinguished from the charismatic revolt of priests and nuns against church and state.

4. RELIGIOUS VIRTUOSI AGAINST CHURCH AND STATE[20]

Historically, priests have been the most important legitimizers of political authority. Today they are rivaled and frequently eclipsed by secular legitimizers, whether they be free-lancing intellectuals or employed party ideologists. This competition has destroyed the clergy's one-time monopoly. In recent years many clergymen have tried to regain their once dominant position as exclusive guardians of faith and morality by involving themselves in social and political issues. Hundreds of young clergymen prefer the campus ministry over suburban assignments, and many of them joined "the Movement" in the sixties. To some extent this development can be understood as a mundane phenomenon, in Weberian terms, as the struggle of monopolist guild interests against competitors. But there has also been a nucleus of genuine charismatics, who incur great personal risks by taking an extreme stand calculated to invite "repression" from the church and the state. "Divine disobedience" has become the slogan of these virtuosi.

Typologically, priests are the preservers of a sacred tradition within an institutionalized setting, such as the bureaucratic Catholic church. Catholic priests are bearers of institutional charisma. Their sacramental acts are valid irrespective of the priest's individual state of grace. But the rebel priests turned themselves into *prophets*—that means, individual bearers of charisma. They did not proclaim a new religious message—prophecy need not be concerned with offering a new religion, but may simply preach the renewal of religion in the spirit of its original revelation. The rebel priests were often willing to experiment with new forms of liturgy and

20. A first version of this section appeared in *Rassegna Italiana di Sociologia*, 13, no. 3 (1972): 448ff.

modes of living, but more important was their harking back to the personal example of Christ and the days of early Christianity with its communal organization. Theirs was a deliberate "raw fundamentalism," as Daniel Berrigan has said of his brother Philip and of himself. The Berrigan brothers have become the most famous of the small group of clerical virtuosi, and their beliefs and actions can be viewed here as prototypical.

Men and women like the Berrigans challenge the church as a worldly institution that has completely failed its spiritual mission. The orders, too, are failing. The Jesuits, for instance, appear as not much more than academic climbers. The Berrigans profess themselves disinterested in many of the internal issues agitating the church and the Catholic community—celibacy, divorce, birth control, and parochial education. Instead, they are preoccupied with the great moral issues of the world—poverty, exploitation, and war. In this supreme perspective the church and most Christians appear self-centered and oblivious, in Daniel Berrigan's words, to the true meaning of "Christ's invitation that all men come join Him, and be with Him—in all their variety."[21] Before Christ's message the church and, a fortiori, the state are found wanting. For this kind of religious virtuosity, as Weber has observed, the fact that

the use of force within the political community has increasingly assumed the form of the constitutional state (*Rechtsstaat*) . . . is merely the most effective mimicry of brutality. All politics is oriented to *raison d'état*, to realism, and to the autonomous end of maintaining the external and internal distribution of power. These goals must necessarily seem completely senseless from the religious point of view [that means] the ethic of brotherliness.[22]

In Weber's terms, such judgments are a form of ethical prophecy. However, virtuosi such as the Berrigans are not content just to carry a message; they also insist on following the path of *exemplary prophecy*. Within the Christian context,

21. Daniel Berrigan and Robert Coles, "Dialogue Underground: Inside and Outside the Church," *New York Review of Books*, April 8, 1971, p. 13.
22. *ES*, p. 600f.

this takes the form of *imitatio Christi*. It is not enough for these virtuosi to *be* right; only by becoming martyrs can they *do* what is right.[23] Although they are, of course, interested in political effectiveness, their kind of "divine diobedience" is first of all an insistence on living an exemplary life. The spiritual attitude is decisive, and for this reason Daniel Berrigan, for one, could discourage others from imitating his particular political tactics. However, rebel priests can become a political force by identifying the suffering of Christ and that of the masses, and by joining their own *imitatio* to them. As Daniel Berrigan succinctly put it:

What is most important to Phil and me, I believe, is the historical truth manifested in the actuality of Jesus, and the community which we believe is in continuity with His spirit and His presence—a presence which makes certain rigorous and specific demands on man at any period of time. . . . I think there is something important to be undergone, something with a certain spiritual value to it; it is almost as if to be cast out can become a way of being cast in. which means I will taste not solely or even primarily the bitterness of being an American locked up . . . but I will also taste a fate millions of others know, millions of people whose historical struggle matters very much, even if not to those who run our military machine and plan our foreign policy and invest money in the semi-colonial countries we still dominate in various parts of the world. . . . I do have the sense that to be right now in some serious trouble with respect to the "powers and principalities" of this nation means to occupy a most important geographical position—if one wishes to struggle with others all over the world for their freedom; and by the same token to be in no trouble at all is to share in what I take to be a frightening movement toward violence and death.[24]

23. This point has also been made by F. Du Plessix Gray: "The Berrigans' actions, and those of some one hundred Catholics who have participated in some twenty different draft board raids to date, are grounded in a very ancient monastic mystique that is as old as the formulation of the rule of St. Benedict. In their view, a man's witness in jail, like a monk's years of passive prayer, can aid to purify society and to abate the violence of its rulers. This view, which implies that man can help to redeem society by searching for suffering in imitation of the suffering Christ, is perhaps too utopian for most of us to bear in the 1970s." Gray, "Address to the Democratic Town Committee of Newton, Conn.," *New York Review of Books*, May 6, 1971, p. 20.

24. Berrigan and Coles, *op. cit.*, pp. 14, 19.

Such exemplary identification with the suffering masses can reactivate the revolutionary potential in Christ's message and passion. Although Jesus was not concerned with social and political matters, his teachings can be used politically for pacifist as well as militarist purposes. As the case of the Berrigans and their charismatic followers once again demonstrates, the insistence on a communism of love can easily turn into the practice of a communism of war. The religious virtuosi may end up using the same means as the revolutionary heroes. The only remaining difference may be one of ultimate orientation—toward the transcendental rather than the immanent legitimation of rebellion. In the end, as Weber warned, the moral dilemma is the same for all "warriors of the faith, whether religious or revolutionary."[25] And the moral antinomies inherent in using or foregoing force for the sake of absolute justice tend to be self-defeating for the religious virtuosi who would do away with "politics as usual."

The revival of religious virtuosity in the highly secularized United States was part of the rise of the counterculture. In the last section, I want briefly to sketch some features of the counterculture from the perspective of Weber's generalizations about ideological virtuosity and of his secular theory of the course of revolutionary beliefs.

5. The Counterculture Revisited

The Western countercultures move between two poles. An ethic of sheer commitment based on one or another version of substantive natural law contrasts with antinomian, anarchist, and hedonist attitudes and sometimes changes into them, as has happened before in the history of virtuosi and sects. There is a wide range of demands, from rights to a minimum standard of living, compatible with liberalism, to the total instinctual liberation of the individual, a kind of libertinism.

If from Weber's perspective the moral insurrection against

25. "Politics," p. 125.

governmental policies and the social status quo in the sixties and early seventies appears in part as a natural rights revival and a rekindling of the charisma of reason, in other respects the rebellions amounted to a return of western European nihilism, although there was almost no awareness of historical precedents among adherents and thus no traditional transmission. Again the enemies are capitalism, bureaucracy, and often enough also constitutional government, with their impersonal order that does not yield easily to notions of material justice. The natural rights revival became possible, among other reasons, because positivism and scientism have declined precipitously as a faith, just as the liberal convictions about continuous and irreversible progress have been shattered. Hence, recourse to fundamental rights and insistence on the ought over the is, positions that once were undermined by scientism, whether Marxist or not, have today been rehabilitated. If there are no iron laws of history and no ethically compelling science of behavior, ethical choices must be made, and basic rights must be asserted, without evolutionary or scientific support.

Thus, a new ethico-political movement emerged within intellectual strata in the United States and some other Western countries. Yet there was an important contrast to the rise of the socialist labor movement of a century ago: no new mass movement founded by intellectuals and adaptable to lower-class interests arose, not even a strongly organized student movement. Instead, small groups of virtuosi, many pacifist, some militant, have come into being, which have their historical precedent in religious sects, utopian communes, and bands of warriors. In general, the members of these charismatic groups, which have variously embraced a new ethic of sheer commitment or a new hedonism, come again from strata without direct economic interests—from the ranks of students, many of whom live on unearned income, and from among the professoriate, which in our scheme can be classified as a group of benefice-holders. This results in the emergence of a group of declassed ideologues, mostly former students and instructors, who decided to "drop out of the system." No matter how exalted the status of a professional-turned-guru may be within his own circle, from the dominant system's perspective he has suffered *déclassement*; conversely, many upper-middle-class dropouts have deliberately undergone *debourgeoisement*, which contrasts vividly with the *embourgeoisement* of many workers. Finally, there are the pariah intellectuals, mostly Blacks, such as Malcolm X, Eldridge Cleaver, George Jackson, and others, who turned themselves into intellectual virtuosi in their prison cells.

The pacifist virtuosi—that means, those who in general prefer to withdraw from the dominant system rather than to fight it directly—usually embrace an eclectic world view with components of Eastern wisdom. There is also a strong Christian wing that favors fundamentalism, patriarchalism, and communalism, and in some cases, such as the Jesus Freaks, can perhaps be understood best in the typical mode of the least rational strata with their hankering after magical salvation. By contrast, political salvation has been pursued by the secular virtuosi, who constitute the political activists and in the extreme case form warlike charismatic communities, like the Weather Underground or the Symbionese Liberation Army.

In spite of the waning of the charismatic mass excitement of the 1960s, it appears in the middle of the "calmer" seventies that a core of militant and pacifist communities are going to persist. Political terrorism and guerrilla warfare are practiced by small groups of ideological virtuosi, just as in the decades after 1870 when there was relative calm on the international scene. At the same time personal virtuosity challenges the institutional charisma of the established churches, from the ethico-political activism of priests and nuns to the so-called charismatic movement of those capable of glossolalia and other signs of personal grace and pneumatic, trance-like powers.

The new revolutionary voluntarism may be as unlikely to succeed against relatively strong governments and in the absence of profound political crises as were its predecessors between the Napoleonic period and the First World War. And the new religious movements may not be able to change basically the prevailing state of affairs, namely the shrinking scope of religious influence (witness divorce and abortion legislation) and the reduction of religion to a personal choice. However, this does not mean that the new virtuosi have no impact on the world. Political and religious revolutions are very rare, but frequent has been the attempt of virtuosi to go it alone. National or world-historical success is not the decisive criterion. What counts is an exemplary way of life and personal testimony, and on this score the ideological virtuosi, whether secular revolutionaries or true religious believers, will not act differently in the future than they have in the past. Directly or indirectly, they tend to influence the ingrained patterns of thought and the life-style prevailing in the dominant culture.

In conclusion, my suggestion has been that one way of comprehending some of the revolutionary challenges to the established political and religious order is through a secular theory of modern revolutionary beliefs and through some sociological generalizations about ideological virtuosi and the propensities of groups with marginal status or without direct economic interests. Weber arrived at these generalizations in the course of his comparative study of the salvation religions and applied them with only minor modifications to modern secular ideologies. In my judgment they are indeed applicable for two reasons, one historical and one analytical: First, secularization does not mean the disappearance of basic attitudes or basic forms of social organization; rather, it does mean profound changes in the content of historical beliefs and in the combination of organizational patterns. Second, as Weber's sociology of religion moves along the path of secularization to his own time, it contributes within the architectural framework of *Economy and Society* to a sociology of the intelligentsia and of radical politics, transcending the confines of the world religions.

V

DURATION AND
RATIONALIZATION:
FERNAND BRAUDEL AND
MAX WEBER

Guenther Roth

1. The French *Annales* School
and German Antecedents

In this chapter I shall be concerned not with the applicability of Weber's models and secular theories but with a comparison between Weber's historical vision and methods and those of Fernand Braudel. Both men have in common a strong interest in the nature and causes of Western capitalism, although they pursue this problem in quite different ways. This alone warrants a comparison. But such a comparison is also desirable because to many scholars today the two men seem to represent quite different historical approaches. My comparison is intended to establish not only their irreducible differences, but also their complementarity and their visible as well as less visible major similarities. I shall conclude the chapter with a consideration of Weber's concept of rationalization from the viewpoint of Braudel's notion of historical persistence (*la longue durée*)—the historical key concepts of the two men.

An early version of this essay was presented at one of the Weber symposia at the University of Wisconsin, Milwaukee, February 22, 1977; an advanced version was given at a Weber colloquium at the University of Constance, September 12, 1977.

The dominant figure of the French *Annales* school from the 1950s to the 1970s, Braudel has become famous as leader of a movement which, according to Traian Stoianovich, has created a paradigm "for the world community of historical scholarship."[1] There is, in fact, no clearly articulated *Annales* paradigm. Much of the *Annales* research consists of "structural" history of the socio-economic variety, from historical demography to extremely detailed regional studies, and this approach has been linked in the United States to the growing interest in quantitative, "cliometric" techniques on the part of younger scholars inside and outside of history departments.[2]

In important respects, however, the *Annales* school has not been a unified phenomenon in spite of its increasing bureaucratic centralization. From its founders Marc Bloch and Lucien Febvre in the 1920s to Emmanuel LeRoy Ladurie today there have been studies of attitudes (*mentalités*) next to the accumulation of demographic and economic data.[3] But it is true that studies of ideological and political structures have been relatively de-emphasized in most of the *Annales* research since the Second World War, when the group took over the decisive academic power positions in France. It is also true that most of the *Annales* research has been limited to the centuries before the French Revolution—a limitation not as strongly shared by foreign sympathizers. Theoretically, the *Annales* school has operated in the ambiance of Parisian Marxism, existentialism, and anthropological structuralism and responded with eclectic flexibility, usually under the flag of the

1. Traian Stoianovich, *French Historical Method: The Annales Paradigm* (Ithaca: Cornell University Press, 1976), p. 236.

2. For an overview of new approaches to history by historians and social scientists, see Daniel Chirot, "Thematic Controversies and New Developments in the Uses of Historical Materials," *Social Forces*, 55, no. 2 (1976): 232–241.

3. See Marc Bloch, *The Royal Touch*, trans. J. E. Anderson (London: Routledge & Kegan Paul, 1973), first published in 1924; Lucien Febvre, *Le Problème de l'incroyance au XVIᵉ siècle* (Paris: Albin Michel, 1942); Emmanuel LeRoy Ladurie, *The Peasants of Languedoc*, tr. John Day (Urbana: University of Illinois Press, 1974).

integration of the social sciences. In England and the United States, the *Annales* school has been attractive to those who want to fuse history and social science and has encountered opposition from those who view history as an integral part of the humanities. Some American researchers have made a rapprochement with the *Annales* school because of their own Marxist interests in the origins of capitalism; they perceive and welcome it as another variant of historical materialism. The Marxist scholar Immanuel Wallerstein, who turned from sociologist into historian with his study of the rise of the capitalist world economy in the sixteenth century, established a Fernand Braudel Center for the Study of Economies, Historical Systems and Civilizations at the State University of New York at Binghamton in 1976.[4] For other scholars demography has provided the major link to the *Annales* school, witness in England the Cambridge Group for the History of Population and Social Structure. Only in Germany has the *Annales* school scarcely made headway. German social and economic history of either Marxian or non-Marxian mold has continued to stress research on modernization, bureaucratization, and democratization in the wake of the French Revolution, and a growing number of German scholars are vigorously criticizing *Annales* research, in the name of an integrated structural history of modernity.[5] In the process German historians are discovering intellectual legacies shared by an earlier generation of German historians and early Annalistes.

Accounts of the history of the *Annales* school, by its members and its American and English interpreters, usually point out that it started with a call for social scientific synthesis and an attack on the reigning Sorbonnistes, the Parisian historians

4. See Immanuel Wallerstein, *The Modern World System* (New York: Academic Press, 1974); see also the papers of the Inaugural Conference of 1977 in the Center's *Review*, 1, no. 3/4, (1978).
5. For chapters on the *Annales* school and recent German historiography, see Georg G. Iggers, *New Directions in European Historiography* (Middletown: Wesleyan University Press, 1975). For citations of the German *Annales* discussion, see also Jürgen Kocka, "Sozialgeschichte—Strukturgeschichte—Gesellschaftsgeschichte," *Archiv für Sozialgeschichte*, 15 (1975): 1–42.

committed to a methodological variant of Prusso-German political and diplomatic historiography. However, it is rarely recognized today that some major *Annales* orientations were anticipated by German social and economic historians who opposed the orthodox Prussian historiography and with some of whom Weber was closely affiliated—such as Eberhard Gothein, Werner Sombart, and Werner Wittich. In fact, what we may call the "prehistory of the *Annales* school," from the 1890s to about 1920, roughly coincides with Weber's scholarly career.

Henri Beer's *Revue de synthèse historique* of 1900, to which Karl Lamprecht and Heinrich Rickert contributed, was the literary precursor of the *Annales* journal of 1929 in its call for interdisciplinary synthesis of the social sciences, but Weber's *Archiv für Sozialwissenschaft und Sozialpolitik* of 1904 was a parallel effort in its interdisciplinary approach. When Lucien Febvre and Marc Bloch launched their onslaught in the 1920s from Strasbourg against the Sorbonnistes and founded the *Annales d'histoire economique et sociale* after the pattern of the *Vierteljahrschrift für Sozial- und Wirtschaftsgeschichte,* they still echoed Gothein's vigorous reply to the apologist of a purely political historiography, Dietrich Schäfer, in 1889.[6] In his massive *Cultural History of the Black Forest* (1892) and other writings on the Reformation and Counter-Reformation, Gothein anticipated much of the economic, social, and cultural history later propagated and practiced by Febvre and Bloch. This included the advocacy of a close connection between *Kulturgeschichte* and geography: "Among the branches of natural science one has established an inseparable relationship with cultural history—geography. Indeed, it also shares with cultural history the fate of being looked down upon as a hodgepodge by some of our proud political historians."[7] If the most basic *Annales* scheme is the study of a phenomenon on

6. On the founding of the journal, see Paul Leuilliot, "Aux origines des 'Annales d'histoire économique et sociale' (1928). Contribution à l'historiographie française," *Méthodologie de l'histoire et des sciences humaines. Mélanges en l'honneur de Fernand Braudel,* ed. Edouard Privat (Toulouse, 1972), pp. 317–324; Eberhard Gothein's pamphlet is entitled *Die Aufgaben der Kulturgeschichte* (Leipzig: Duncker & Humblot, 1889).

7. Gothein, *op. cit.,* p. 41.

the geographic, economic, and cultural (or political) levels, Werner Wittich's *Deutsche und französische Kultur im Elsass* was an exemplary anticipation.[8] In the 1890s Karl Lamprecht, who was close to Pirenne, an acknowledged precursor of the *Annales,* almost managed to capture the leading German historical journal, *Historische Zeitschrift,* for the cause of cultural, social, and economic history. Two of the most successful historians of Prussian political and administrative history, Kurt Breysig and Otto Hintze, moved toward comparative world history, eliciting much antagonism from their peers. Thus, in his study of the origins of German social historiography, Gerhard Oestreich could remark: "If one reads today the leading organ of French social history, the *Annales,* if one listens to the debates abroad about the concepts of contemporary social history, one could think that he hears the voice of German social history between 1880 and 1890: type, condition, lawful development, statistical method, structure—all of the concepts with which the present is still preoccupied."[9]

Weber's own work was a special case, however. In his substantive and methodological concerns Weber transcended the German economic and social history that anticipated the *Annales* school. The range of his "global" historical vision and the accomplishment of his historical sociology made him stand apart from, and above, the two major currents of German historiography. Weber pursued a *Universalgeschichte* of a particular kind: he rejected the old evolutionary schemes of a unified history of mankind with its regular stages of development, and instead tried to construct empirically a grand

8. See Werner Wittich, *Deutsche und französische Kultur im Elsass* (Strasbourg: Schlesier & Schweikhardt, 1900); French transl., "Le Génie national des races française et allemande en Alsace," *Revue internationale de sociologie,* 10, no. 11 (1902): 707–907.

9. Gerhard Oestreich, "Die Fachhistorie und die Anfänge der sozialgeschichtlichen Forschung in Deutschland," *Historische Zeitschrift,* 208 (1969): 362; on Hintze and Breysig, see also Oestreich, "Otto Hintzes Stellung zur Politikwissenschaft und Soziologie," in Otto Hintze, *Gesammelte Abhandlungen,* vol. 2, *Soziologie und Geschichte,* ed. G. Oestreich (Göttingen: Vandenhoeck, 1964), pp. 7–67, esp. p. 56.

secular theory of the uniqueness of Western rationalism as it had developed historically (rather than necessarily) over the last 2,500 years. More precisely, he studied *universalgeschichtliche Probleme* rather than elaborated yet another old-fashioned universal history.[10]

Braudel also stands apart from his peers and assumes an almost solitary position by virtue of his tenacious pursuit of *la longue durée*–phenomena of long duration. He is the only Annaliste to have developed a sweeping vision that sometimes approaches Weber's, both in his *La Méditerranée et le monde méditerranéen à l'époque de Philippe II* and in *Civilisation matérielle et capitalisme, 1400–1800*.[11] I shall compare Braudel and

10. Cf. "Author's Introduction," p. 13: "It is inevitable and justified that as products of modern European culture we will deal with problems of universal history with the question in mind: What concatenation of circumstances has brought it about that only in the Occident did cultural phenomena emerge which have followed a developmental direction of universal significance—at least so we like to think."

11. See Braudel, *The Mediterranean and the Mediterranean World in the Age of Philip II*, trans. Sian Reynolds (New York: Harper, 1972), after the second revised French edition of 1966, first published in 1949; and *Capitalism and Material Life, 1400–1800,* trans. Miriam Kochan (New York: Harper, 1973), first published in 1967; volumes 2 and 3 are scheduled for 1978. Braudel has provided a summary of the unpublished volumes in *Afterthoughts on Material Civilization and Capitalism,* trans. Patricia Ranum (Baltimore: Johns Hopkins Press, 1977). In English the title *Civilisation matérielle et capitalisme* has been reversed in a misleading way; therefore I retain the French title in the text, although I cite from the English edition.

The *Mediterranean* is roughly as long—about 1,300 pages—as Weber's *Economy and Society*; the complete series of *Civilisation matérielle* may be as large—about 1,400 pages—as Weber's *Collected Essays in the Sociology of Religion*. Apart from these two works, which are based on very detailed archival research, Braudel has written several programmatic and polemical treatises. The most important are two contributions to the section on "Débats et Combats" in the *Annales*, "Histoire et sciences sociales: La longue durée," 13 (Oct. 1958): 725–753 (English in *Economy and Society in Early Modern Europe,* ed. Peter Burke. New York: Harper, 1972, pp. 11–42); "Sur une conception de l'histoire sociale," 14 (1959): 308–316 (a critique of Otto Brunner's *Neue Wege der Sozialgeschichte*); see also "Histoire et sociologie," *Traité de Sociologie,* ed. Georges Gurvitch (Paris: Presse Universitaire, 1958), pp. 84–98.

Weber's oeuvre, written in half the productive life span of Braudel's, is at least twice as large as Braudel's, but this difference is in part attributable to

Weber not in their broad scholarly context but as creatively independent scholars in their own right. The intellectual history behind the two men is exceedingly complex and requires long and detailed research, for which there is no room here.

2. Two Approaches to Structural History

The first and most obvious similarity between Braudel and Weber is their lack of interest in diplomatic and political history: Philip II does not come on stage until page 900 of *The Mediterranean,* and the three hundred pages on "Events, Politics and People" are a conventional appendix in the style of older French dissertations. In Weber's scholarly works the high and the mighty appear only as bit players, serving as mere examples or typological illustrations. The disciplinary base line common to both men is economic history. Braudel turned himself from a conventional Sorbonniste into an economic geo-historian under the influence of Lucien Febvre.[12] Weber began his career as an economic and legal historian, working on Mediterranean statutes and other legal documents, before branching out from ancient and medieval to modern history and finally the comparison of civilizations.[13]

In *Economy and Society* Weber deals only in passing with geo-historical issues, in contrast to Braudel's 300-page treatment of the role of the environment in *The Mediterranean.* Weber was fully aware, however, of the importance of geographic factors and the basic mode of production—witness his voluminous writings on antiquity, China, and East Elbia.[14]

---

the difference between digging into vast amounts of archival materials and working with a very large secondary literature.

12. See Lucien Febvre, *La Terre et l'évolution humaine* (Paris: La Renaissance du Livre, 1922). The book appeared in Henri Beer's series "L'Évolution de l'humanité."

13. See Weber, *Zur Geschichte der Handelsgesellschaften im Mittelalter. Nach südeuropäischen Quellen* (Stuttgart: Enke, 1889). See also my introduction to *ES*, pp. XXXIV-LI.

14. See Weber, *Die römische Agrargeschichte in ihrer Bedeutung für das Staats- und Privatrecht* (Stuttgart: Enke, 1891; The Agrarian Sociology of Ancient Civilizations, trans., R.I. Frank. London: Routledge & Kegan Paul, 1976. For

Regrettably, this point must be made because Weber continues to be frequently mistaken for representing a basically "idealist" interpretation of history. We must keep in mind that *Economy and Society* was part of a division of labor: it was conceived by Weber as part of the *Grundriss für Sozialökonomik* (*Outline of Social Economics*), of which he was editor-in-chief. While he purposively omitted a "general economic history . . . in view of the systematic character of the work," he provided room for geography, demography, and technology in the *Grundriss,* which dealt with the nature and origins of modern capitalism, the basic idea being "to study economic development particularly as part of the general rationalization of life."[15] In fact, there is a threefold division of the part in the *Grundriss* which deals with "Economy and . . .": (1) "Economy and Nature"; (2) "Economy and Technology"; (3) "Economy and Society." In the section on "economy and nature" Alfred Hettner contributed "The Geographic Conditions of the Human Economy," a systematic treatise on the surface of the earth, the coasts, the mountains and seas, the quality of the land, crops and animals, and the climate, concluding with an historical overview of "The Geographic Course of Economic Culture." He took a stand against Friedrich Ratzel, just as Febvre did in *La Terre et l'évolution humaine.*[16] In the second

---

Weber's early writings on East Elbian agrarian issues, see R. Bendix, *Max Weber* (Berkeley and Los Angeles: University of California Press, 1977), chap. 11.

15. Cited in *ES,* p. LVIII.

16. See *Grundriss der Sozialökonomik,* II. Abteilung, I. Teil: Wirtschaft und Natur; II. Teil: Wirtschaft und Technik (Tübingen: Mohr, 1923). The other contributions deal with "economy and population," with sections on "Demography," by Paul Mombert, and on "Economy and Race," by Robert Michels, who discussed what is today called the cultural division of labor in developed and underdeveloped countries. Weber originally had planned to write this section himself, and the chapter on ethnic groups in *Economy and Society* may be a version of what he had in mind (cf. the "Stoffverteilungsplan" printed by the Mohr/Siebeck publishing house in 1910 for distribution among the contributors). Karl Oldenberg wrote on "Consumption," and Heinrich Herkner on "Labor and Division of Labor." The contribution on "Economy and Technology" was written by Friedrich von Gottl-Ottlilienfeld.

edition of 1923 Hettner also cited the geographer Vidal de la Blache, who is considered a major inspiration by the Annalistes. Braudel, in turn, acknowledged Hettner in *The Mediterranean,* not his contribution to the *Grundriss,* to be sure, but a study on "Islam and Oriental Culture" (1932), adding that "to this article as indeed to the whole German school of geographers I am much indebted."[17]

There is, then, no basic difference between Weber and Braudel on the issue of the importance of geographic factors in history. Geographic factors constitute powerful constraints on human action. They are relatively enduring and in this sense "structural" limitations. The two men are similar, too, in pushing beyond the boundaries of conventional social and economic history. Braudel goes beyond conventional economic history by insisting that the starting point of research be the long term (*la longue durée*): "The fact is that economic history has to be rethought step by step, starting from these slow, sometimes motionless currents."[18] In *The Mediterranean* the long term is primarily the role of the environment, the mountains, plateaus, plains, seas and coasts, islands, the land and sea routes, transhumance and nomadism, and the climate. In *Civilisation matérielle* the long term is demography, the reproduction of daily life, and the slow spread of technology. Weber transcends economic and social history by aiming at a comprehensive "social economics," which "considers actual human activities as they are conditioned by the necessity to take into account the facts of economic life,"[19] hence the original title which Weber gave *Economy and Society*: "The Economy and the Arena of Normative and de facto Powers." This required the study of the interdependencies between the economy and all major areas of institutionalized social life— politics, law, religion, social stratification, and "culture."

Approaching history in terms of underlying continuities, of almost immobile and very slowly changing conditions, constitutes Braudel's structuralism. Here is a clear difference from

17. Braudel, *The Mediterranean,* p. 1274.   18. *Ibid.,* p. 1241.
19. *ES,* p. 312.

Weber, for whom the essence of Western history is a radical transformation along the lines of rationalization, irrespective of the slowness of the process. Braudel and Weber, then, are structural historians in different senses of the term.

The term *l'histoire structurale* seems to have arisen in the 1940s[20] and suffered an inflationary spread in the 1950s, much to the chagrin of Febvre, who complained about "structure": "It is a word I do not much care for . . . a fashionable term . . . which even in the *Annales* on occasion is flaunted too much for my liking. For what real 'structure' is there among the multiplicity of structures which meet the eye? After all, why talk of structures and not rhythms, pulses, currents and cross-currents?"[21] Braudel, however, has an answer to the question about what constitutes a "real" structure. It is the long term: "In our imperfect language we designate by the name of *histoire structurale* . . . phenomena of trends with imperceptible slopes . . . a history of very long periods, a history slow to take on curvature and for that reason slow to reveal itself to our observation."[22] Braudel is committed to the missionary viewpoint that most of modern historiography before the ascendancy of his own school has been merely skirting the surface of history, but he acknowledges that some of the great historians have been concerned with the long run—Michelet, Ranke, Burckhardt—and he even points to recent studies of the long term in intellectual history, to E. R. Curtius, Alphonse Dupront, and Pierre Francastel.[23] He also reminds the reader at the very outset of his *Afterthoughts* that "Lucien Febvre himself planned to write *Western Thought and Belief,*

---

20. See Dieter Groh, "Strukturgeschichte als 'totale' Geschichte?" *Vierteljahrschrift für Sozial- und Wirtschaftsgeschichte,* 58, no. 3 (1971): 312.

21. Lucien Febvre, preface to Huguette and Pierre Chaunu, *Séville et l'Atlantique* (Paris, 1959), p. 11, cited in Maurice Aymard, "The Annales and French Historiography," *Journal of European Economic History,* 1, no. 2 (1972): 505.

22. Cited in J. H. Hexter, "Fernand Braudel and the Monde Braudellien," *Journal of Modern History,* 44, no. 4 (1972): 504 (from *Revue économique,* 9 (1960): 41).

23. Braudel, "Histoire et sciences sociales," p. 732.

1400–1800 as a companion piece that was to accompany and complete my own book. Unfortunately, his book will never be published. My own work has thus been irrevocably deprived of this extra dimension."[24] But for Braudel himself *la longue durée* is primarily a matter of geographic and demographic constraints.[25]

Braudel's notion of historical persistence has not remained unchallenged among Annalistes. On empirical grounds Georges Friedmann, a well-known member of the *Annales* editorial board, has argued (in Stoianovich's words) "that the unprecedented transformation of the function of technological change since 1850 has provoked so much and such rapid change in the other functions that there is no longer much point to studying any of these functions in the framework of Fernand Braudel's *longue durée*."[26] However, the question must also be raised whether for Braudel *la longue durée* is an ontological rather than an historical phenomenon. It seems to me that he pushes his conception onto the plane of an unfalsifiable personal philosophy of history when he claims that "the long run always wins in the end. Annihilating innumerable events—all those which cannot be accommodated in the main ongoing current and which are therefore ruthlessly swept to one side—it indubitably limits both the freedom of the individual and even the role of chance. I am by temperament a 'structuralist,' little tempted by the event or even by the short-term conjuncture."[27]

24. *Afterthoughts*, p. 3.

25. A recent critic remarked that "it is perhaps not simply the accident of death that left Febvre's book on thought and belief unwritten and Braudel's on capitalism and material life complete. It may indicate in an over-simple but nevertheless neat way what has happened to this historiographic tradition since *Annales* was first published forty-eight years ago. The end of the Annalistes may remain the illumination of *mentalités* but their means have become increasingly statistical and even mechanistic." Peter Scott, "Master Navigator on Sea of History," *The Times Higher Education Supplement,* Dec. 9, 1977, p. 9f. Symbolic as the absence of Febvre's book may be, it must be remembered that he was seventy-two in 1950 when he and Braudel (born in 1902) wanted to embark on their joint venture.

26. Stoianovich, *op. cit.* (n. 1 above), p. 186.

27. Braudel, *The Mediterranean*, p. 1244.

We can now ask in what sense Weber may be said to have had a structural approach to history. Braudel's last sentence could also have been written by Weber, who focuses on "the structural forms of social action" which follow laws of their own, which have *Eigengesetzlichkeit*. In a key passage of *Economy and Society* Weber elaborated his structuralist notion of "social economics," with a thrust against monocausal determinism and systemic functionalism:

Groups that are not somehow economically determined are extremely rare. However, the degree of this influence varies widely and, above all, the economic determination of social action is ambiguous—contrary to the assumption of so-called historical materialism. . . . Even the assertion that social structures and the economy are "functionally" related is a biased view, which cannot be justified as an historical generalization, if an unambiguous interdependence is assumed. For the structural forms (*Strukturformen*) of social action follow "laws of their own," as we shall see time and again, and even apart from this fact, they may in a given case always be co-determined by other than economic causes. However, at some point economic conditions tend to become causally important, and often decisive, for almost all social groups, at least those which have major cultural significance; conversely, the economy is usually also influenced by the autonomous structure of social action within which it exists. No significant generalization can be made as to when and how this will occur. However, we can generalize about the degree of elective affinity between concrete structures of social action and concrete forms of economic organization. . . . Moreover, at least some generalization can be advanced about the manner in which economic interests tend to result in social action of a certain type.[28]

Weber presents the latter kind of generalization in his exposition on open and closed economic relations, monopolist and expansionist tendencies, and the types of want satisfaction and taxation, especially in relation to capitalism and mercantilism. But the bulk of *Economy and Society* is concerned with a typology of the structures that follow "laws of their

28. *ES*, p. 341. On the importance and the historical background of the notion of "elective affinity," which Weber never defined, see Richard Herbert Howe, "Max Weber's Elective Affinities: Sociology Within the Bounds of Pure Reason," *American Journal of Sociology*, 84: 2 (1978): 366–385.

own," ranging from the more universal to the historically more specific ones, from the household, the neighborhood, the kin group, and the ethnic group through the oikos and the enterprise to the major religious, legal, and political forms of association. The notion of "laws of their own" refers not to any developmental scheme or any inherent laws of evolution but to institutionalized logics and rationales—this is the core of Weber's structural approach. Thus, this notion is related to the concept of rationalization. In Weber's view "the economy and the arena of normative and de facto powers" can be understood as a heterogeneous process of various kinds of rationalization which create new forms of structural differentiation and integration. Rationalization may be a response to built-in conflict in a given structure. In patrimonial regimes, for instance, in which there is a perennial struggle between ruler and staff over the appropriation of the means of civilian and military administration, the ruler may try to bureaucratize his administration and to promote a monetary economy. Rationalization may also result from external pressures, such as military threats. Moreover, there are intellectual strains toward consistency, and here scribes, priests, and jurists become important: "It happens to be a fact, and it has always been true, that the rational in the sense of the logical or teleological 'consistency' of an intellectual-theoretical or practical-ethical position has power over human beings, no matter how limited and precarious this power has everywhere been in relation to the other forces of historical life."[29] Finally, rationalization tends to develop different logics for different spheres, and this process too creates historical tensions with unpredictable outcomes, either new syntheses of varying duration or historical breaks of a revolutionary nature.

3. Duration, Model, and Secular Theory

A comparison of Braudel's and Weber's levels of analysis cannot be expected to find a close correspondence

29. Cf. "Theory," p. 324.

between the two schemes, but it may help illuminate both. Braudel has introduced a well-known threefold distinction among levels of historical time. He finds "that nothing comes closer to the heart of social reality than [the] lively, intimate, constantly recurring opposition between the instant and the long term." He recognizes a plurality of durations (and histories), but reduces them to three levels for the sake of simplification: (1) "A history . . . embracing hundreds of years; it is the history of very long time periods"; (2) social and economic history, "the description of the 'conjuncture,' enquiring into large sections of the past: ten-, twenty-, or fifty-year periods"; (3) the conventional "history of the event," *l'histoire événementielle,* as François Simiand had called it.[30]

As we have seen in chapters three and four, Weber's sociohistorical models (or general ideal types) are summaries of historical experience assembled from different times and places, and as such cannot have any material duration, but as dynamic models they have a time perspective built into them. They have a general duration at the same time that Weber refused to link them to a sequence and periodization in the manner of the older evolutionary schemes. The models cannot be compared directly to the specific *longue durée,* for example, of the Mediterranean as an historical entity. But most of the models in Weber's sociology of domination— patriarchalism, domination by notables, political patrimonialism, feudalism, hierocracy, and caesaropapism—deal with traditionalist and hence persistent forms, which as institutions have had a long historical life, even if personnel changes were frequent, as in the palace coups under sultanism. (One of Braudel's critics has made the obvious point that monarchy persisted in the Mediterranean for centuries, although it does not appear as one of his forms of *la longue durée.*) Charisma alone belongs to the realm of *le temps court,* being subject to either disappearance or routinization, in which case it joins again the medium or the long term. Braudel and Weber actually agree that traditionalism is a per-

---

30. Braudel, "History and the Social Sciences" (n. 11 above), p. 13f.

vasive force and established structures are hard to change. Just as Braudel speaks of "those age-old habits of thought and action, those tough resilient frameworks of life that often defy all logic,"[31] so Weber asks "how anything new can ever arise in this world, oriented as it is toward the regular as the empirically valid."[32] For Weber, too, man is a creature of habit, but innovation is possible through empathy and inspiration, which he later conceptualized as a charismatic relationship; it is also possible through rationalization in the various spheres of life—a matter of secular theory.

The correspondence between Braudel's and Weber's levels of analysis seems closest in the case of "conjuncture" and secular theory, since in most instances both concern medium-range historical changes. Hexter has pointed out the difficulties of translating *conjoncture* and remarked that "fairly consistently Braudel seems to use *conjoncture* to signify cyclical transformation or, less precisely, changes in society, sciences, technology to which he ascribes cyclic changes (undefined) over times (not clearly specified)."[33] Weber's secular theories tend to comprise several generations and hence are usually also medium-range, although sometimes they may stretch to include the long term. Finally, in a superficial sense Weber's political writings deal with the "history of events," such as the Russian revolution of 1905, but they remain structural analyses in their own right and never turn into the kind of historical narrative with which Braudel ends his work on the Mediterranean in the age of Philip II. In relation to Weber's three levels of analysis, then, we may add that they are structuralist also in the following ways: on the level of the socio-historical models Weber establishes his sociology as a body of type concepts; on the second level, he causally explains the medium-range transformation of organizational and mental structures; and on the third he looks beyond the sequence of political events to the basic class and constitutional structure of a polity.

31. *Ibid.*, p. 19.   32. *ES,* p. 321.
33. Hexter, *op cit.* (n. 22 above), p. 503.

Since I am using the term "model" for Weber's general types, I should add that Braudel uses the term partly in a generalized and partly in a particular sense. At the beginning of *Civilisation matérielle* Braudel emphatically cites Werner Sombart: "No theory, no history." However, he rejects a "general theory," as it was once propagated by the sociologists of progress. Instead he limits himself to a "schéma d'ensemble," under which he subsumes models.[34] In his portrayal of the city, where he comes closest to Weber and even cites him twice positively, he formulates "the big problem: How can one classify the urban forms or construct a model?"[35] He distinguishes three basic types or models of the Western city—the open city, the closed city, and the city under the control of the prince or the state—and compares them to the situations outside Europe. Next to these general socio-historical models, he puts particular models that apply to only one case. In the second edition of *The Mediterranean* (1966) Braudel inserted a new section with the questioning title: "Is It Possible to Construct a Model of the Mediterranean Economy?" He had in mind a "national accounting" procedure which would "draw up a tentative balance sheet of the Mediterranean in the sixteenth century . . . in short, to form a picture of the major structures of its material life."[36] After an accumulation of descriptive statistics Braudel concluded that "as yet quantitative history is unrewarding, where all the valid statistics are hidden from our gaze."[37] In this case, then, it is a matter of detailed fact-finding before the model can be more complete and reality more adequately described.

Although Braudel's approach has been called an example of *histoire globale* or *totale*, he has almost completely neglected

---

34. *Civilisation matérielle*, p. 9. Cf. *Capitalism and Material Life*, p. xi. The translator uses "model" for "schéma d'ensemble."

35. *Civilisation*, pp. 397ff; *Capitalism*, pp. 401ff. Braudel seems to accept at least in part Weber's theory of the distinctiveness of the occidental city (cf. pp. 391 and 403, English pp. 396 and 410). The translator used the empty heading "Urban Patterns" for "Le grand problème: les formes urbaines, ou un 'modèle.'"

36. *The Mediterranean*, p. 420.   37. *Ibid.*, p. 461.

the institutional and ideological levels in *The Mediterranean* and in *Civilisation matérielle*. When he asserts the unity and coherence of the Mediterranean world, he disregards the Turkish and Christian institutions: "Of the religious structures Christianity and Islam, that at once held each together and divided it, we see nothing from the inside. They are recurrent names, but what gave them life—their interlaced institutions, practices and beliefs—is nowhere to be found."[38] In fact, Braudel has been critical of Sombart for emphasizing *mentalités* at the expense of economic explanations. In referring to the victory of the nouveaux riches in Florence in 1293, Braudel remarks: "Sombart, as usual, preferred to place the problem on the level of states of mind and the development of rational spirit, rather than on the plane of societies, or even of the economy, where he was afraid of following in Marx's footsteps."[39] The mercurial Sombart indeed moved from a Marxian variant of historical materialism—capitalism as a result of the ground rent—to an extreme spiritualism, but Weber always maintained a balance between material and intellectual factors.

There is some indication in Braudel's *Afterthoughts on Material Civilization and Capitalism* and from public statements that he is now more cognizant of the permanence of political and religious hierarchies.[40] Moreover, from his *Afterthoughts* we can understand his views on the rise of capitalism better than from his previously published work, although we do not yet have before us the last two volumes of *Civilisation matérielle*. We now have enough of a basis to compare Braudel's and Weber's account of the nature and causes of capitalism.

4. Two Views of Capitalism

Braudel's account of the nature and rise of capitalism has some distinctive features, but it also amounts to an unin-

---

38. Hexter, *op. cit.*, p. 520.
39. *Capitalism and Material Life*, p. 400.
40. See *Afterthoughts*, p. 64f. If mass media accounts can be trusted at all,

tentional restatement of some of Weber's insights—another instance of scholarly discontinuity. After searching for *la longue durée* in the Mediterranean, Braudel turned in 1950 to a general historical work in the series *Destins du Monde,* of which he took charge after Febvre's death in 1956. Braudel's plan was a general economic history of the European "world economy" during the *ancien régime* from 1400 to 1800, to the early stages of the Industrial Revolution in England. He adapted economic history to his view of historical time, and herein lies his innovative contribution. Braudel distinguishes three levels of economic activity: material life, the market economy, and capitalism, each of which has a different historical speed. On the level of material life he perceives *la longue durée* as "repeated actions, empirical processes, old methods and solutions handed down from time immemorial." Market-oriented activities appear as "a higher and more privileged level of daily life. . . . It is born of trade, transport, differentiated market structures." The "awkward word *capitalism*" refers to "the more sophisticated capitalist mechanism, which encroaches on all forms of life, whether economic or material. . . . Capitalism . . . has betokened modernity, flexibility and rationality from its earliest beginnings."[41]

This reconceptualization of economic history results from Braudel's basic conception of history: "Mankind is more than waist-deep in daily routine." He reminds the English reader that the translation of the first volume of *Civilisation matérielle* omitted the subtitle "The Possible and the Impossible: Men Face to Face with Their Daily Life," and suggests that he really should have selected the title "Structures of Daily Life." He chooses a geographic metaphor for the enduring structures of daily life: "Ancient, yet still alive, this multicenturied past

---

Braudel is supposed to have conceded recently: "I don't think of society the way I did forty years ago. There is no society without hierarchy. You have economic hierarchy—the rich and the poor; cultural hierarchy—the knowledgeable and the ignorant; political hierarchy—the rulers and the ruled. The hierarchies maintain themselves. The permanence of hierarchies—I didn't see this problem with enough depth." *Time Magazine,* May 23, 1977, p. 78.

41. *Capitalism and Material Life,* p. xiif.

flows into the present like the Amazon River pouring into the Atlantic Ocean the vast flood of its cloudy waters."[42]

The exchange economy very slowly arose from the level of material life. Market-oriented activities at first centered on public markets, which were under traditionalist controls, and then developed into private markets or what Braudel likes to call "counter-markets"—"very long, autonomous commercial chains that acted freely."[43] The bourse and various credit instruments had their ups and downs during the *ancien régime*, but in the end proved stronger than in the non-European world-economies. Braudel ranks the world-economies according to this criterion. This permits him to employ another geographic metaphor: "One might say that the economy of the entire world is a succession of different altitudes, as in a relief map."[44]

The next step for Braudel is the distinction between market economy and capitalism. There are two possible forms of the market economy, the A and the B categories. The first form comprises regular exchange, including long-distance trade, the second form, speculative exchange leading to the counter-market. This latter category encompasses the capitalist process. Hence, Braudel deals primarily with merchant capitalism, in his own terms, and with adventure and political capitalism in Weber's terms. Therefore, he can say that capitalism unfolded "at the very summit of society . . . on the level of the Bardis, the Jacques Coeurs, the Jakob Fuggers, the John Laws, or the Neckers." In Braudel's view, capitalism was not a mode of production that seeded itself, rather it was "rooted" in the two underlying layers; it remained essentially conjunctural: "In reality, everything rested upon the very broad back of material life; when material life expanded, everything moved ahead, and the market economy also ex-

42. *Afterthoughts*, p. 6f.   43. *Ibid.*, p. 28.

44. *Ibid.*, p. 35. Braudel distinguishes between the economy of the whole world and world-economies, a translation of the German term *Weltwirtschaft*, that is, economies that form an economic whole, such as the Mediterranean in the sixteenth century (cf. p. 80f.).

panded rapidly and reached out at the expense of material life. Now, capitalism always benefits from such expansion. . . . I persist in my belief that the determining factor was the movement as a whole and that the extensiveness of any capitalism is in direct proportion to the underlying economy."[45] Thus does Braudel maintain the primacy of *la longue durée.*

Braudel ventures into new territory when he tries to spell out the social and political preconditions of capitalism. In a surprising agreement with Weber, he recognizes that society consists of "ensembles—the economy, politics, culture, and the social hierarchy. . . . Capitalism can only be fully explained in the light of these contiguous 'ensembles' and their encroachments."[46] In what Braudel mistakenly takes to be a critique of Weber, he declares that "the real fate of capitalism was determined by its encounter with social hierarchies."[47] There must be enough stability in the social order to permit the accumulation of family fortunes, and the state must be neutral, weak, or permissive—subjects extensively covered by Weber.[48]

Even before the end of the *ancien régime* the expansion of the European world-economy drew in a substantial part of the economy of the whole world and invaded more and more non-European world-economies. Here Braudel sketches the by now familiar theory of the division of the European world-economy into center, intermediate zone (or semi-periphery), and periphery and of the geographical shifts within this economy. Instead of the old evolutionary scheme of the transitions from slavery to feudalism to capitalism, he

45. Both quotes from *Afterthoughts*, p. 63.
46. *Ibid.,* p. 64.   47. *Ibid.,* p. 67.
48. See *ES*, pp. 1059–64, 1109; "Parliament and Government" (in *ES*, p. 1395); *EH*, p. 93. Braudel follows Weber unknowingly in arguing that capitalism can prosper only if family property is protected and that in non-European societies "capitalism generally encounters social obstacles that are very difficult or impossible to hurdle" (*Afterthoughts*, p. 71). That, after all, is a major theme of Weber's "The Economic Ethic of the World Religions."

points to the simultaneity of these phenomena in the expanding European economy.

Braudel concludes with the Industrial Revolution in England, the only country that managed to create a national market at an early date. He makes two points consistent with his overall scheme: the Industrial Revolution, too, was "a slow-moving phenomenon," and it had "deep-down origins." It was created from below, if in a way different from merchant and financial capitalism, which had nothing to do with its origin. "The cotton revolution . . . burgeoned from the lower level, from the level of ordinary life. . . . Its inventions were generally the work of artisans. Industrialists were quite often of humble origin. . . . Industrial capitalism . . . could only grow . . . to the degree permitted by the underlying economy."[49] This view is compatible with Weber's insofar as Weber, too, emphasized the gradual accumulation of small amounts of capital in the absence of the monopolist advantages of adventure and political capitalism, and pointed to the important role of decentralized government—an extremely attenuated form of patrimonial rule by the English gentry—which denied justice to the poor and thus proved permissive to the industrial capitalists.[50]

There is a very sketchy critique of Weber in the *Afterthoughts*. Braudel's sparse references to Weber in his writings suggest that he barely knows Weber's work. It is not surprising, therefore, that he falls victim to some misconceptions. His critique is twofold: (1) "For Max Weber, capitalism in the modern sense of the word was no more and no less than a creation of Protestantism, or to be even more accurate, of Puritanism. . . . All historians have opposed this tenuous theory . . . it is clearly false." (2) "All things considered, I believe that Max Weber's error stems essentially from his exaggeration of capitalism's role as promoter of the modern world."[51]

49. Braudel, *Afterthoughts*, pp. 108 and 109.

50. See *ES*, p. 1064; *EH*, p. 228.

51. Braudel, *Afterthoughts*, pp. 65 and 67. Weber's works, which in the United States have attracted so much diffuse (and confused) attention over

A very brief summary of Weber's theory of capitalism and of the modern world must suffice as a contrast to Braudel's views. In *The Protestant Ethic and the Spirit of Capitalism* Weber presented no more and no less than a secular theory which attempted to make plausible how intensely held sectarian convictions of a rationalist kind promoted methodical conduct in all spheres of life, including the economic realm, where it became secularized in time as "the spirit of capitalism." In contrast to Braudel, whose vision of history is focused on the simultaneity of phenomena with different historical duration, Weber wanted to identify the causal concatenation that for over two and one-half millennia had led to the present rationalized world. Again in contrast to Braudel, who minimized the difference between merchant and industrial capitalism by virtue of their presumed common origin in the layers of material life and market economy, Weber endeavored to establish the nature of the old capitalism, which in Braudel's terms belongs to the realm of *la longue durée,* and the distinctiveness of modern industrial capitalism. He concluded that modern capitalism differed from the older forms (tax-farming, trade speculation, money-lending, slaves as capital goods) in two crucial respects: (1) It operated with the rational permanent enterprise and rational accounting procedures, which presupposed "a rational organization of labor which had nowhere previously existed"; (2) there was no barrier between the internal and the external economy, between insiders and outsiders. Weber rejected all monocausal explanations: neither demographic growth nor precious metals nor Roman law nor geographic conditions nor war nor luxury goods could be considered the major cause (*Ent-*

---

the last three decades, have been noticed within *Annales* circles only since the 1970s. The French classicist Pierre Vidal-Naquet, for example, pronounced Weber "notre père à tous" in Braudel's seminar in the early seventies, a reference to Weber's explanation of the economy of the ancient city in terms of its political institutions. At the same time the *Annales* critic Paul Veyne called Weber's "the most exemplary historical work of the century" (citations in Stoianovich, *op. cit.* [n. 1 above], p. 143). Previously only Raymond Aron and Julien Freund had persistently tried to promote an understanding of Weber in France.

stehungsgrund) of capitalism. Rather, a multitude of historical factors had combined in a unique constellation. Among these were the rational state with its professional officialdom, rational law created by jurists, the occidental city and its burghers, rational science and technology, and finally a rational ethic for the conduct of life which had originally been religiously inspired.[52] Thus, Weber did not consider Puritanism the sole creator of modern capitalism, nor did he exaggerate capitalism's role as promoter of the modern world—Braudel's second charge.

The modern world was the result of a long process of rationalization, of which economic capitalism was only a part. While Braudel is fascinated by the historical "weights" that make basic historical change a matter of excruciatingly slow and almost imperceptible transformations, Weber is preoccupied with the forces of rationalization which have pushed Western civilization along its world-revolutionary path. Therefore, in the final section I shall look at Weber's concept of rationalization from Braudel's viewpoint of *la longue durée*. In what sense can it be argued that rationalization is part of a *longue durée* or a dynamic force overcoming the forces of persistence?

5. RATIONALIZATION AND *LA LONGUE DURÉE*: CHINA AND THE WEST

The Chinese case is important for our comparison because a particular kind of rationalization led to the stabilization of the social and political order for many centuries and thus to a long duration. Weber's chapter on China in "The Economic Ethic of the World Religions" was analytically prepared by the chapter on religious groups in *Economy and Society*. There he sketched his socio-historical models of religious leadership and organization, of the religious affinities of the various social strata, and of the intellectuals and their relations to salvation religion. This he followed with a typology of

52. Cf. *EH*, pp. 232, 246, 292, 301.

orientations toward salvation and a comparison of the typical relation between religious ethics and the "world" (of economics, politics, sexuality, and art). On the level of secular theory he concluded with a comparison of Judaism, Islam, Buddhism, and Christianity, especially Puritanism. In his study of China he ultimately aimed at a comparison of Confucianism and Puritanism in relation to economic capitalism, but he arrived at this comparison only after a comprehensive analysis of Chinese economy and society, which also presupposed the political and economic typologies (or models) of *Economy and Society*.

The purpose of Weber's studies in the economic ethics of the world religions was neither "a systematic typology of religions" nor a "purely historical presentation." His analysis was meant to be "typological only in the sense that it focuses on what is typically important about the historical realities of the religious ethics with regard to the great differences in economic mentality." Weber specified that he was interested not just in the economic ethics of the world religions but in their relation to economic rationalism; in fact, he was even more specifically concerned with "economic rationalism of that type which began to dominate the West as a part of the native bourgeois rationalization of life since the 16th and 17th centuries. Once more we must keep in mind that 'rationalism' can mean very different things."[53] Thus, he was interested in a

---

53. "Introduction," p. 292f. When Weber wrote the last version of the "Intermediate Reflections: Stages and Directions of Religious World Rejection" in 1920, he added the term "theory" to the title. He had in mind not a secular theory but a typology or model of asceticism and mysticism, "an ideal-typical means of orientation." With his "attempt at a sociology of religion" he meant to make a "contribution to the typology and sociology of rationalism itself." However, his historical purpose was "to identify the degree to which certain theoretically feasible rational conclusions were indeed drawn in reality"—and this refers to the level of secular theory, the "developmental" (*entwicklungsgeschichtliche*) dimension, which he mentions three times in the same passage (cf. "Theory," pp. 323 ff.). In comparison with the models or typologies of the "Intermediate Reflections" the preceding last chapter of the study on China is largely concerned with the secular theory of Confucianism and Puritanism (cf. *China*, pp. 226–249).

secular theory, a causal explanation, of the ways in which Western bourgeois rationalism and Confucian rationalism either furthered or hindered economic capitalism.

In his study of China, Weber gives considerable attention to what are for Braudel the levels of material life, market economy and capitalism. In his investigation of the social foundations of Chinese rationalism, he deals with the basic geographic feature of China as an inland (rather than a maritime) economy; the archaic monetary system and its instability; and the cities and their guilds, which lacked the occidental political features of an autonomous political community. He traces the rise of the patrimonial administration and of the central role of the pontifical ruler after a period of feudalism and political capitalism, and he discusses the modes of taxation in the increasingly demilitarized and pacified empire. The struggle for imperial unification involved a rationalization of the civilian and military administration. It is here that the literati came into their own and created Confucian rationalism. Now the material forces which militated against an economic capitalism of the Western kind were reinforced by motivational factors (*innere Gründe*), an ethic of world adjustment and world affirmation on the part of the scholar-administrators. The religious heterodoxies were even more hostile to economic capitalism. In Weber's view the impact on the masses of the ideology of pious submission to the worldly power was a negative one: it prevented ethical prophecy and suppressed orgiastic animism.

Weber concludes his study with two lessons in his final comparison of Confucianism and Puritanism: (1) Sobriety, thriftiness, "acquisitive drive" and high estimation of wealth, as they prevailed in China, do not amount to a "capitalist spirit in the sense of the specifically modern economic professionalism" (*Berufsmenschentum*). (2) Both the Chinese and the Western ethic were rational, but only the "Puritan rational ethic with its transcendental orientation pushed innerworldly economic rationalism to its [full] consequences." Instead of rational adjustment, the West achieved a rational domination of the world. As a minimal claim for his conclusion, Weber asserted:

"The pacification of the [Chinese] world empire directly explains the absence of political capitalism, which we find in occidental Antiquity (up to the Imperial period), in the Orient and in the Middle Ages, but not the absence of purely economic capitalism. It can scarcely be denied that the basic features of the mentality—in our case of the practical attitude toward the world—strongly codetermined the barriers to economic capitalism by virtue of their autonomous effects (*Eigengesetze*), although these basic features were codetermined in turn by political and economic forces (*Schicksale*)."[54]

Rationalization in the form of Confucian ideology and administration thus contributed to the very persistence of the Chinese imperial system. In the West, however, rationalization of a different kind destroyed the *ancien régime* and created a new world. In Weber's grand secular theory of the uniqueness of the Western development, modern Europe was the product of a long series of rationalizations and of five revolutions that transformed it and made it different from the other parts of the world. In contrast to the Chinese world empire, which did not need technical rationalization, "in the Occident there were autonomous powers, with which the central power either had to ally itself and break the traditional barriers or which, under very particular conditions, could defeat the patrimonial ruler with their own military might, as it happened in the five great revolutions that have been decisive for the Occident—the Italian revolution of the twelfth and thirteenth centuries, the Dutch of the sixteenth, the English of the seventeenth, and the American and French of the eighteenth century."[55] Moreover, only in the West did a crucial compatibility between economic and religious rationalization occur, which lasted long enough to "break the traditional barriers" to the thoroughgoing rationalization of all spheres of life. European rationalization finally put traditionalism on the defensive and led to many revolutionary changes all over the world.[56]

54. Cf. *China*, pp. 247ff.   55. Cf. *China*, p. 62.

56. For a parallel treatment, see Benjamin Nelson, "On Orient and Occi-

It is well known that Weber was ambivalent toward some aspects of rationalization and looked with great apprehension toward the future. Bureaucratization had been a revolutionary process vis-à-vis the *ancien régime,* but "once fully established, bureaucracy is among those social structures which are hardest to destroy.... Once administration has been completely bureaucratized, the resulting form of domination is practically indestructible."[57] Western history had not followed any laws of development, nor was its course irreversible. Complete bureaucratization had not yet occurred, but both capitalism and socialism tended toward pervasive bureaucratization. Thus, a new *longue durée* appeared possible, a long-term sentence in the iron cage of modern economic life as well as a new slavery under "Egyptianization."

The belief in progress was first shaken in Weber's generation in Germany. Weber himself became one of the first scholars to study the long-range vicissitudes of an ambiguous rationalization which once had looked innocuously like "progress" toward inevitable human betterment. Even though he opposed *Kulturpessimismus* as another fashion of the literati, his scholarly and political perceptions were affected by a fear of stagnation and decline. This may have been an attitude typical of the epigoni of empire-builders, but it also became a realistic view from a larger perspective.

In France, England, and the United States it took longer to shake the belief that material life would always improve in spite of occasional setbacks through economic crises and wars. The fairly quick recovery of western Europe and of the capitalist world economy after the Second World War gave a big boost to the belief in the self-perpetuating powers of a growth economy. But today declining economic growth and even stagnation, coupled with political instability, raise the spectre of a world in which the rich become poorer and the poor more wretched, as it has happened before in Western

---

dent in Max Weber," *Social Research,* 43, no. 1 (1976): 114–129, esp. the section on China, pp. 121ff.

57. *ES,* p. 987.

history. We must worry about what will happen when "the last ton of fossil fuel has been used up," as Weber put it in the conclusion of *The Protestant Ethic and the Spirit of Capitalism*.[58] Suddenly we may find ourselves in a position in which Weber's *apprehensions* may appear to be compatible with Braudel's vision of history as the story of material constraints, of politics as an evanescent superstructure powerless before the geographic, demographic, and economic substructures of long duration. However, in contrast to his apprehensions, it was the *essence* of Weber's scholarship and partisanship to help human beings gain greater control over their destinies and make them less dependent on unperceived forces.

58. Cf. *PE*, p. 181.

Epilogue

WEBER'S VISION OF HISTORY

Guenther Roth

1. Levels of Historical Analysis: Sociological, Historical, Situational

Weber's levels of historical analysis resulted from his perception of the purpose of historiography, its contemporary possibilities and limitations, and this perception was influenced by the intellectual situation in which he found himself. He came to stand at a crucial juncture in modern historiography, the point at which disillusionment with the evolutionary views of the preceding three generations (whether Deist or naturalist) made a methodological reorientation strongly desirable. This disillusionment came about partly because of changes in intellectual climate—ongoing secularization, but also the incipient skepticism toward scientific laws as all-explanatory devices; partly it was the result of rapidly accumulating research that did not seem to support the various evolutionary-stage theories. If there was no deterministic scheme of evolutionary development, the only empirical alternative seemed to be the construction of "type concepts" or socio-historical models and of secular theories of long-range historical transformation.[1]

1. On the genesis of Weber's typological approach, see my essay in *Scholarship and Partisanship: Essays on Max Weber* (Berkeley and Los Angeles: University of California Press, 1971), chap. 13.

This historiographic crisis occurred in the years before the First World War when European hegemony reached its zenith. The capitalist world system enveloped nearly the whole globe, yet the future did not appear to Weber as certain and benign as it had to believers in progress among earlier European generations and contemporaries. This setting has been described by Beetham and Mommsen,[2] and I shall limit myself to the methodological observation that Weber began to ask the kind of questions that are indicative of a reflective stance in a situation of reorientation: Who are we that we have come that far? How did we get there? Where are we likely to go? And where should we go from here? The answers to these questions seemed best given from the perspective of universal history. The question of our identity, of who we are, had previously been answered largely in terms of European legacies, especially the Judeo-Christian tradition. In view of the worldwide impact of Western civilization, it seemed appropriate to answer this question, in addition, through research-oriented comparison with the other civilizations of past and present. The problem was one of configuration, the first level of historical analysis. The question of how we did get that far had to be answered on the second, the "historical," level of analysis and was a causal problem; it was feasible only after identifying the phenomenon to be explained. The answer to the first query was couched in terms of the distinctiveness of Western rationalism, a unique configuration; the answer to the second question was given in terms of historical concatenations that had brought it about. The question of where we stand and are likely to go is dealt with on the level of situational analysis and of extrapolating from perceived trends. In the absence of a belief in determinism and evolutionism, this is an open-ended trend analysis. Where should we go? The answer involves all three levels of empirical analysis, but it requires also a moral choice, either a

2. See David Beetham, *Max Weber and the Theory of Modern Politics* (London: Allen and Unwin, 1974); W. Mommsen, *The Age of Bureaucracy: Perspectives on the Political Sociology of Max Weber* (Oxford: Blackwell, 1974).

reaffirmation or a modification of one's own commitments. For this last answer Weber did not claim the protective mantle of science and scholarship—since values cannot be legitimated by science—but a rational decision had to be based on as clear a grasp of universal history as possible.

The three levels are all historical in a general sense, but in Weber's terminology the first is that of sociology—of type or model construction and of rules of experience—whereas the second level, the causal explanation of past events, is labeled by him "historical" in quotation marks, or sometimes "developmental" (*entwicklungsgeschichtlich*). Here we find his secular theories. Occasionally he calls the third level, which we find mostly in his political writings, an analysis of the "general social and political situation," as when he disclaims in "Russia's Transition to Pseudo-Constitutionalism" (1906) that he had intended to provide "something like a 'history' of the last half year."[3] (By "history" Weber here meant "chronicle" rather than causal explanation.) His own phrasing, then, may justify naming this third level "situational analysis."

Mommsen is right in saying that Weber became a sociologist by retreating from "history," the level of causal analysis. But this was only a strategic retreat. Although *Economy and Society* was not meant to explain the uniqueness of Western rationalism, it offers a typological framework for its study; thus it is sociology strictly as a "preliminary" and "preparatory" exercise. Its typology consists of models such as bureaucracy, patrimonialism, charismatic rulership and community, hierocracy, church, sect, and others that are constructed from different times and places. But even in *Economy and Society* there are many historical explanations that amount to sketches of secular theories about the genesis and consequences of particular historical phenomena, from the Protestant ethic to the modern state.[4]

3. "Russlands Übergang zum Scheinkonstitutionalismus," *Archiv für Sozialwissenschaft*, 23 (1906); partially reprinted in *PS*, p. 106.

4. In a methodological essay, which does not specifically deal with Weber, Mommsen has suggested a distinction similar to the one proposed here: he contrasts structural models (*Strukturmodelle*) with processual models (*Ver-*

The socio-historical models as well as the secular theories are not intended to explain what is happening in a given situation. One model alone cannot adequately describe a given case; a battery of models or hyphenated types, such as patrimonial bureaucracy, can provide a better approximation. Their utility lies in serving as base lines for identifying the distinctiveness of a case. While secular theories attempt to trace a long line of causation, they too have limited usefulness with regard to a given situation. Theories such as those of democratization and industrialization diminish in explanatory value when we look at the relatively short time span of a few years or even two or three decades, because they are concerned with long-range structural changes. Phenomena like the charismatic eruption of an ethic of conviction during the 1960s cannot be sufficiently explained by recourse to the secular theory of corporate capitalism, since that theory covers the time span of "the silent fifties" as well as the waning of charismatic mass excitement in the early seventies. Hence the need for situational analysis, which probes into the contem-

---

laufsmodelle). The former are exemplified by "epochal concepts" such as feudalism, renaissance, bourgeois society, and fascism. Thus he thinks of what in an older terminology were called "individual ideal types," in contrast to the "general ideal types" on which I focus. But the logic of their construction is the same in this respect: "Such explanatory models are primarily static and accentuate the elements that are dominant in a social structure. However, they always contain implicitly a specific pattern of social change. This is evident from the simple fact that most of the time they constitute a contrast to older social formations or emphasize certain trends. . . . Processual models are rarely explicated to the same degree as structural models. As a rule, they serve as guidelines for narrations of a predominantly chronological kind." Wolfgang J. Mommsen, "Gesellschaftliche Bedingtheit und gesellschaftliche Relevanz historischer Aussagen," *Die Funktion der Geschichte in unserer Zeit*, ed. Ernst Weymar and Eberhard Jäckel (Stuttgart: Klett, 1975), p. 218. As examples of processual models Mommsen cites Tocqueville's theory of democratization and the Marxist theory of historical stages. However, the degree to which Marx was also a structural-model builder in his comparative studies unpublished during his lifetime has been examined by R. Stephen Warner, "The Methodology of Marx's Comparative Analysis of Modes of Production," *Comparative Methods in Sociology*, ed. Ivan Vallier (Berkeley and Los Angeles: University of California Press, 1971), pp. 49–74.

porary play of forces—apart from the necessary recourse to models such as the charismatic community. The construction of models and secular theories can have ideological overtones, just as situational analysis can be relatively neutral in partisan struggles. However, situational analysis is also the vehicle for political analysis proper, which is concerned with the assessment of a given distribution of power with a view toward changing or preserving it, not with secular change or differences between civilizations. In his voluminous writings on agrarian and industrial capitalism and constitutional reform, Weber dealt explicitly with questions of how to bring about change—just as Marx did. When David Beetham synthesized Weber's secular theory of modern politics from his more political rather than his more academic writings, he also showed that the two kinds of writing differ in their analytical emphasis, not just their manifest intent. Much more is involved here than the difference between political evaluation and scholarly "freedom from value judgment." It is true that "the point of [Weber's] political writings is to be sought in the political context, and that of his sociology, in the first instance at least, within a particular scientific tradition."[5] However, because the focus of political analysis is on how to bring about (or prevent) change, "it is possible to find in Weber's political writings a sense of the interrelationship of forces in society which is frequently lacking in his academic work."[6] In his political writings, then, the crucial issue is the relationship between a given state and society, the clash of the major social groupings in the political arena—in other words, for him, too, political analysis must be class analysis in one way or another.

When Beetham claims that in *Economy and Society* "there is little politics as Weber himself defined it,"[7] he seems to mean that the overall frame of analysis is not the struggle for power among the social classes. This would be true especially of the sociology of domination, which, after all, was an attempt to extend Georg Jellinek's social theory of the state. It was an

5. Beetham, *op. cit.*, p. 30.   6. *Ibid.*, p. 252.   7. *Ibid.*, p. 15.

undertaking within the "particular scientific tradition" of comparative constitutional theory, which is not directly concerned with class struggles. Yet part of Weber's achievement lies in the fact that he treated empirically the "validity" of modes of legitimation in relation to the perennial power struggles between rulers and staffs (and partly also the subjects).

There is, of course, a considerable thematic and analytical overlap between Weber's political and scholarly studies, quite apart from the fact that some of his writings are difficult to classify, for instance, the studies on the agrarian conditions in East Elbia and on Russia. Some of his self-declared political writings, such as "Parliament and Government in a Reconstructed Germany," are heavily freighted with the results of his historical researches, while most of his scholarly writings, beginning with those on antiquity, are more or less clearly linked to his political interests. But Beetham is right in pointing to significant differences: in the scholarly writings, modes of legitimation and the technical superiority of bureaucracy in relation to other forms of administration are given special attention; in the writings on the political situation, the German and Russian bureaucracies appear as vested interests, if not as outright parasites, preventing needed social change and reflecting the class structure of the two societies. In the scholarly writings capitalism is treated as part of Western rationalism, whereas in his political studies Weber stresses the ways in which capitalism creates class conflicts.

Most of Weber's extensive political writings dealt with Imperial Germany and Imperial Russia, especially with the impact of industrialization and the difficulties of establishing liberal democracy in countries that lacked the historical preconditions for it. Beetham sees clearly that Weber's analyses were not merely institutional in spite of his great interest in the varieties and technicalities of constitutional reconstruction; Weber always looked for the social basis of a political movement. He recognized that the introduction of advanced capitalism into "underdeveloped" countries such as Germany and Russia, in which the bourgeoisie had not played its Western historical role of promoting religious, political, and economic liberties, militated against the growth of liberal democracy by reinforcing traditionalist sentiments, such as archaic agrarian communism (in the Russian case), propelling radical socialism, and frightening the weak bourgeoisie into submitting to authoritarian rule.

2. LESSONS OF HISTORY: SWIMMING AGAINST THE STREAM

Weber's political writings contain a combination of situational analysis, elements of models (such as agrarian communism), and sketches of secular theories. They also deal with the possible shapes of the future and offer a trend analysis. What is distinctive about Weber's historical vision is his insistence on keeping "the future as history" open to human will and resolution. Neither in theory nor in practice did he accept any "iron laws" of history. Indeed, it was important to employ rules of experience, configurations, and secular theories—the whole assembly of the lessons of history— exactly for the purpose of "swimming against the stream." Here we arrive at the last level of analysis, which transcends the purely empirical realm: What are we to do now and in the future? In 1906 Weber gave an eloquent answer in his essay "On the Situation of Bourgeois Democracy in Russia," which I shall quote at length, since it can give us a final illustration of the way in which he bound together the observation of a trend, a rule of historical experience, a model, a secular theory, and a declaration of political commitment in taking his stand on the issue of the conditions for liberal democracy. Half a century before American social science embraced the now discredited theory that economic development tends to promote political pluralism, Weber warned:

Today the chances for democracy and individualism would be very poor indeed, if we relied for their development upon the social laws of the effects of material interests. . . . May those rest assured who live in continuous fear that in the future there could be too much democracy and individualism in the world, and not enough authority, aristocracy and office prestige and such things. As matters stand, the trees of democratic individualism will not grow skyhigh. According to all experience, history relentlessly recreates aristocracies and authorities, to whom can cling whoever finds it necessary for himself—or for the people. If the material conditions and the resultant interest constellations were predominant, every sober analysis would have to draw the conclusion that all economic weather vanes point in the direction of increasing lack of freedom. It is utterly ridiculous to attribute elective affinity with democracy or even freedom (in any sense of the word) to today's advanced capitalism—that inevitability of our economic development—as it is now imported into Russia and as it exists in the United States. Rather, the question can be phrased only in this way: How can democracy and freedom be maintained in the long run under the dominance of advanced capitalism? They can be maintained only if a nation is always determined not to be ruled like a herd of sheep. We individualists and partisans of democratic institutions are swimming against the stream of material constellations. Whoever desires to be the weather vane of a developmental tendency may abandon those old-fashioned ideals as quickly as possible. The rise of modern freedom presupposed unique constellations which will never repeat themselves. Let us enumerate the most important ones: First, the overseas expansion. In Cromwell's armies, in the French Constituent Assembly, in our whole economic life, even today, there blows that wind from beyond the seas. But a new continent is no longer available. Just as in antiquity, the population centers of Western culture are moving irresistibly to large inland areas, the North American continent and Russia with their monotonous plains which favor uniformity. The second constellation was the nature of the economic and social structure of the early capitalist epoch in western Europe, and the third the rise of science. Finally, there were certain values that grew out of the concrete historical distinctiveness of a religious body of thought. These religious conceptions shaped the ethical quality and the "higher culture" of modern man, in combination with several equally peculiar political constellations and with those material preconditions.[8]

Since Weber did not claim the powers of scientific prophecy, the total course of events could not prove him wrong, but his vision and foresight could not help but be blurred in many

8. "Zur Lage der bürgerlichen Demokratie in Russland," *Archiv*, 22 (1905/6); partially reprinted in *PS*, pp. 63ff.

particulars. He took it for granted that "our weak eyes" cannot see far into "the impenetrable mists of the future of human history."[9] Inevitably, he observed trends and made extrapolations that did not turn into historical reality because of counter-trends. Weber was certainly right in anticipating that the trees of democratic individualism would not grow skyhigh, when that hope had not yet diminished as much as it has by now. Since he wrote the passage, the rule of experience about the relentless renascence of "authorities" has been buttressed by the proliferation of authoritarian governments after both world wars.[10] What may today strike us particularly about his assertion that advanced capitalism does not inherently or necessarily promote democracy is the observation over the last seventy years that liberal democracy has survived mainly in its own heartlands, which also happen to be the centers of the capitalist world economy. Weber's hope that Germany would turn into a liberal democracy as a result of internal party struggles proved vain. Only western Germany and Japan became liberal democracies by virtue of conquest. Weber did not foresee the defeat of capitalism in Russia, but he anticipated that Marxism would grow stronger at the expense of populist romanticism. He understood that Marxism could not theoretically cope with the "tremendous and fundamental agrarian problem" in Russia, and he applied to the Russian revolutionaries the historical maxim that "the mortal folly not only of every radical but of every ideologically oriented policy is its capacity to miss opportunities."[11] But he

9. *Ibid.*, p. 65.
10. See my essay on "Personal Rulership, Patrimonialism, and Empire-Building" in *Scholarship and Partisanship*, pp. 156–169.
11. *Ibid.*, pp. 59 and 62. Trotsky seems to have taken a similar position, both in his overall assessment of the character of Russian capitalism and in his judgment of his fellow revolutionaries. See Baruch Knei-Paz's remark that "Trotsky's analysis of the Russian bourgeoisie and of Russian liberalism may be seen as an attempt to carry the generally accepted argument about the feebleness of the Russian middle classes to its logical conclusion. If the bourgeoisie was indeed so impotent a force, if it resembled its Western counterpart only in name, then it was incumbent, in his view, to draw practical, political conclusions which would take account of this anomaly. Not to do so

did not anticipate that Lenin would be pragmatic enough to see his opportunity and take it. However, he realized that a European war would spell the end of tsarism and was aware that the feeble forces of Russian liberal democracy would have to face either bureaucratic or Jacobin centralism. When he claimed, on the basis of a geo-historical argument, that America and Russia seemed to turn inward, he could not foresee that Russia would indeed withdraw from the capitalist world system and that the United States would retreat into isolationism in the wake of one world war, before the next one would change all of that because of historical counter tendencies.

The survival of liberal democracy in recognizable forms and in spite of many counter-trends seems to be related to certain historical legacies. Each of the factors Weber enumerated as historical conditions of the rise of liberal democracy can be elaborated into a secular theory. Several of these theories can be synthesized into an overview of Western and universal history, but they cannot amount to a total theory of society, since the process of additions of secular theories is theoretically limitless. Insofar as Marxism, which is one of the targets of Weber's passage, has tried to offer a total theory of the course of Western history, its claims about the necessary relationships of all parts have been beyond the realm of historical verifiability, and many of its specific predictions have been proven wrong by the course of events over the last century.

To sum up: In Weber's practiced methodology "sociology" is the generalized aspect of the study of history and contrasts

---

meant to deny the relevance of social history to political events and this is precisely what he accused his Marxist colleagues of doing, that is, misunderstanding and ignoring the political reality which was taking shape around them, thereby also remaining fixed within theoretical preconceptions which did not conform to that reality" (*The Social and Political Thought of Leon Trotsky*, Oxford: Clarendon Press, 1978, p. 31). In the same context Knei-Paz refers to Weber (p. 32). Trotsky's analysis is contained in *1905* (New York: Random House, 1971), a collection of articles written between 1905 and 1908.

with the causal analysis of individual phenomena—the task of "history." Both sociology and historiography proceed from the causality inherent in social action. When Weber defined sociology as "a science concerning itself with the interpretive understanding of social action and thereby with the causal explanation of its course and consequences," he meant to affirm that in history only men act, not social organisms or reified collectivities.[12] The construction of socio-historical models, such as patrimonialism or rule by notables, is possible because, in principle, we can understand the intentions of men and causally explain the course and consequences of their actions. Of course, such structural types transcend the task of "history" to explain causally a given event; model construction synthesizes the historical observation of many individual actors. The main point about interpretive sociology was that we should try to understand the ideas and intentions of historical actors rather than search for "scientific" laws of social evolution, as Marx and other evolutionists had done. However, on the levels of both model and secular theory history provided many lessons in unintended consequences. Revolutionary charisma tends toward routinization; rule-oriented bureaucracy tends toward becoming a vested interest; and political patrimonialism, an effort at centralized control, tends toward decentralization. The paradoxes and ironies are built right into the models. The same is true of Weber's most famous secular theory, "The Protestant Ethic and the Spirit of Capitalism": the transition from the Protestant ethic to the spirit of capitalism and in turn to the "iron cage" of advanced capitalism was one of the secular developments, fateful for Western history, which poignantly demonstrated the "heterogony of purposes."

Weber's philosophy of history was pragmatic rather than pessimistic. Unless we save ourselves, nothing and nobody will save us. Historical knowledge, which comprises the levels of

12. *ES*, p. 4.

analysis discussed here, is necessary for self-clarification, for deciding what we want and where we want to go. But that knowledge cannot lead to the kind of science of society that would unlock the secrets of history and provide a master key to the future.

ACKNOWLEDGMENTS

The following previously published essays appear here in revised form:

Chapter I, W. Schluchter, "Die Paradoxie der Rationalisierung: Zum Verhältnis von 'Ethik' und 'Welt' bei Max Weber," *Zeitschrift für Soziologie*, 5, no. 3 (July 1976): 256–284.

Chapter II, W. Schluchter, *Wertfreiheit und Verantwortungsethik: Zum Verhältnis von Wissenschaft und Politik bei Max Weber.* Tübingen: Mohr, 1971.

Chapter III, secs. 2–5, G. Roth, "Socio-historical Model and Developmental Theory: Charismatic Community, Charisma of Reason and the Counterculture," *American Sociological Review*, 40, no. 2 (April 1975): 148–157. By permission.

Chapter IV, G. Roth, "Religion and Revolutionary Beliefs: Sociological and Historical Dimensions in Max Weber's Work—In Memory of Ivan Vallier (1927–1974)," *Social Forces*, 55, no. 2 (Dec. 1976): 257–272. By permission.

Chapter III, sec. 1, and Epilogue, G. Roth, "History and Sociology in the Work of Max Weber," *The British Journal of Sociology*, 27, no. 3 (Sept. 1976): 306–318. (Special issue on History and Sociology.) By permission.

INDEX OF NAMES

Composition Lehmann Graphics
Lithography Malloy Lithographing, Inc.
Binder Malloy Lithographing, Inc.
Text VIP Baskerville
Display VIP Baskerville
Paper 50 lb Glatfelter natural
Binding Joanna Oxford 19990